I0810151

IMAGES of America

# PERU

## CIRCUS CAPITAL OF THE WORLD

*On the cover*: In 1935, the Peru winter quarters was owned by Ringling Brothers and called the Ringling Circus Farm. The country was in a time of depression, and hoping to increase ticket sales, Ringling management decided to send the Hagenbeck-Wallace Circus out with the title Hagenbeck-Wallace–Forepaugh-Sells Combined Circus. The Forepaugh-Sells name had not been used in nearly 25 years. (Courtesy of the Miami County Historical Society.)

IMAGES
*of America*

# PERU

## CIRCUS CAPITAL OF THE WORLD

Kreig A. Adkins

ARCADIA
PUBLISHING

ISBN 978-0-7385-6071-7

Published by Arcadia Publishing
Charleston, South Carolina

Printed in the United States of America

Library of Congress Control Number: 2008943131

For all general information contact Arcadia Publishing at:
Telephone 843-853-2070
Fax 843-853-0044
E-mail sales@arcadiapublishing.com
For customer service and orders:
Toll-Free 1-888-313-2665

Visit us on the Internet at www.arcadiapublishing.com

*To all the circus families past and present that called Peru home*

# Contents


| | | |
|---|---|---|
| Acknowledgments | | 6 |
| Introduction | | 7 |
| 1. | The Great Wallace Shows | 9 |
| 2. | Hagenbeck-Wallace Circus | 19 |
| 3. | The Winter Quarters | 27 |
| 4. | Birth of a Circus Empire | 33 |
| 5. | "How's the Crowd in the Big Show?" | 49 |
| 6. | Welcome Home | 61 |
| 7. | The End of the Street Parades | 73 |
| 8. | The Steel Arena | 83 |
| 9. | Madison Square Garden in 1930 | 95 |
| 10. | The Reckoning | 103 |
| 11. | The Last Hurrah | 115 |

# ACKNOWLEDGMENTS

I would like to thank Arcadia Publishing for giving me this wonderful opportunity to tell the story of how Peru became "the Circus Capital of the World" and share with circus fans everywhere photographs of circus days gone by, many of which have never been published. I would also like to thank the Miami County Historical Society Board of Directors for its continued confidence in my work and for accommodating me at the museum by giving me access to the circus archives. Thanks also to the late Carl "Snowy" Hartisch, who took the time to save everything he could about the circuses in Peru. A special thanks to Malcolm McCarter for allowing me to once again tell Peru's history, featuring photographs from the Malcolm McCarter Photo Collection, and to Ellen Harvey for helping make this book the best it could be.

Unless otherwise noted, all photographs are from the Miami County Historical Society.

# INTRODUCTION

Peru, located on the banks of the Wabash River in north-central Indiana, has always been a special place. The area in and around modern-day Peru played a major role in American history and the development of Indiana as a state. The Miami Indians' Osage village was near the confluence of the Mississinewa and Wabash Rivers. It was here that Tecumseh asked the Miami Nation to join his confederacy of Native Americans and fight the U.S. Army to preserve this land for all Native Americans. The Miami people declined to join the confederacy, and Tecumseh was later killed fighting for his cause in the War of 1812. Indiana became a state in 1816, but the northern part of the state was still unsettled and occupied by Native Americans. It was not until 1829 that the United States government would sign a treaty with the Native Americans to cede the land on the north bank of the Wabash River for the government's new project, the Wabash and Erie Canal. Almost immediately new settlements were being platted all along the proposed route of the canal. The first settlement was called Miamisport and was platted by Joseph Holman in 1829. The boundaries were from present-day Lafayette Street to Holman Street and from Canal Street to Main Street. Miamisport grew quickly, with the Miami Indians being the best customers. The Miami people were receiving annuities from the federal government and were eager to spend it on conveniences and services now available in the area. Locks No. 18, 19, 20, and 21 as well as dam No. 3 were planned to be built in Miami County for the Wabash and Erie Canal. As the canal got closer to Miamisport, more and more canal workers arrived in the area and fueled the local economy.

By 1832, Miamisport needed to expand and plans were made to expand to the west. This decision infuriated William Hood, who owned the property east of Miamisport. He vowed to plat his own town, so he hired engineers from the Wabash and Erie Canal to plat the town of Peru. Hood was committed to Peru's success and offered free lots to any church that would build in Peru. He also offered free lots to anyone that would move from Miamisport to Peru. Other lots were offered as cheap as $50. Hood wanted Peru to be the county seat, so he donated the property for a courthouse and jail and donated $150 for the county books. A vote was taken, and Peru became the county seat of the newly formed Miami County. In 1841, another vote was taken and the name Miamisport was dropped and the settlement was made a part of Peru.

Around this time, the Miami Indians suffered a great loss. In 1840, the last Miami war chief, Francis Godfroy, passed away and just one year later civil chief Jean Baptiste de Richardville passed away. These two men were chiefs during one of the most trying times in the tribe's history. The U.S. government expected the Miamis to move to a reservation in Kansas. The new civil chief, Francis Lafontaine, did all he could to keep the Miamis in Indiana. In 1846, soldiers came to Peru and gathered up the Miamis and put them on canal boats. The Miami people with American and French heritage were allowed to stay and, although Lafontaine was of French heritage, he escorted his people to Kansas. On the chief's return trip, he became ill and passed away in Lafayette. Chief Francis Lafontaine was the last federally recognized chief in Indiana. From the time Lafontaine died to present, the Miami people of Indiana have fought to regain their recognition.

In 1848, Peru was incorporated, and the first train rolled into Peru in 1854. The Central Canal, that was proposed to operate from Indianapolis to Peru in 1839, failed one year later. Since that time, the people of Miami County longed for a direct route from Peru to the state capital. Several prominent men in Peru came together to form the Peru and Indianapolis Railroad. Trains would continue to run in and out of Peru on this line for the next 140 years. Although the last train ran out of Peru in 1992, there are still sections of this line in operation today.

When the Civil War broke out in 1861, the young men of Peru anxiously stood in line to be mustered into the Union army. From Gen. Ulysses S. Grant's siege on Vicksburg, George Meade's battle at Gettysburg, and William Tecumseh Sherman's march to the sea, the young men of Peru fought for the Union in nearly every major battle in the eastern theater. The Civil War was a turning point in American history. The hundreds of thousands of men who marched and fought across the country would learn much in their ventures, and upon returning home after the war, they were eager to apply their lessons. In the postwar years, Peru would see many changes. Log cabins were replaced by framed and brick homes and brick buildings were erected on Broadway. Telegraph lines and another railroad were added. Over the next 20 years, Peru would see many improvements, and there would be little sign of the pioneer village that it once was. Even the Wabash and Erie Canal had outlived its usefulness and the water had become still and stagnant. The local townspeople were using the canal for no more than a landfill.

By the 1880s, the Civil War generation had grown up, rebuilt the country, and started the Industrial Revolution. They built fortunes and created empires, and during this time period, the first circus was launched in Peru. Benjamin E. Wallace was discharged from the Union army and returned to Peru eager to put the war behind him and become a successful local businessman. Wallace entered into the livery business at the corner of Miami and Second Streets. He did very well in the business and soon owned the largest livery in town. In the early 1880s, Wallace acquired some circus equipment from a circus that had been in the area and fallen on hard times. This must have given Wallace the bug because he began buying animals and circus equipment from other circuses that had failed. Soon he had collected enough equipment and animals to launch his own show. All was well until January 25, 1884, when a fire broke out in the building where Wallace kept his animals and stored equipment. The loss totaled more than $2,000 in animals and equipment, but it did not destroy his dream. Wallace and his partner, James Anderson, quickly began replacing the equipment and animals. On April 26, 1884, Wallace and Company's Great World Menageries, Grand International Mardi Gras, Highway Holiday Hidalgo and Alliance of Noveltics opened in Peru. The show did so well that on May 1, 1884, the *Miami County Sentinel* printed on the front page of the newspaper, "The Wallace and Company Show was advised on its next visit to Peru to bring a canvas of sufficient dimensions to hold the population of Miami County."

# *One*

# The Great Wallace Shows

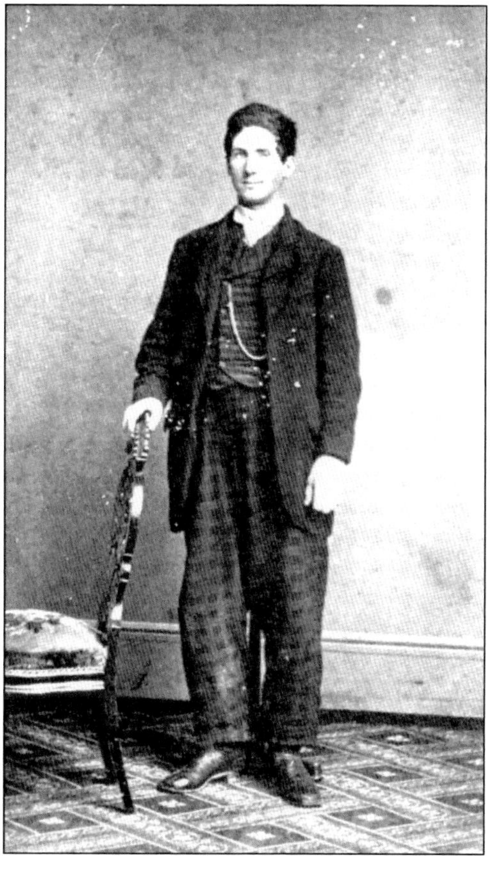

Benjamin E. Wallace, age 21, discharged from the Union army and was eager to take his place in the local business community. The look of confidence and ambition is clearly written on his face. In the years to come Wallace not only would become the "Circus King," but he would start the Wabash Valley Trust Company, partner in the Senger Dry Goods Company, own many farms, and build over a dozen homes in Peru.

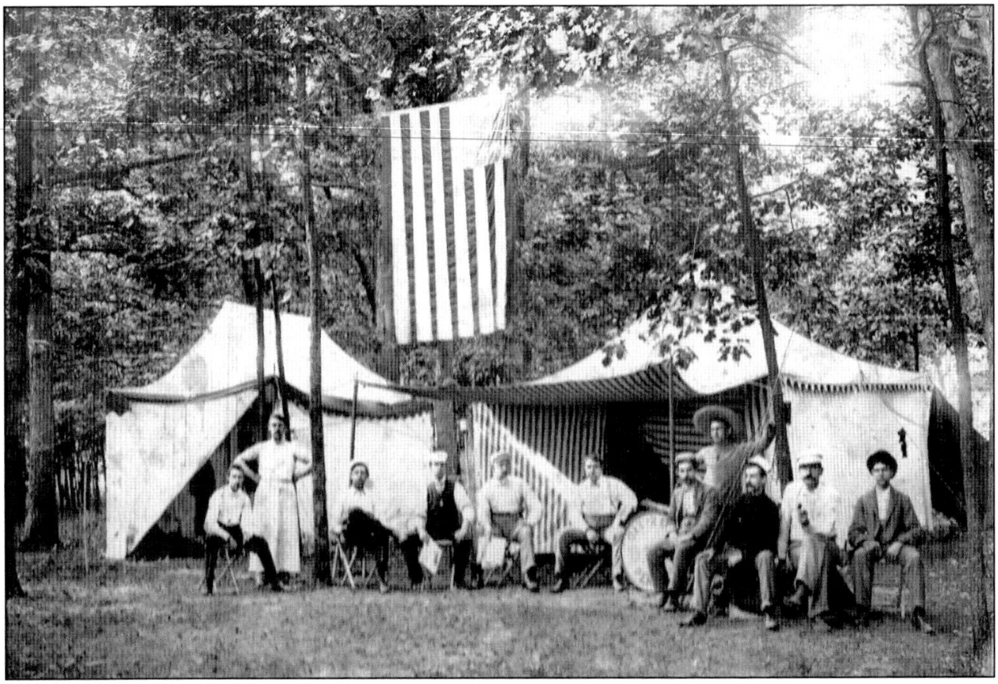

Opening day of Wallace and Company's Great World Menageries, Grand International Mardi Gras, Highway Holiday Hidalgo and Alliance of Novelties was on April 26, 1884; the Peru 3rd Regiment Band dressed in new uniforms and marched in a parade before thousands of spectators. The matinee was a sell-out. Management quickly arranged for additional seating for the sold-out evening performance. The Peru 3rd Regiment Band would open the Wallace and Company's Great World Menageries and International Circus in Peru for many years to come.

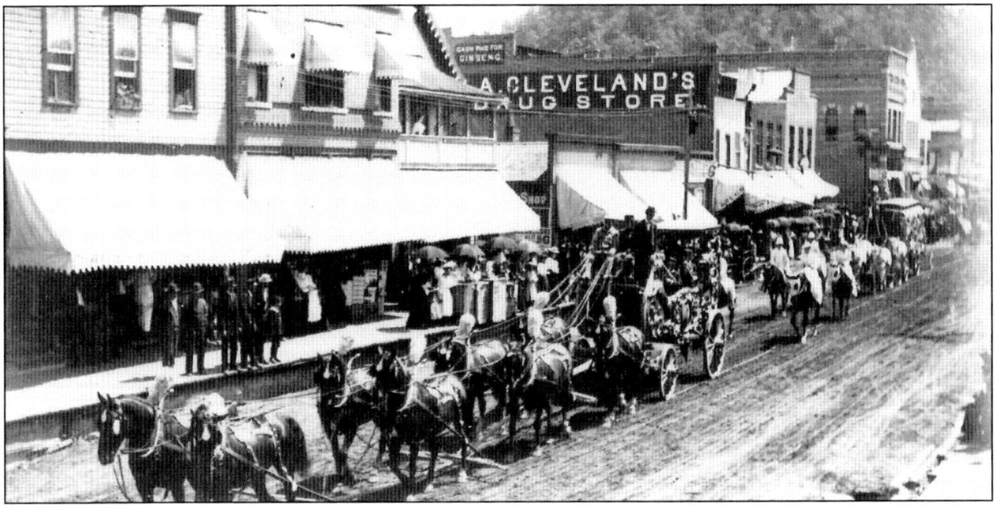


In 1884, the Wallace and Company's Great World Menageries, Grand International Mardi Gras, Highway Holiday Hidalgo and Alliance of Novelties left Peru by horse and wagon, touring Indiana, Kentucky, and Virginia. The show was received well at all stops, and after a profitable first season, the show came back to Peru to winter. The 1884 season was also the first season for Benjamin E. Wallace's competition, the Ringling Brothers Circus and Buffalo Bill's Wild West Show.

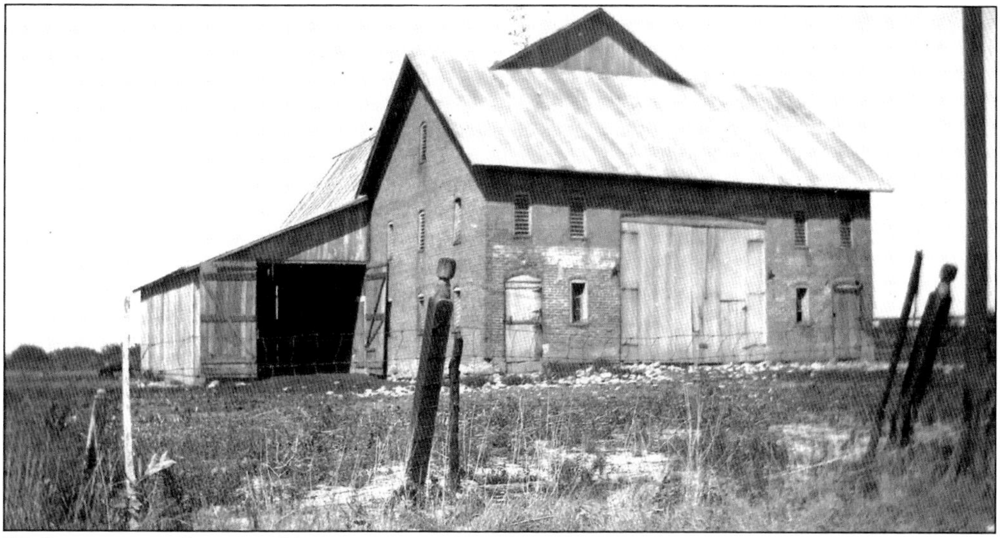

Wallace wintered some of his circus animals on his farm east of town in Butler Township, considered to be the first winter quarters. Other animals were put up in the old Peru and Indianapolis Railroad shops at Third and Lafayette Streets. Wallace was already planning the next season. He wanted the show to be bigger, better, and grander than the first.

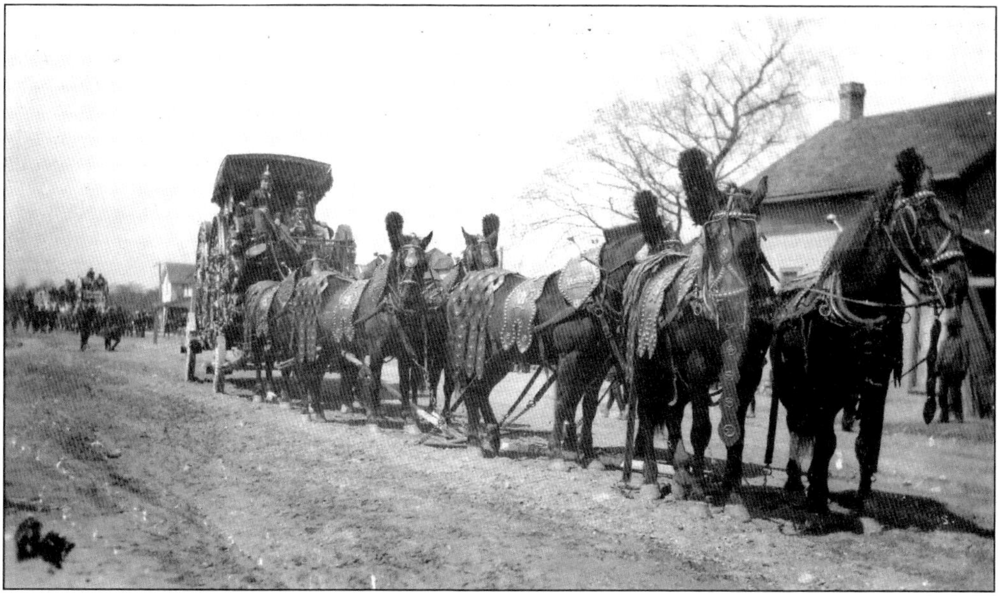

The 1885 season again opened in Peru on a rainy, muddy day. There was no parade, but the shows were well attended and met everyone's expectations. The circus would tour by horse and wagon for its second season. The shows were profitable, went off without a hitch, and returned to Peru to winter.

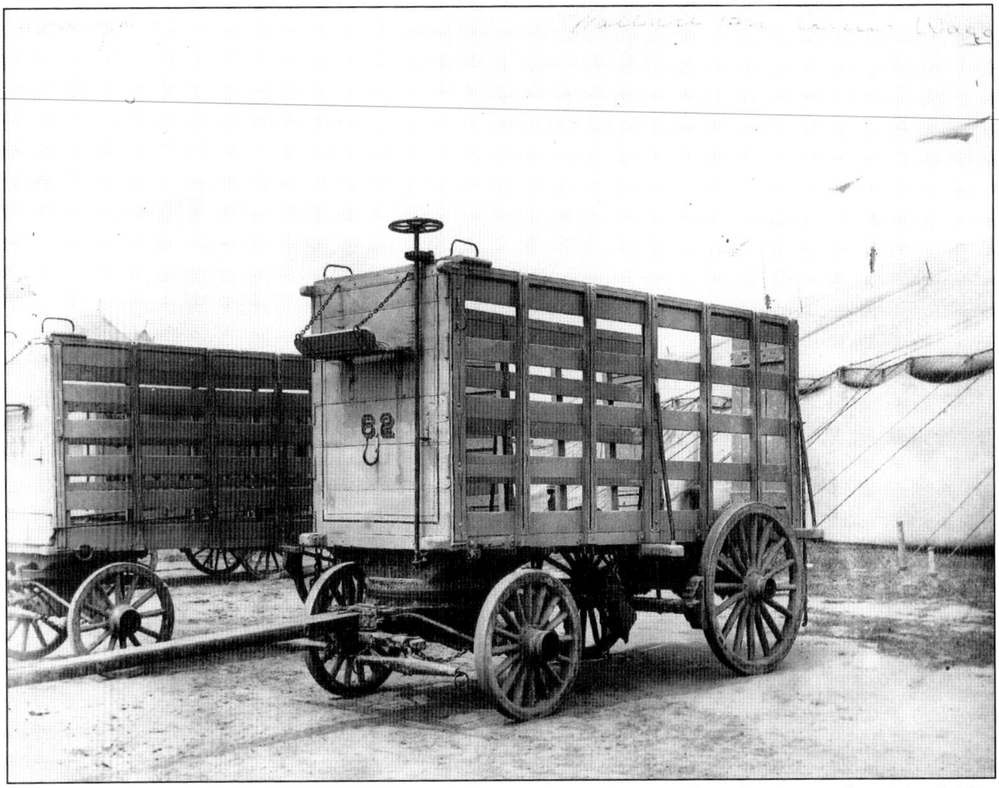

In the spring of 1886, the Great Wallace Shows left Peru on 15 railroad cars. Each car had "the Great Wallace Shows" painted on the side. The circus could now reach more and bigger markets, ensuring its profitability. The circus was beginning to make quite a name for itself.

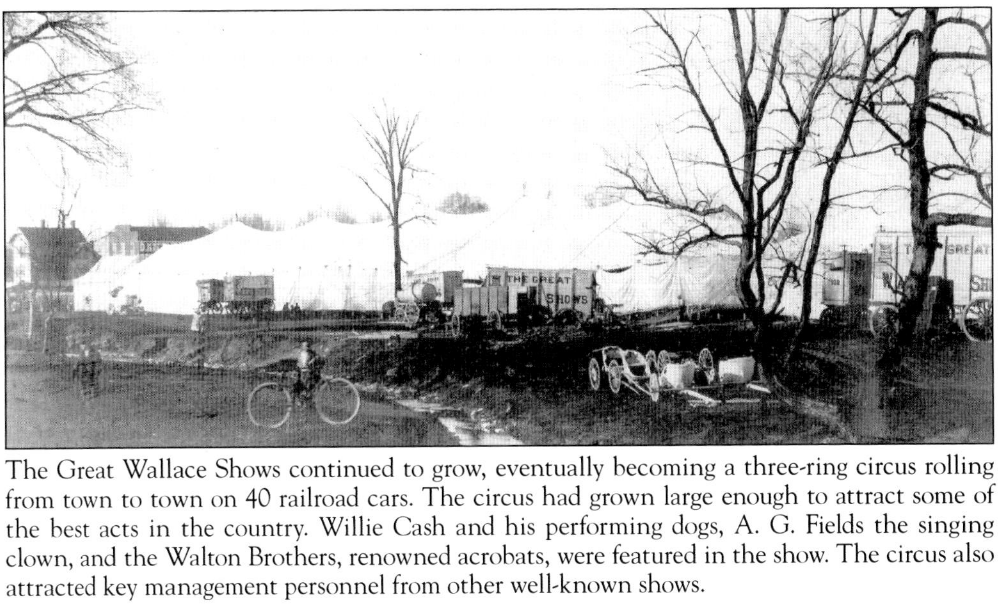

The Great Wallace Shows continued to grow, eventually becoming a three-ring circus rolling from town to town on 40 railroad cars. The circus had grown large enough to attract some of the best acts in the country. Willie Cash and his performing dogs, A. G. Fields the singing clown, and the Walton Brothers, renowned acrobats, were featured in the show. The circus also attracted key management personnel from other well-known shows.

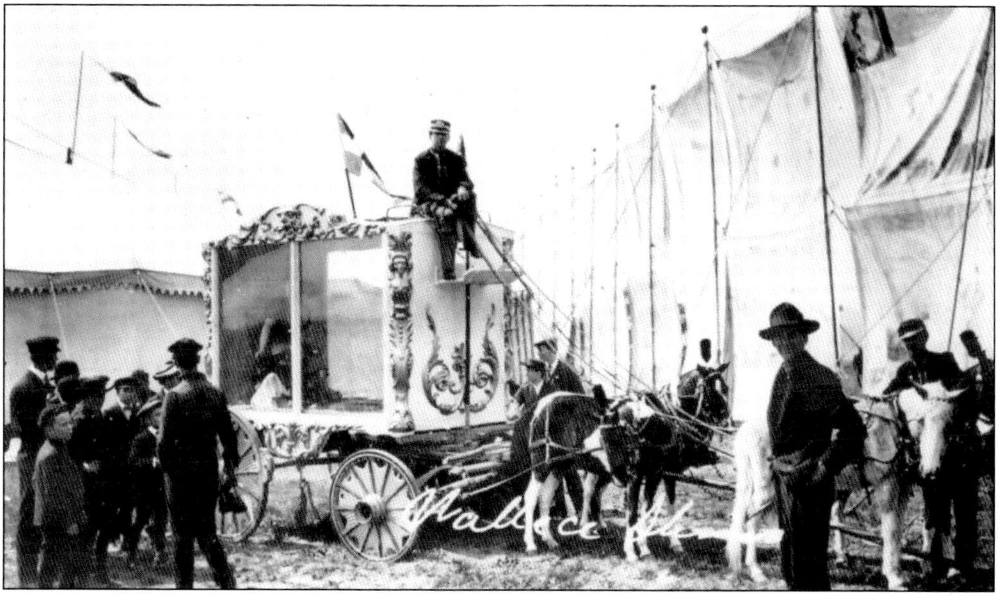

Benjamin E. Wallace bought out his partner, James Anderson, in 1890 and became the sole owner and manager of the show. Anderson returned to Columbus, Ohio, where he was the chief of police for several years. Wallace was reinvesting his profits and had plans to buy a farm large enough to build a winter quarters where he could house, repair, and manage his circus each winter.

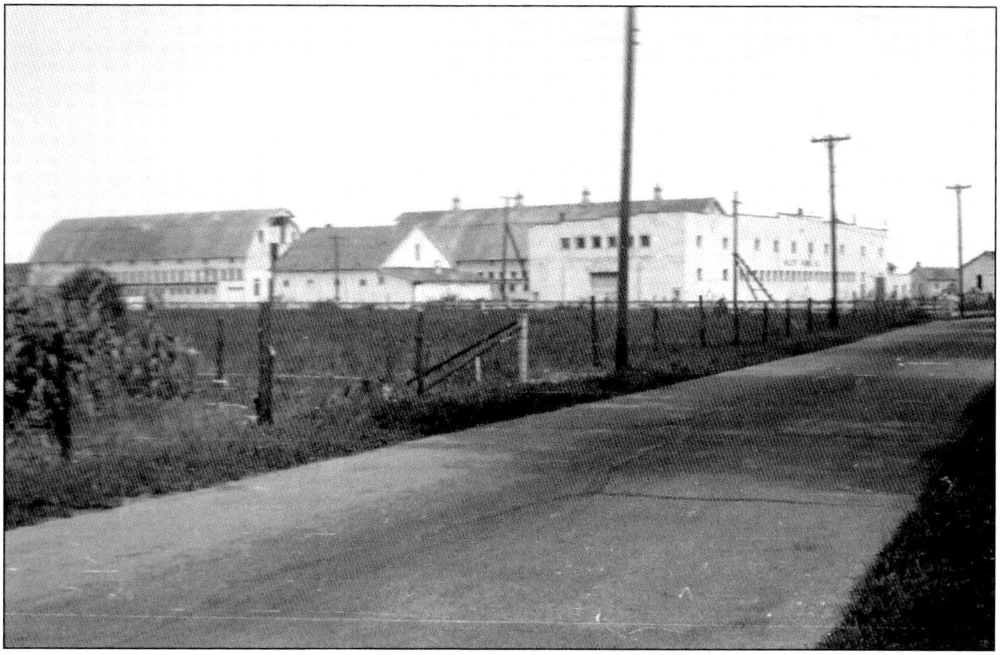

In 1892, Wallace bought 220 acres along the bank of the Mississinewa River. The last Miami Indian war chief, Francis Godfroy, originally owned this land. He had left it to his son, Gabriel Godfroy, who sold it to Wallace. Wallace would erect many barns and buildings on the property over the years, including a cat barn, an elephant barn, a wagon shed, a carpenter shop, and even a foundry. All the buildings were painted yellow.

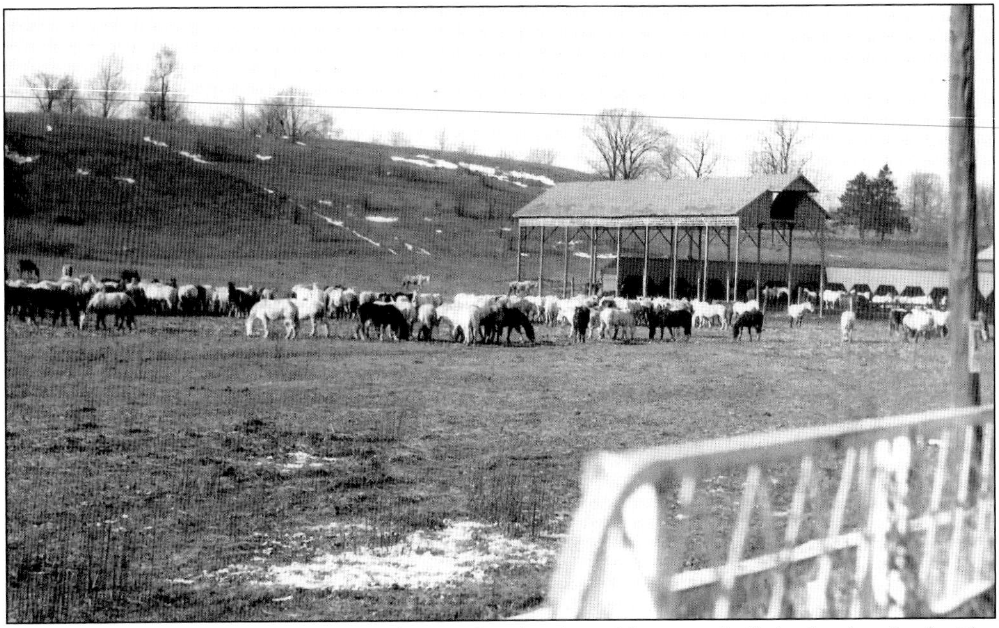

Benjamin E. Wallace would continue buying farmland until he owned all the land on both sides of the road between the new winter quarters and the eastern edge of Peru—more than two miles away. The land was needed for growing crops to feed his large menagerie and hundreds of horses. He also built many houses for his employees along the way.

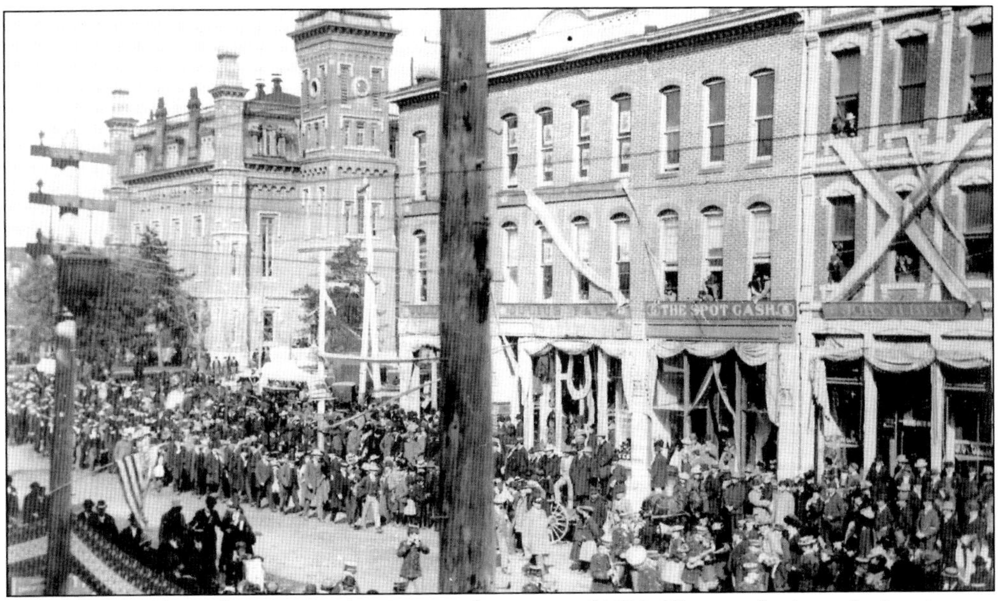


The Great Wallace Shows opened in Peru in the spring of 1892. The parade through the city was the largest and grandest the town had ever witnessed. In eight short years, the Great Wallace Shows had become one of the most respected circuses in the country. It would again leave Peru by rail. Continuing to receive great reviews, it was said that the show was the cleanest and classiest that ever traveled and, furthermore, that no act would shock the modest or cause a blush.

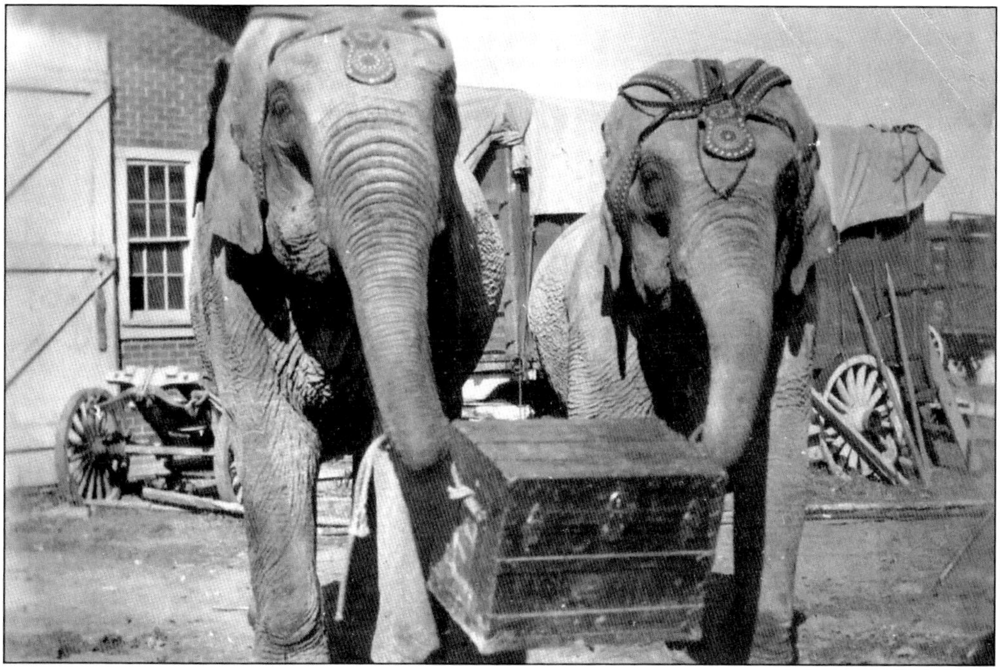

At this time Wallace owned eight elephants—four males and four females. The females were rented to other shows during the circus season. However, Gipsy returned early to the winter quarters after her summer engagement with another show. Four bull elephants were pining for her attention while they were chained in the barn. A tussle broke out, and one elephant was knocked through a brick wall, suffering many battle wounds and a broken tusk. They all took a beating that day although none won Gipsy's affection.

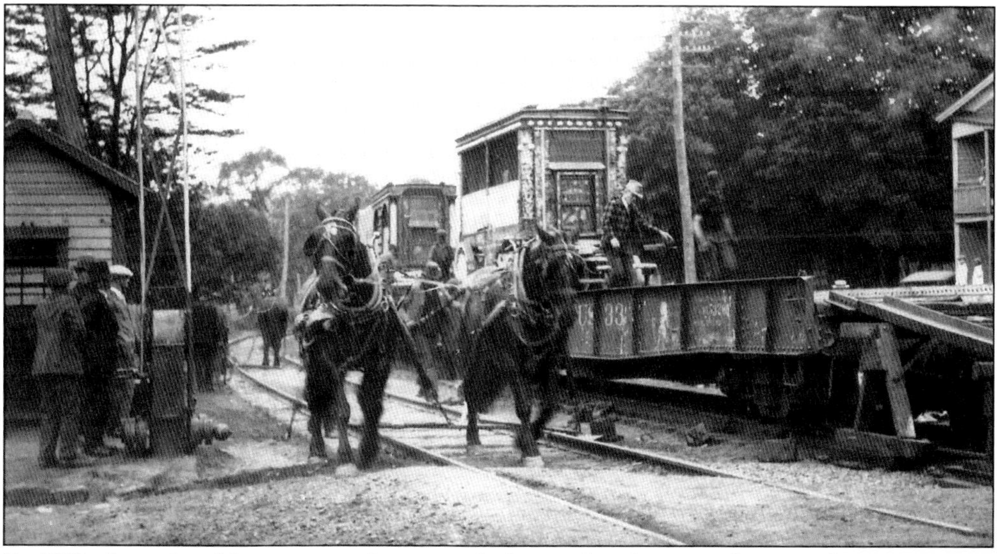

By 1900, the railroad business was booming. In fact, railroads, interurbans, and streetcars were springing up all across the country. Circuses were given rates in five-car increments. The average steam engine of the day could pull 40–45 cars and travel at about 40 miles per hour. Compared to the speed that the horse and wagon shows traveled, this was lightning fast. Circuses could now perform before a sold-out crowd in a new city every day.

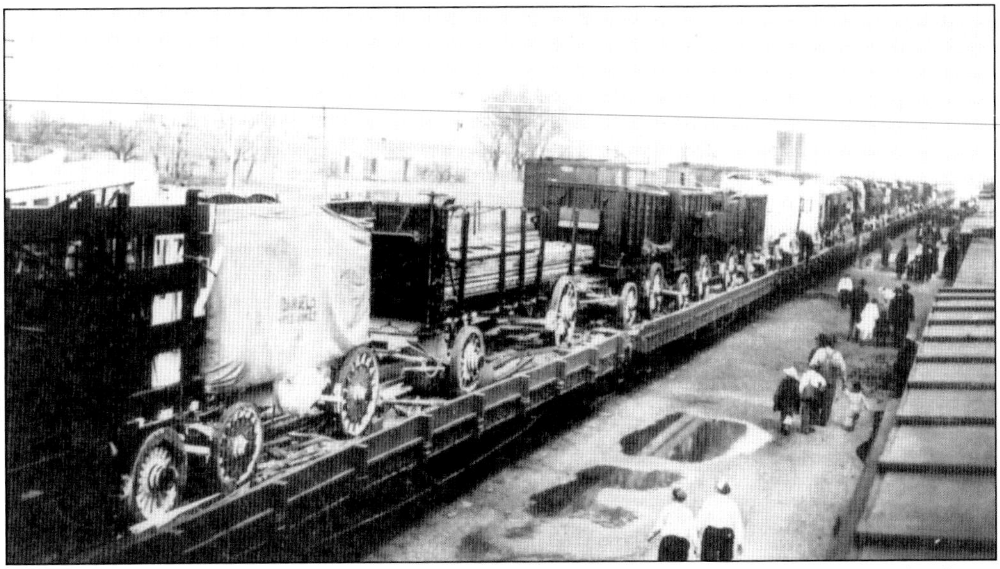

Traveling by rail was not without risk. On August 7, 1903, the Wallace Show was involved in a horrific train wreck in Durant, Michigan. Twenty-four circus employees were killed as well as a variety of livestock. With great sorrow, Benjamin E. Wallace personally supervised the salvage of the wreck. By telephone, Wallace was able to acquire staff and livestock and put his show back on the road, missing only two engagements.

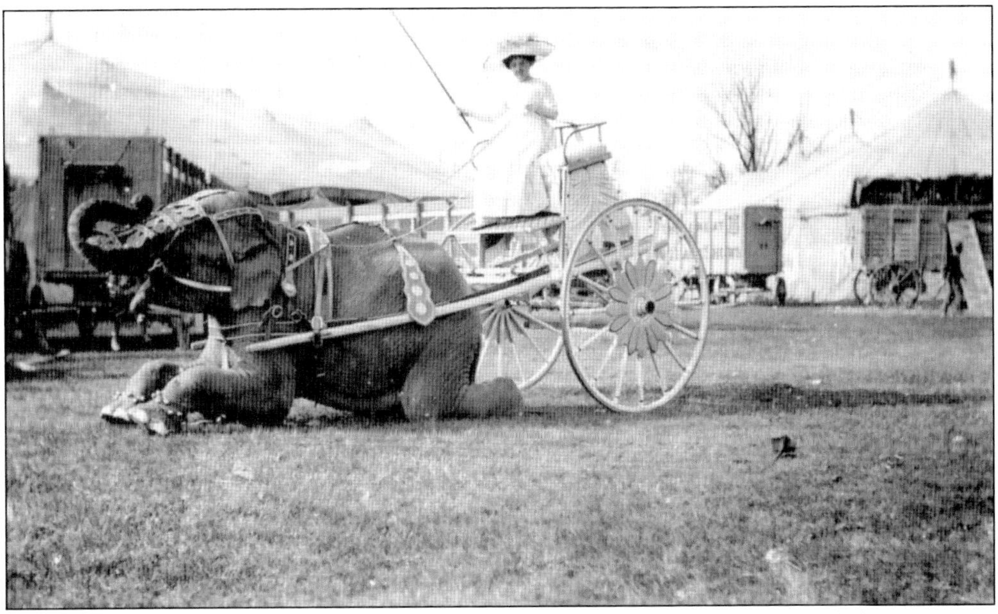

With his show back on schedule, Benjamin E. Wallace returned to Peru and filed suit against the Grand Trunk and Western Railroad, claiming it was directly responsible for the accident. Wallace argued that he lost $48,000 in equipment and livestock and an additional $10,000 each for the two engagements missed. Train wrecks and derailments would haunt nearly every major circus in America for the next 50 years.

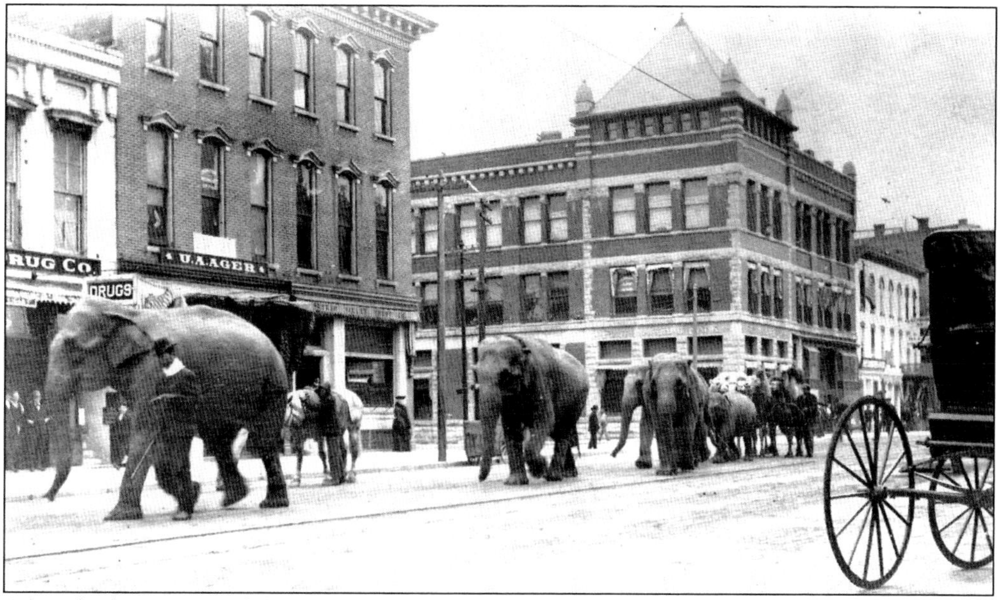


After the beginning of the 20th century, Wallace had a tiff with the Peru National Bank. It decided it no longer wanted to count the thousands of nickels shipped back from the circus in kegs marked "nails." Wallace's solution was to open the Wabash Valley Trust Company and count his own nickels. The bank would stay in operation for more than 80 years.

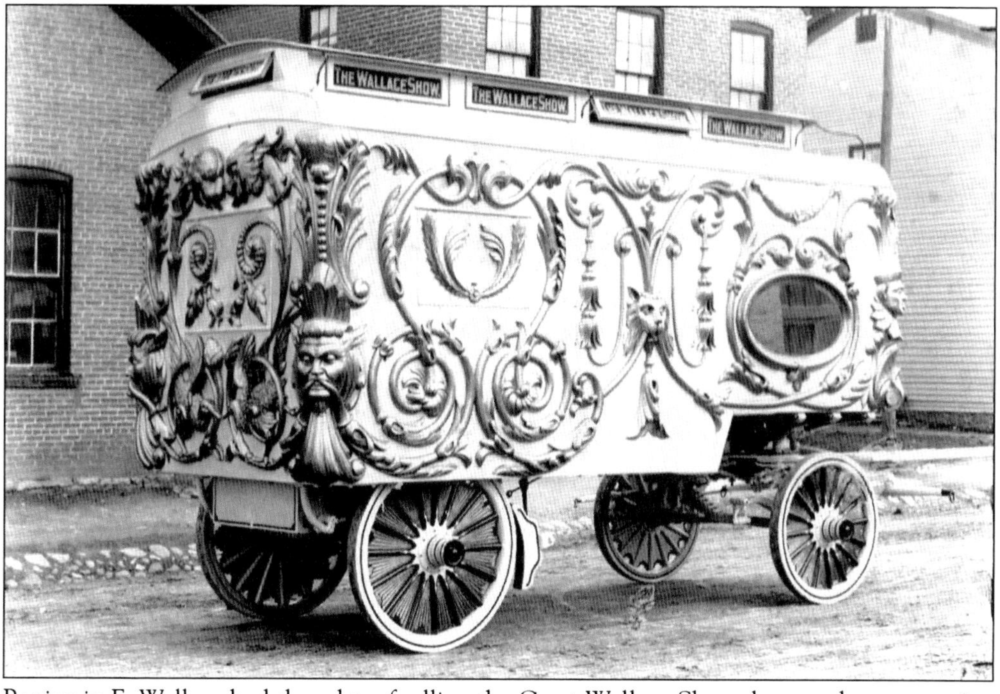


Benjamin E. Wallace had thoughts of selling the Great Wallace Shows because he was nearing 60 years old, and, besides, the show was now worth a small fortune. He could easily sell the show and, with his other interests, live very comfortably the rest of his life. And although he had in fact put his circus up for sale, within weeks he would make the biggest deal of his life and earn his title "Circus King."

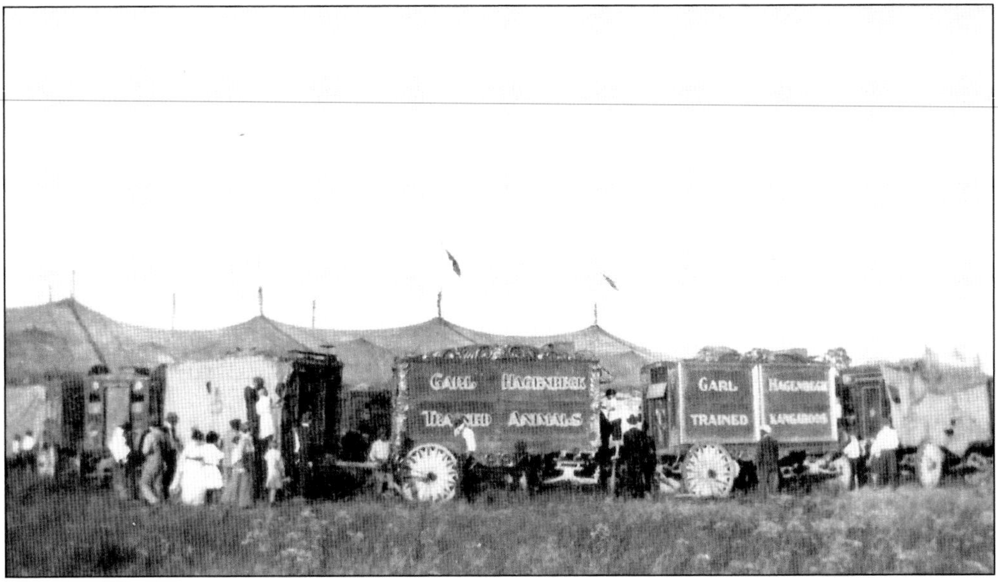


In January 1907, Benjamin E. Wallace closed a deal that would give him controlling interest in the Carl Hagenbeck Circus. The Hagenbeck was internationally renowned and featured the finest menagerie in the world. Merging with the Hagenbeck created one of the largest circuses ever to tour the country. It took three 30-car trains to move the combined show.

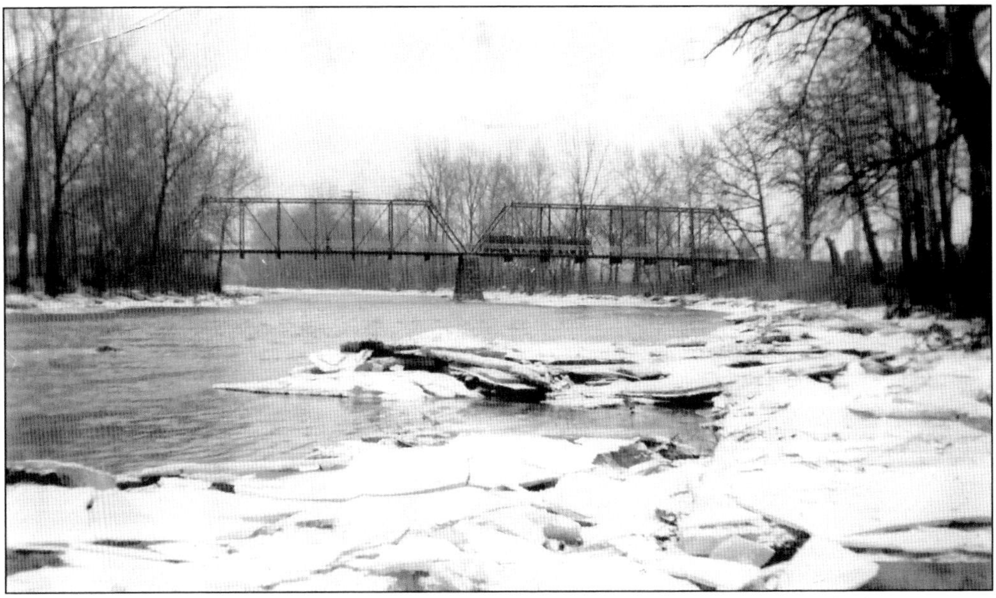

With much work to be done before opening day, Wallace ordered the Hagenbeck show to Peru. Canvases were enlarged and new buildings were built at the winter quarters. The 58 railcars that had moved the Hagenbeck show were painted and repaired. The animals were paraded down Broadway to the winter quarters. When the 16 Hagenbeck elephants entered the barn, a fight broke out with Wallace's 5 elephants, and much damage was done to the barn and elephants before the handlers stopped the brawl.

# *Two*

# HAGENBECK-WALLACE CIRCUS

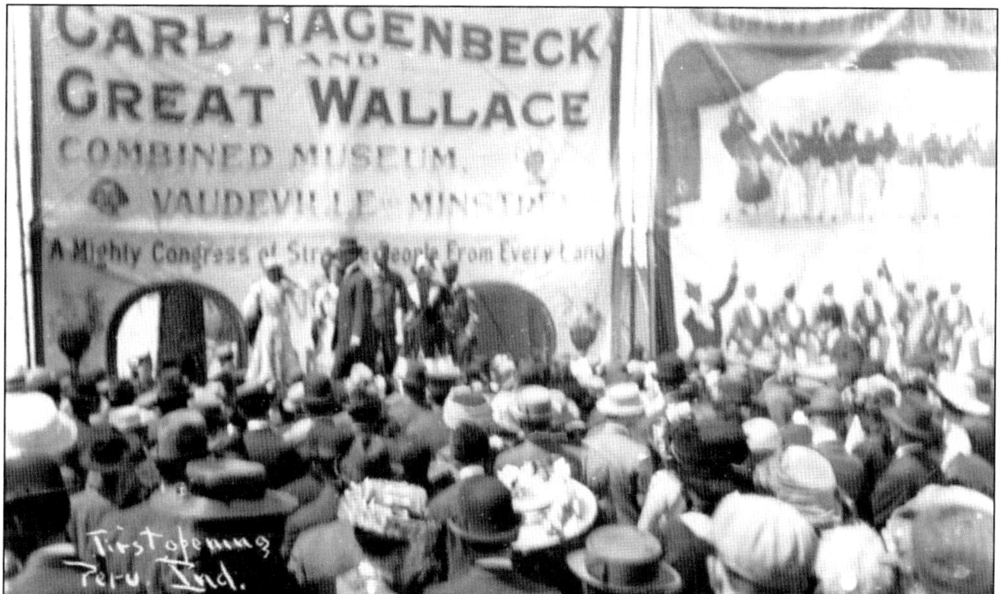


In the spring of 1907, Benjamin E. Wallace owned the grandest circuses in the country. By the fall of 1907, the Ringling brothers purchased the Barnum and Bailey Circus. The Ringling brothers would not combine the two giant shows until the season of 1919. The show would tour with the title Ringling Brothers and Barnum and Bailey Circus for the next 90 years.

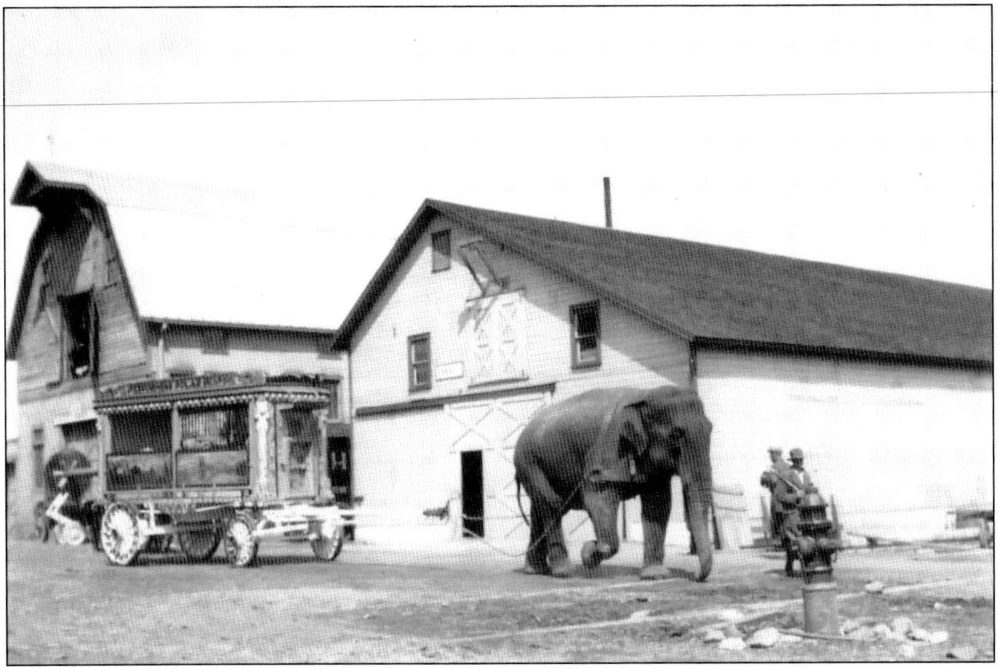

While the winter quarters was busy preparing for opening day of the new Hagenbeck-Wallace Circus, Carl Hagenbeck had taken legal action against Benjamin E. Wallace. Hagenbeck argued that his partners made a deal without his knowledge and Wallace had bought the animals and equipment but not the Hagenbeck name. The court ruled in Wallace's favor and the Hagenbeck-Wallace Circus opened in Peru as planned in the spring of 1907.

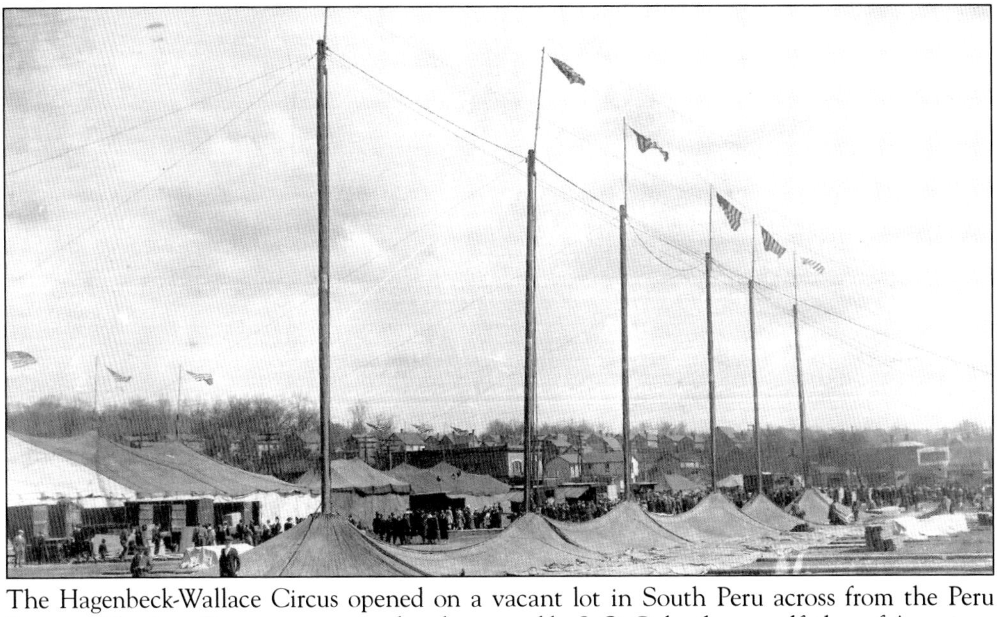

The Hagenbeck-Wallace Circus opened on a vacant lot in South Peru across from the Peru Brewery. The Peru Brewery was owned and operated by J. O. Cole, the grandfather of American music legend Cole Porter. Like most little boys, Cole loved the circus, watching the parades on Broadway and visiting the winter quarters. Marsh Hometown Market now occupies the circus lot.

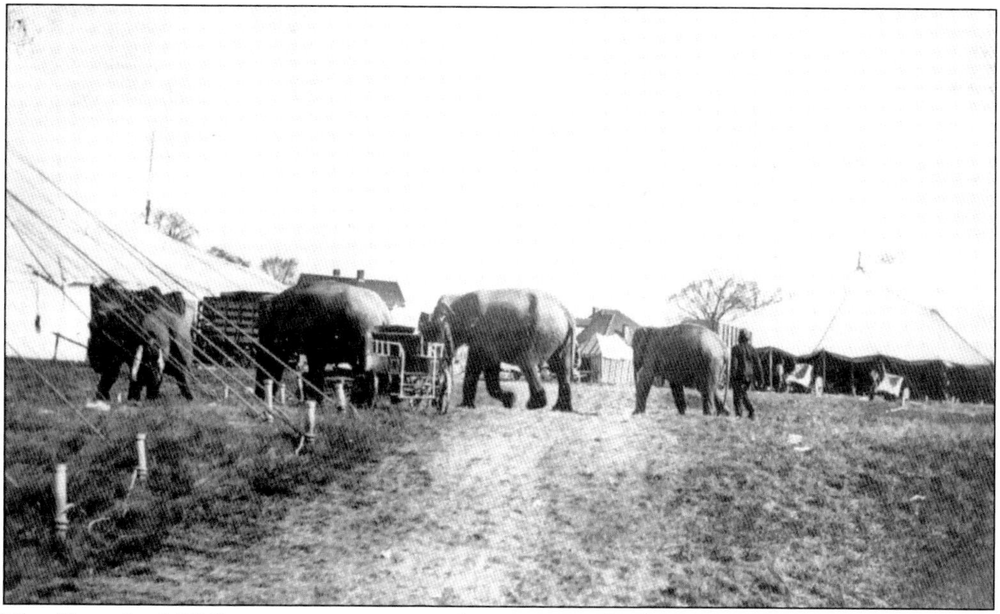

The Hagenbeck-Wallace was a tent city when set up. The big top was 500 feet long with a hippodrome track, three rings, and two stages. The menagerie tent was 400 feet long plus there were tents for dining, wardrobe and dressing rooms, a sideshow, and much more. More than 1,000 men, women, and children traveled with the circus each season.

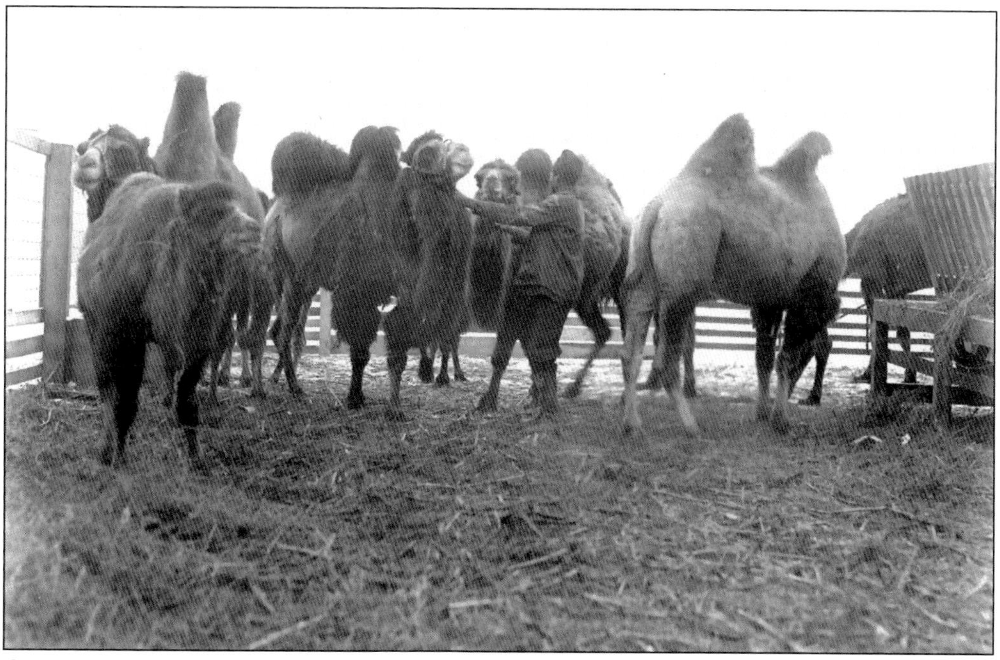

Operating a circus the size of the Hagenbeck-Wallace was a feat in itself. Every day, in each new town, scores of animals and hundreds of employees had to be fed. The animals were fed tons of hay and grain each day, meat was butchered for the cats, and hundreds of employees visited the mess tent when its flag was flying. The circus became so proficient that the U.S. Army studied its traveling routines.

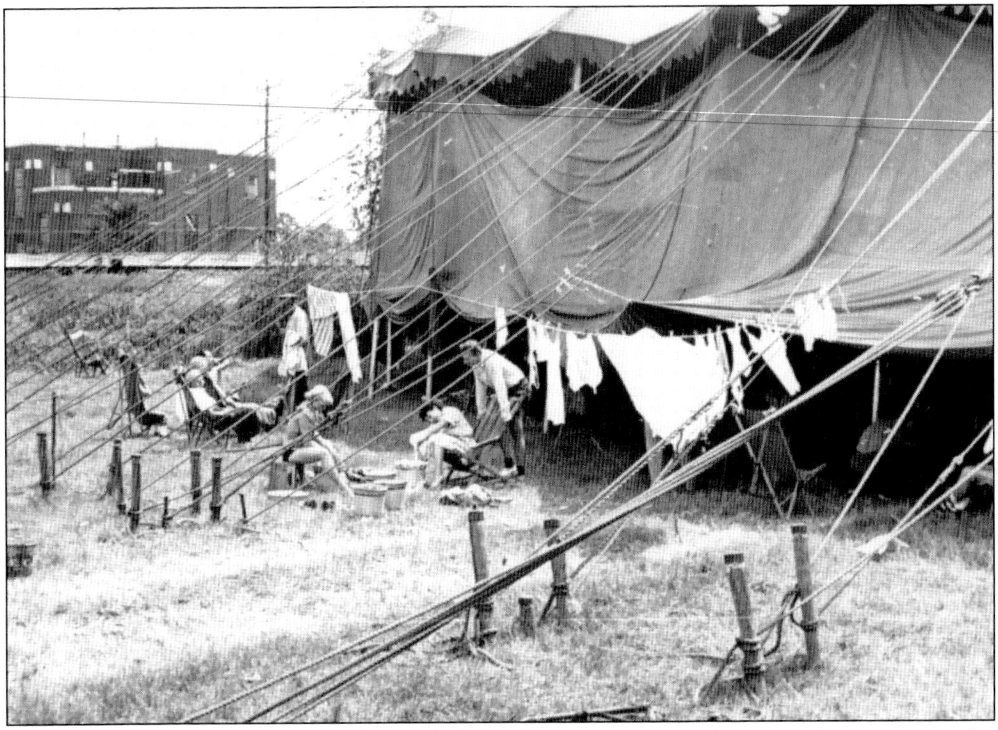

There were few conveniences on the road. Some performers got to sleep in a sleeper car on the train while the roustabouts sometimes slept in or under a wagon. When there was time to bathe, it was most often done with a bucket of water and, if lucky, it might be warm. Laundry was done as needed between shows and hung in the back lot to dry. It was most important that the costumes be kept clean.

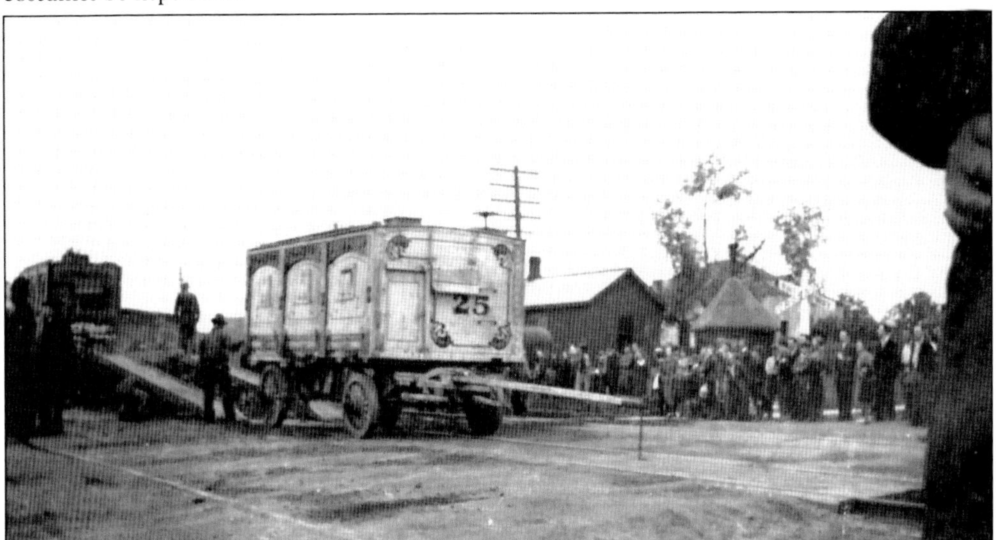


After the evening performance, the tents came down and everything was put back on the wagons and returned to the rail yards. The animals, wagons, and performers were all quickly loaded and left for the next engagement. By sunrise there was scarcely a sign that a circus had been to town. It was the same routine day after day and month after month with few days off.

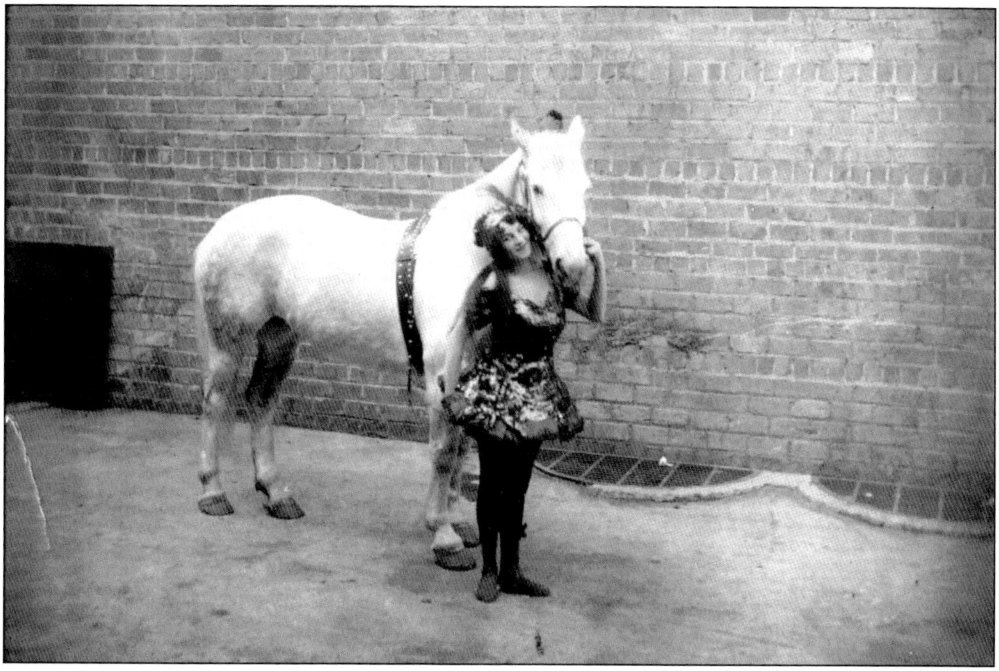

By the end of the season, the tents, wagons, equipment, and costumes were in need of repair. Upon returning to the winter quarters in the fall, work began immediately on the neglected property. Some performers moved on, while others rehearsed new acts for the upcoming season. The winter quarters was a very busy place in the off-season. Men were on the property 24 hours a day keeping the hundreds of animals warm and fed.

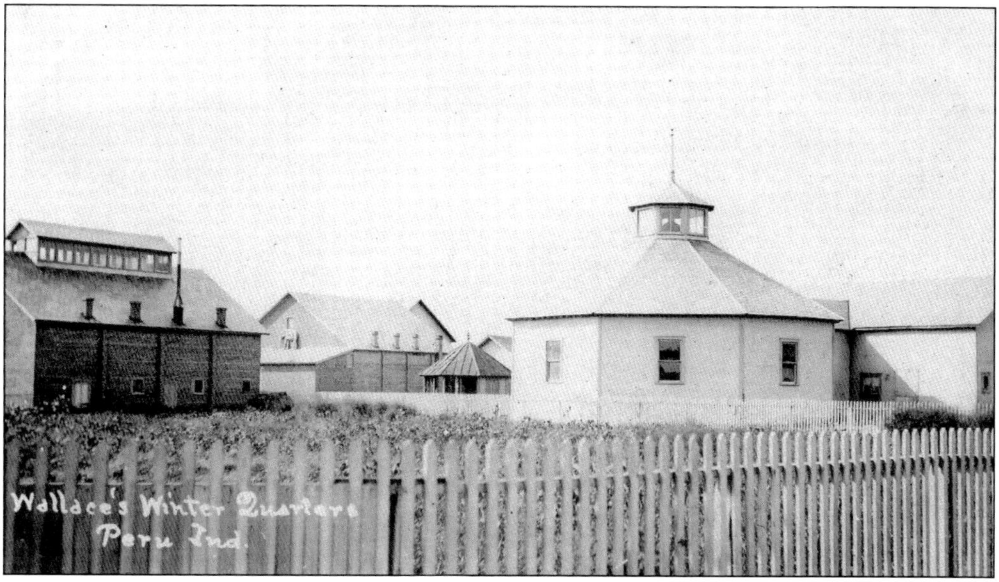


The winter quarters had more than 30 barns, sheds, and shelters built for every purpose and animal imaginable. Building No. 5 was for ostriches and giraffes; No. 8 was for camels, tigers, lions, and a harness shop. There were buildings for all the equipment and rigging, wagon sheds, and a wagon repair shop. Building No. 23 housed a paint shop, a clubroom, a hospital, and even a barbershop.

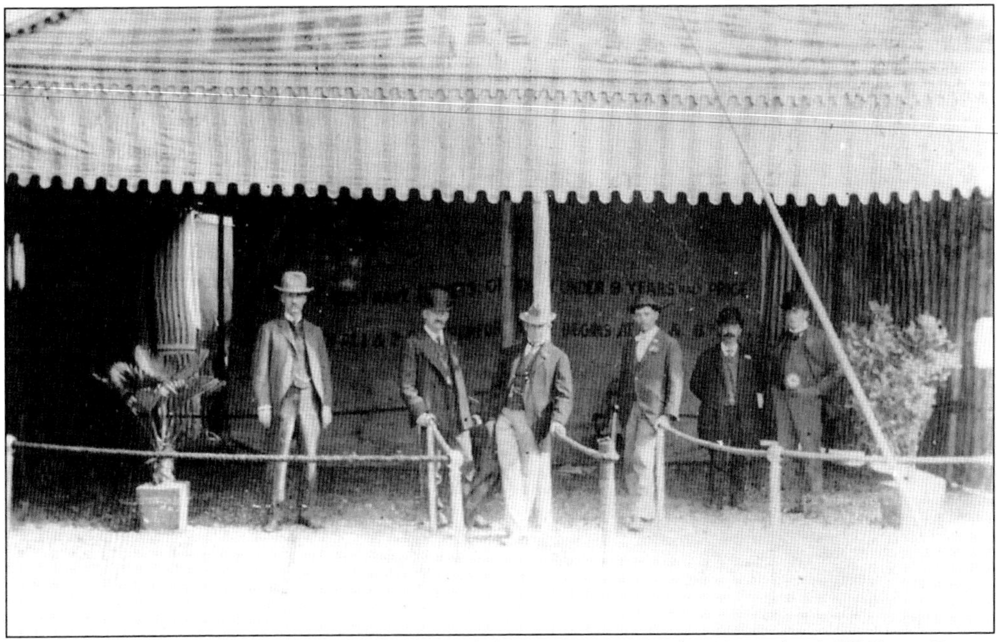

Benjamin E. Wallace (far left) bought out all his investors in the Hagenbeck-Wallace Circus except for John C. Talbot of Denver, Colorado. Wallace was without exception the most successful showman in the world. His cunning business sense had paid off in spades, and he was now enjoying the best years of his career. But nothing would prepare Wallace for the tragedy that was about to strike.

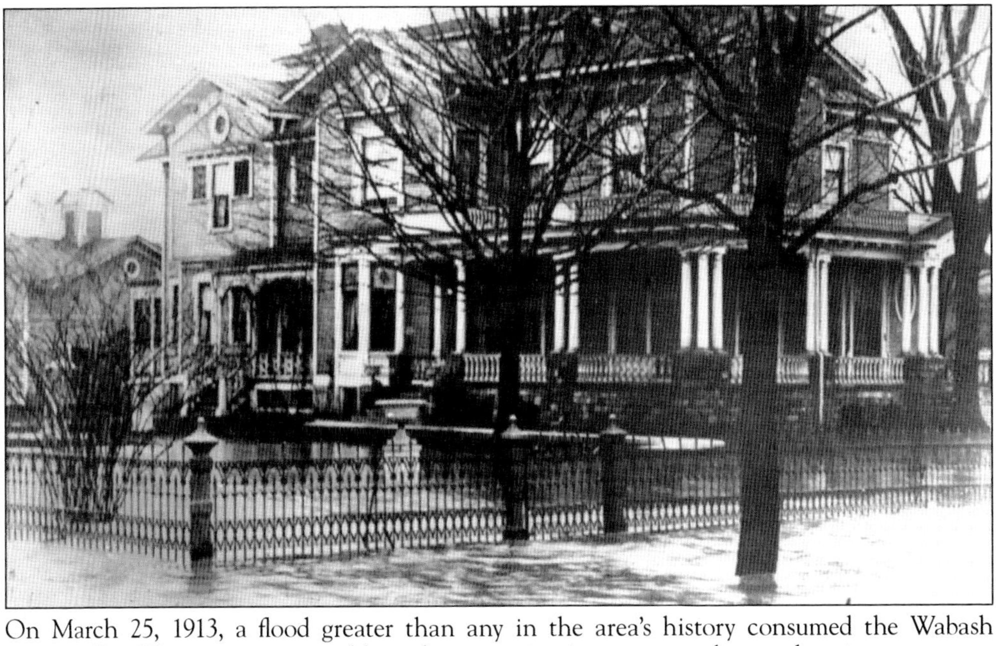

On March 25, 1913, a flood greater than any in the area's history consumed the Wabash River valley. The water rose quickly and communication was soon lost at the winter quarters. The water was knee deep around Wallace's house on Broadway in Peru. Wallace feared the worst; the Hagenbeck-Wallace Circus, all the circus animals, and 75 men were trapped at the winter quarters.

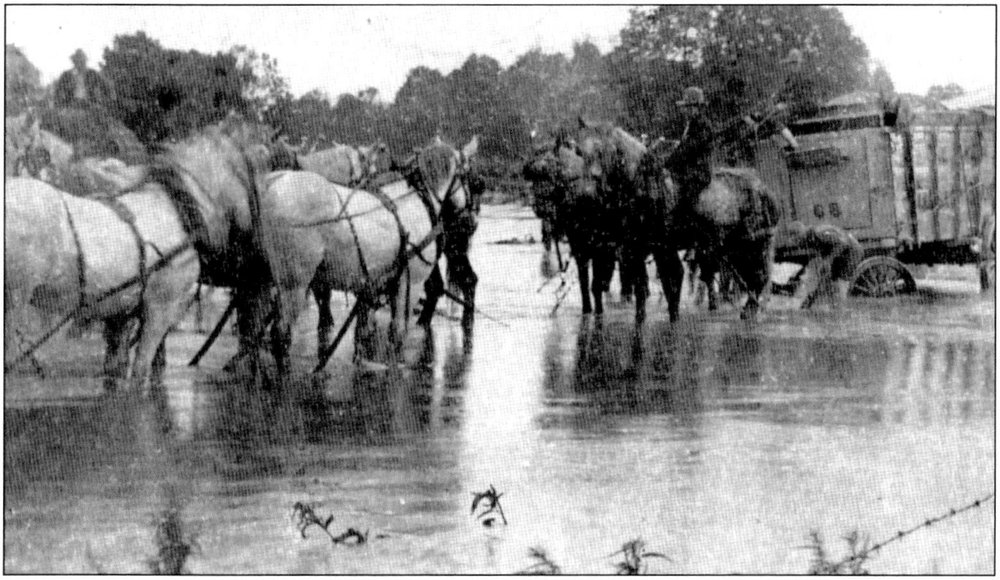

At the winter quarters, the water was rising several inches an hour. The workers did all they could to free the animals. The elephants were chained to the floor, and when the workers set them free, the water was waist deep. Nellie carried the handler back to the brick house as some of the elephants followed. The elephants made a futile attempt to enter the house. The handlers watched as the elephants succumbed to the raging water.

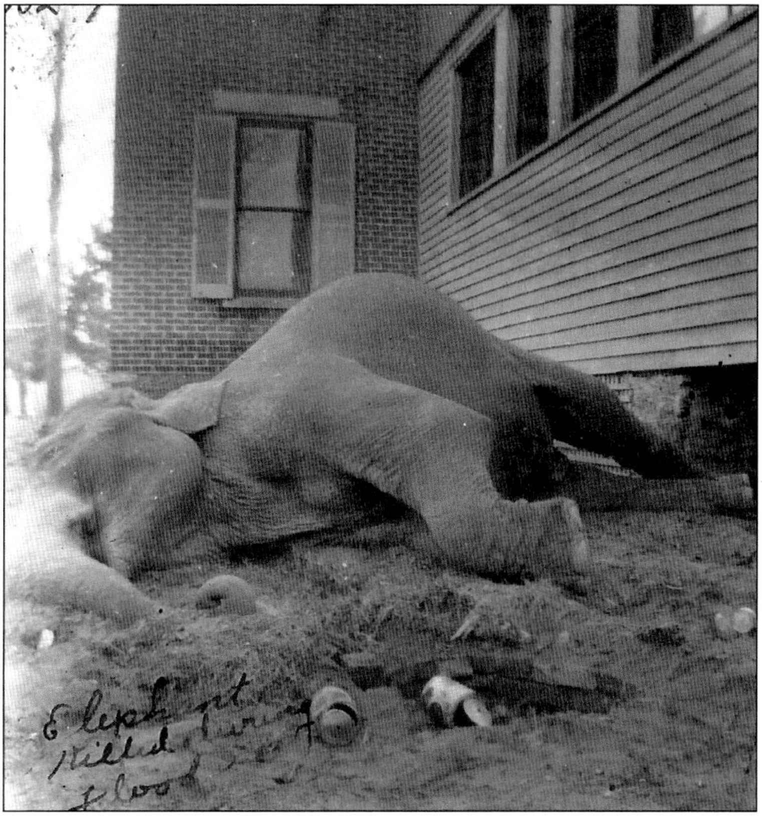

When the water finally receded, they found four dead elephants within a few feet of the house, one dead in the barn, and three others washed downstream. The handlers were happy to see that most of the horses survived. Three camels and three lions were also found alive. The only animal that was no worse for wear was Big George the hippo. He emerged from the river with a big smile as if he had been on vacation.

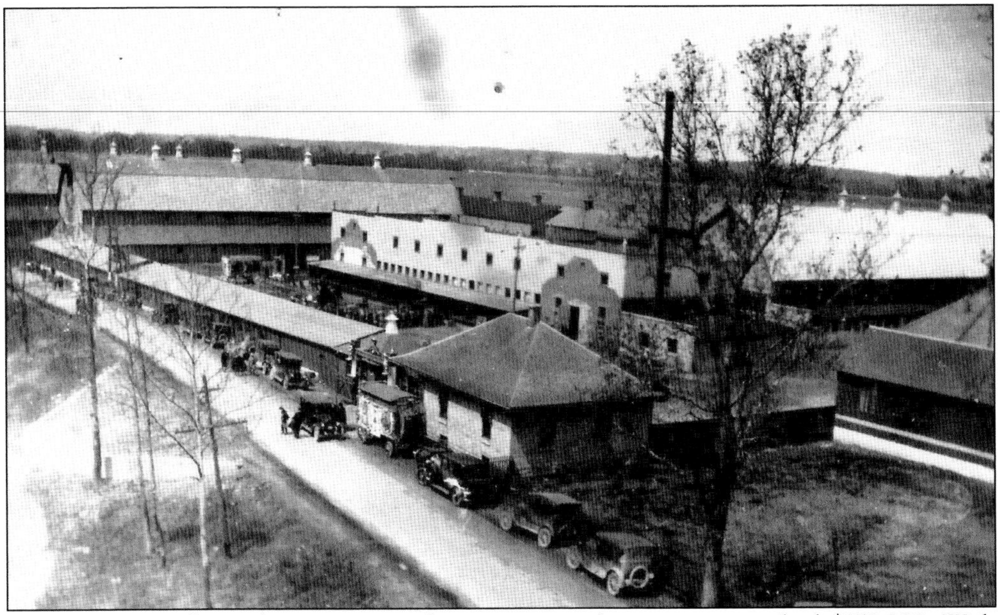

Benjamin E. Wallace's losses in animals, property, and equipment reached $150,000. With opening day only a few weeks away, it looked as if it might have been the end of the great show. Wasting no time, Wallace ordered the repair of the damaged equipment and leased animals so the show could open. Showing no signs of distress, the great show left the winter quarters to tour the 1913 season.

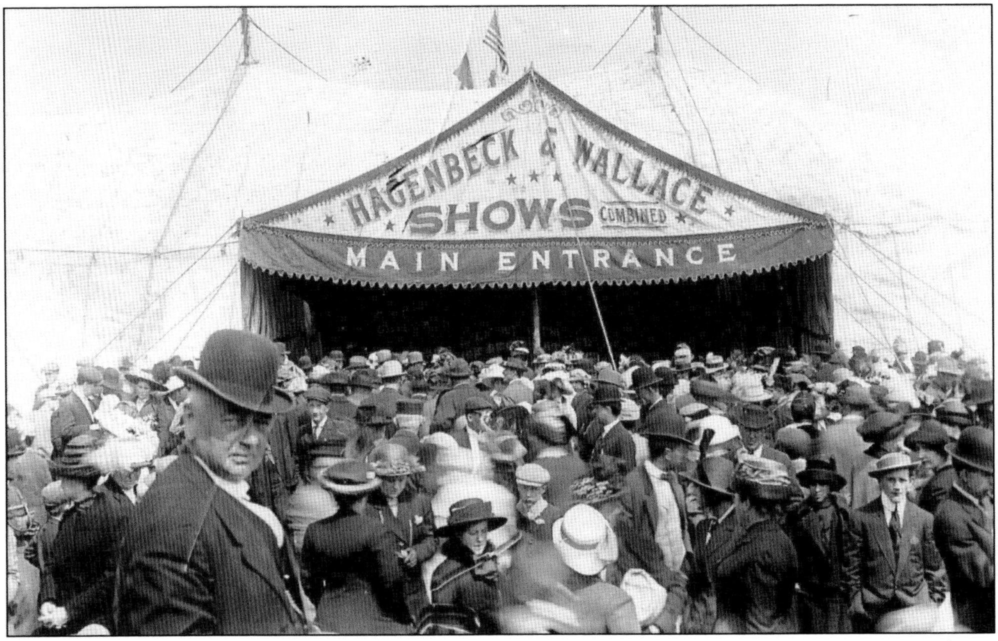


On June 30, 1913, Wallace sold the Hagenbeck-Wallace Circus to an interest in southern Indiana. There were rumors that the great show would not return to Peru. A reporter from the *Peru Evening Journal* asked Wallace if the show would winter elsewhere. Wallace replied, "Is the *Journal* going to move out of the city? The *Journal* is not moving and neither is the circus." As promised, the circus did return to Peru.

*Three*

# The Winter Quarters

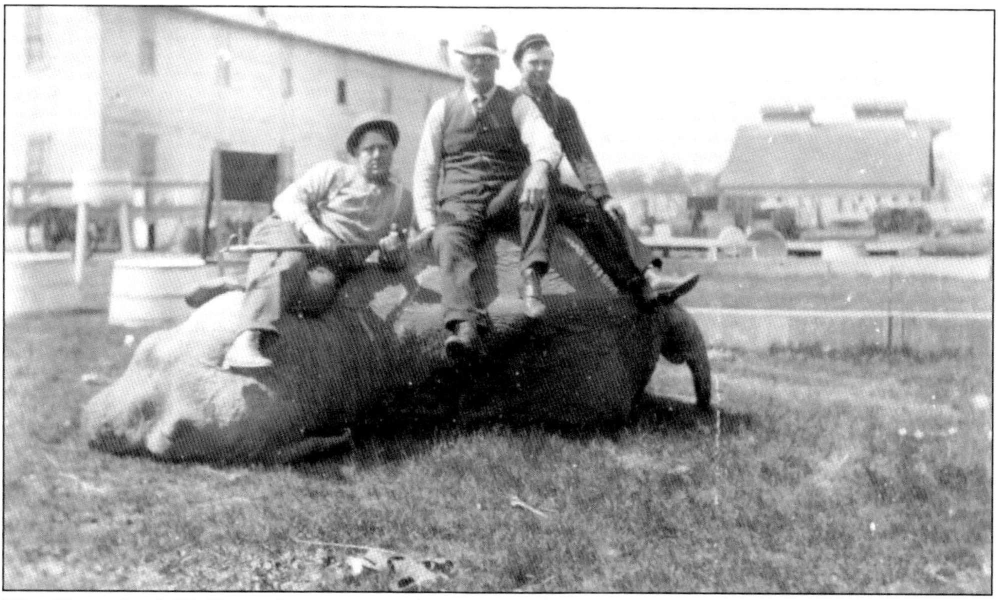

The Hagenbeck-Wallace Circus spent the winter of 1913–1914 in Peru. The new organization leased the second and third floors of the Wabash Valley Trust Company from Benjamin E. Wallace. The second floor was used as a business office, and the third was used as a wardrobe department. In the spring of 1914, the big show rolled out of Peru as it had so many times before. It was the last time Peru saw the circus for many years.

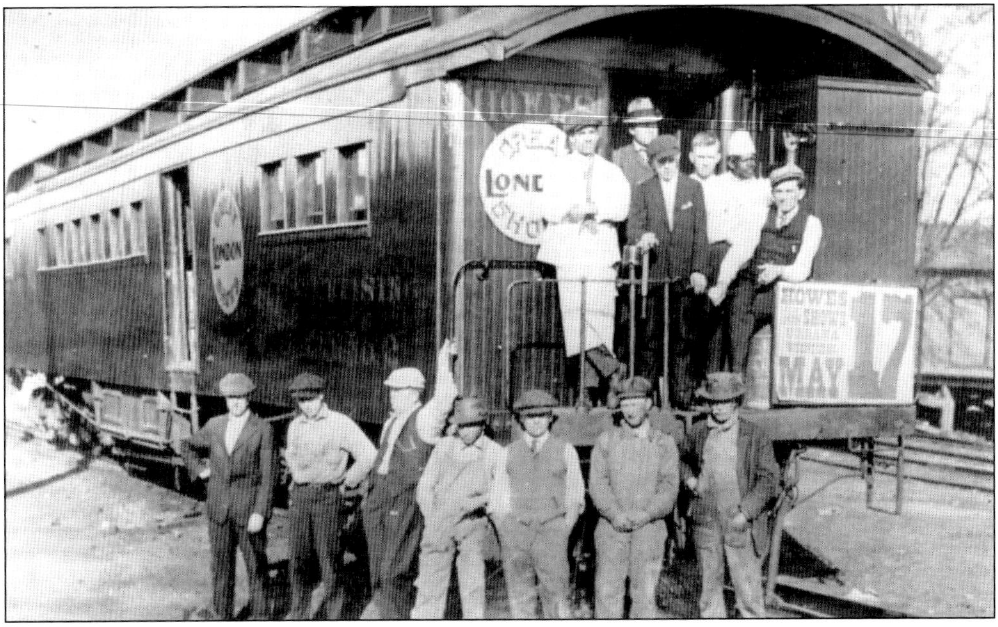



When the 1914 season ended, the Howe's Great London Shows rolled into town and marched to the Wallace winter quarters. Benjamin E. Wallace had rented the property to the owners of the Howe's Great London and Robinson's Famous Shows, Jeremiah Mugivan and Bert Bowers. The Robinson's show also wintered in Peru that year. The new owners of the Hagenbeck-Wallace Circus sent their circus to winter in Carthage, Ohio.

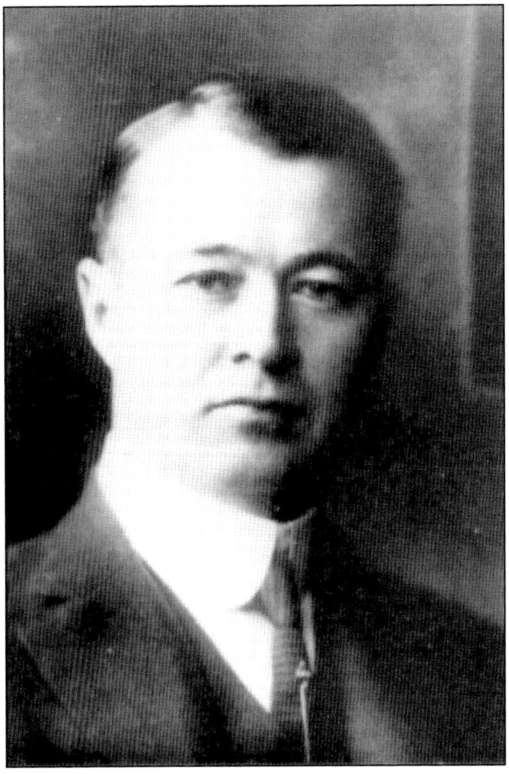

Jeremiah Mugivan was no stranger to Peru or to Wallace. Mugivan managed the dining car for the Great Wallace Shows in the 1901 and 1902 seasons. He had also bought animals and equipment from Wallace for his own circus venture. Mugivan and John Talbott later purchased half of the Great Wallace Shows, and Mugivan would also hold interest in the Hagenbeck-Wallace Circus.

Whenever one would hear Mugivan's name, Bert Bowers's name soon followed. Mugivan and Bowers were friends and partners since they trouped together with the Sanger and Lentz Show in 1893. These two men launched the Great Van Amburg Shows in 1904 and later changing the title to Howe's Great London Circus in 1908. Mugivan and Bowers were extraordinary showmen, and their partnership had an everlasting effect on the circus world.

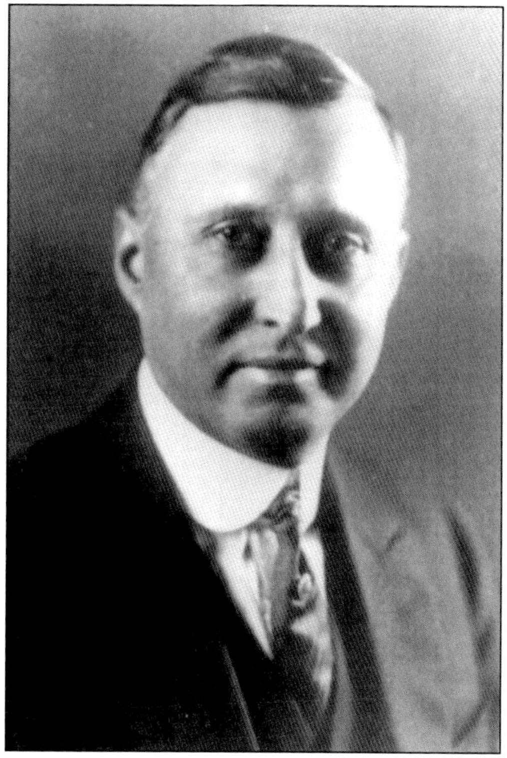

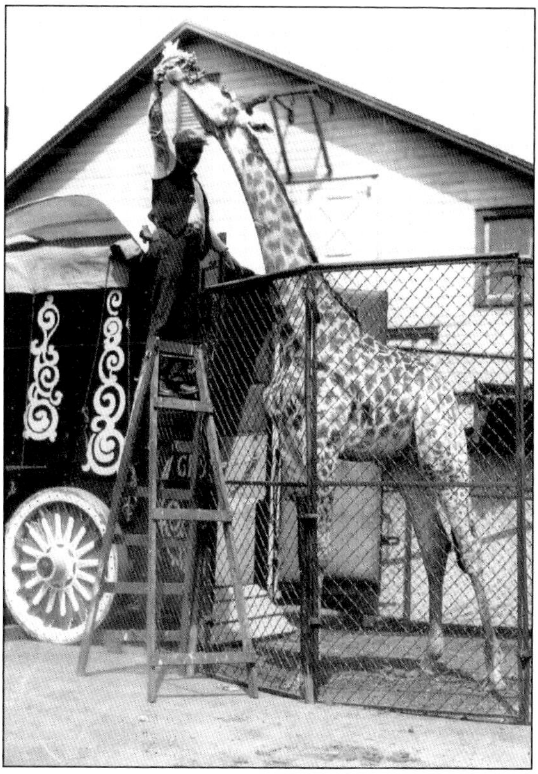

The winter of 1915–1916 marked the first time in 32 years that no circus came to winter in Peru. Mugivan's and Bowers's circuses wintered in Montgomery, Alabama, and the Hagenbeck-Wallace Circus wintered in its new West Baden home. Wallace continued to use the winter quarters for storing used equipment and keeping the animals that he leased to other shows.

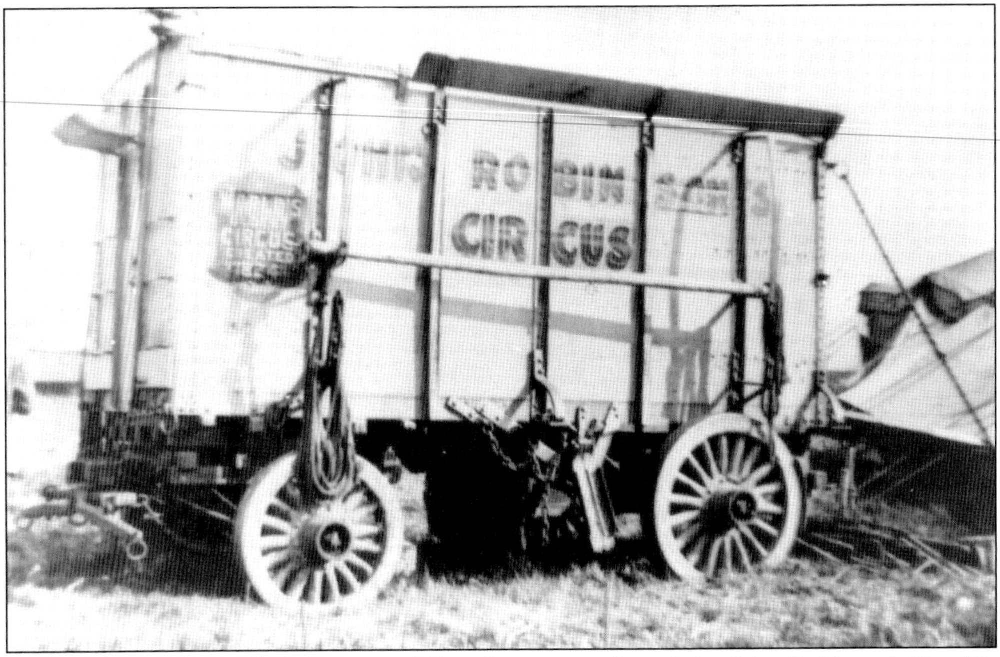

In March 1916, Jeremiah Mugivan and Bert Bowers purchased the John Robinson's Ten Big Shows and quickly sold the equipment from the Robinson's Famous Shows to Benjamin E. Wallace. Mugivan and Bowers considered the purchase a great deal. The equipment was in good shape and the name John Robinson's was respected and well known. At the end of the 1916 season, no circuses rolled into Peru, and the winter quarters was once again without a tenant.

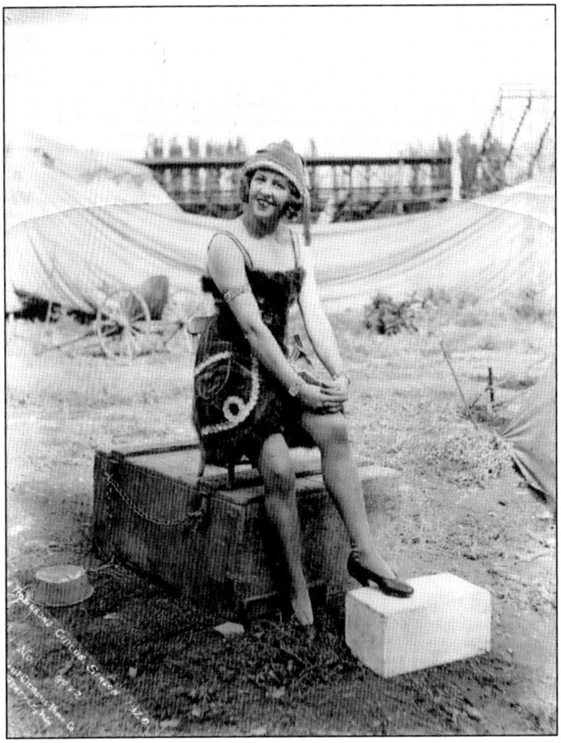

Mugivan and Bowers combined the Howe's Great London and the John Robinson's Ten Big Shows for the 1917 season. They titled the show the John Robinson's Circus and sent it out on 45 railcars. This was the largest circus the partners ever operated. That year the John Robinson's wintered in Peru at Wallace's winter quarters.

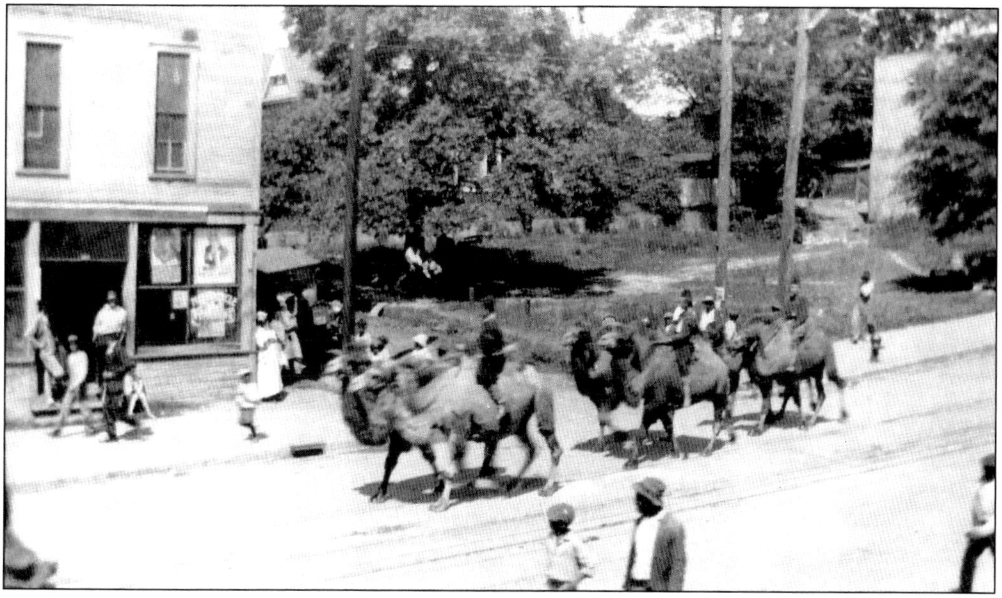

By the spring of 1918, the country was involved in World War I. The John Robinson's Circus rolled out of Peru on 30 railcars. The season was cut short in Elizabeth City, North Carolina, because of the Spanish flu epidemic. The show was once again sent to Peru to winter. While in Peru, Mugivan and Bowers purchased the Hagenbeck-Wallace Circus in a receiver's sale, following a horrific train wreck in northern Indiana that killed 84.

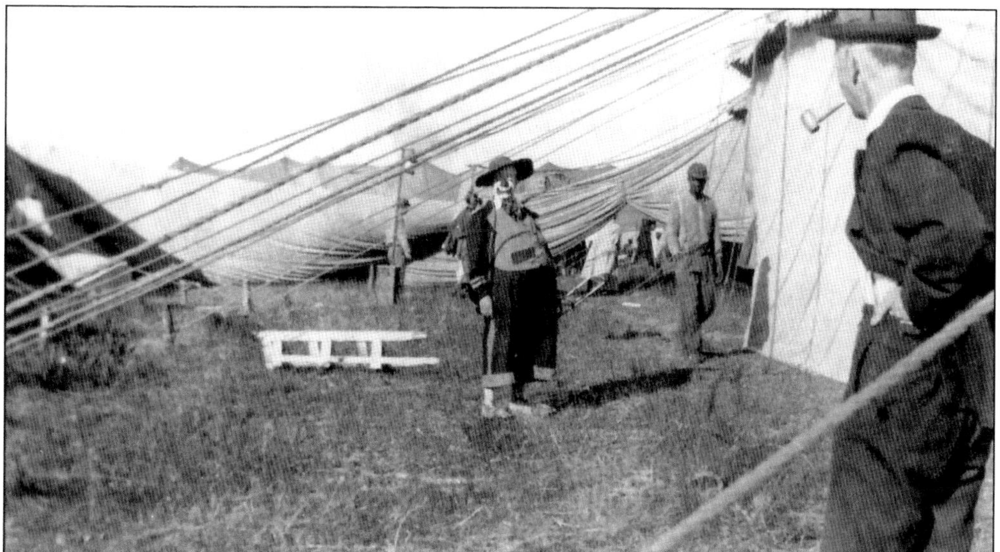

Mugivan and Bowers sent the John Robinson's Circus and the Hagenbeck Wallace Circus out as 30-car troupes for the 1919 season. Managed by Bert Bowers, the Hagenbeck-Wallace closed in Jackson, Tennessee, and the John Robinson's closed in Holly Springs, Mississippi. The John Robinson's returned to Peru, and the Hagenbeck-Wallace returned to West Baden.

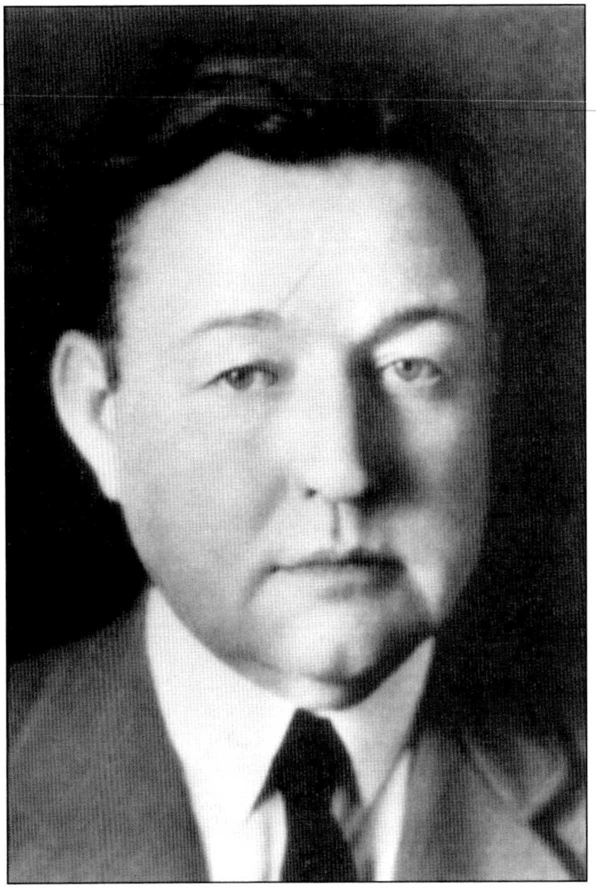

In late 1919, Edward M. Ballard partnered with Jeremiah Mugivan and Bert Bowers. Ballard secured his wealth operating casino resorts in French Lick. Ballard was one of the original members of the syndicate that bought the Hagenbeck-Wallace Circus from Benjamin E. Wallace in 1913. Over the next few years, Ballard bought out all his partners except for C. E. Corey, a nephew of Wallace.

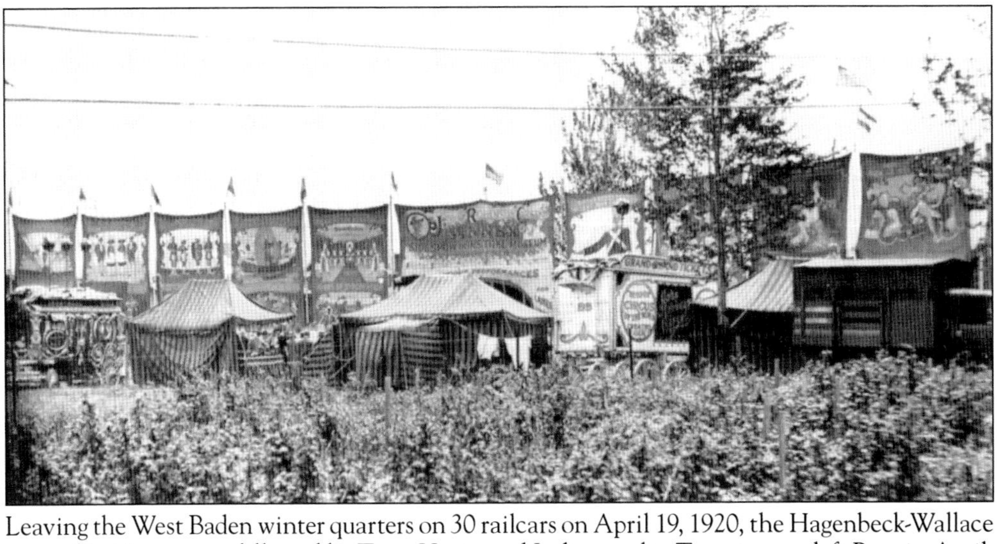

Leaving the West Baden winter quarters on 30 railcars on April 19, 1920, the Hagenbeck-Wallace opened in Vincennes, followed by Terre Haute and Indianapolis. Two circuses left Peru in April, the John Robinson's Circus on 30 railcars and the Howe's Great London Circus on 15 railcars. The three shows did very well that season and each returned to their previous winter quarters except for the Howe's Great London, which wintered in Missouri.

*Four*

# Birth of a Circus Empire

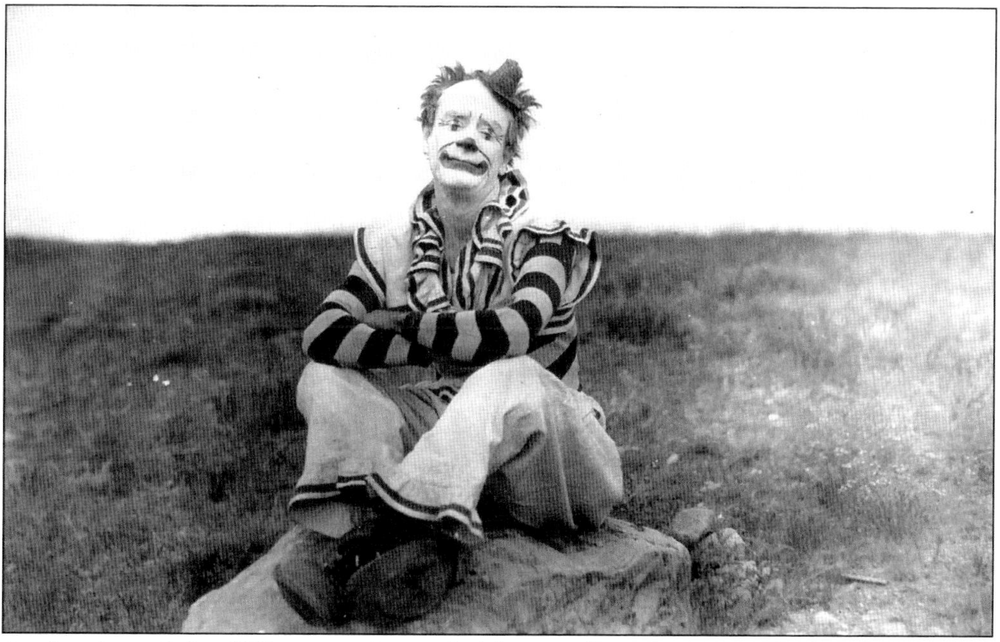

At the close of the 1920 season, Jeremiah Mugivan, Bert Bowers, and Edward M. Ballard purchased the Sells-Floto Circus, Yankee Robinson Circus, and Buffalo Bill's Wild West titles. Along with the Hagenbeck-Wallace Circus, John Robinson's Circus, Howe's Great London Circus, and Great Van Amburg Shows, the trio now held the titles to some of the largest circuses in America. These titles would be the makings of a true circus empire.

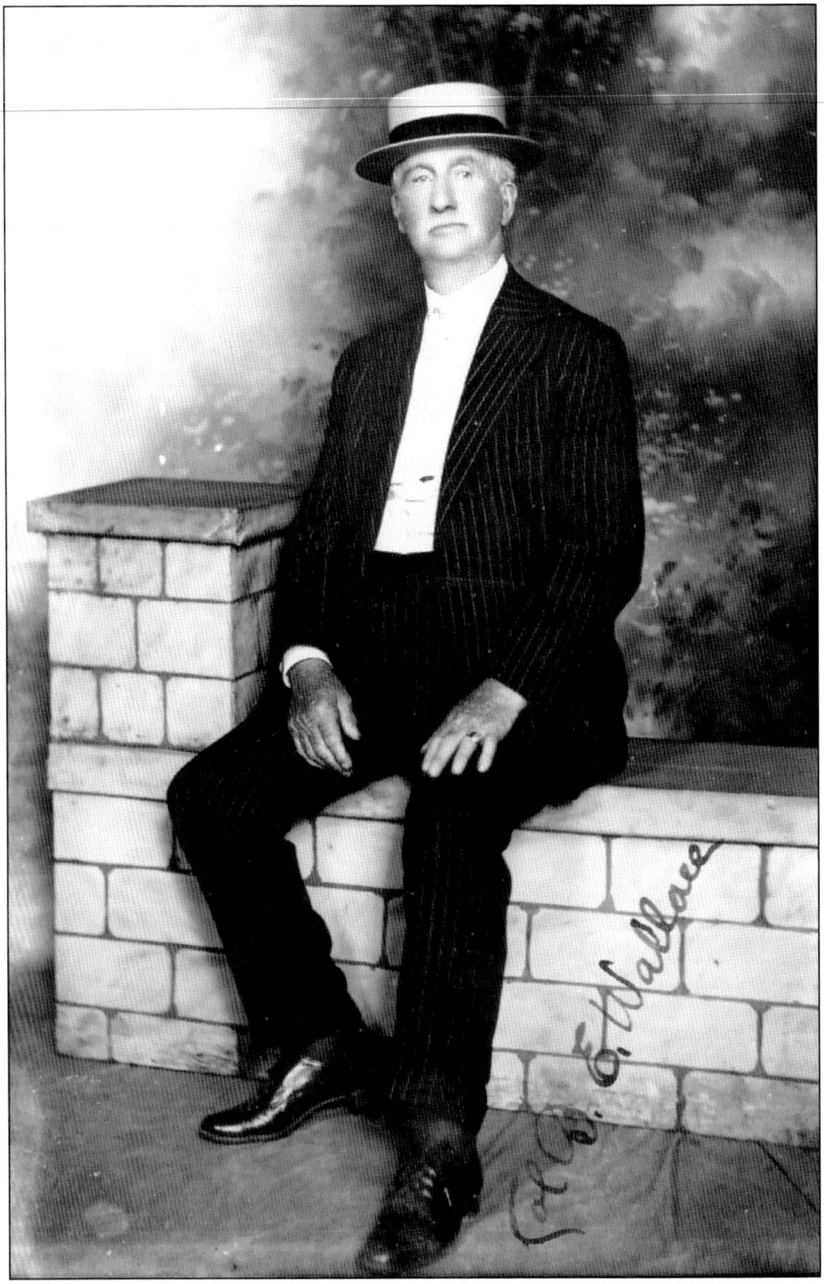

The people of Peru were shocked and saddened upon hearing the news that Benjamin E. Wallace had passed away on April 8, 1921. Wallace had taken a few animals and wagons and turned them into one of the finest circuses in American history. He was one of the best showmen of his time, not to mention a successful businessman and entrepreneur. He gave much to the town of Peru and was respected and appreciated by the townspeople. All who knew him would miss his friendship, wisdom, and generosity. The passing of the "Circus King" opened the door for Jeremiah Mugivan, Bert Bowers, and Edward M. Ballard to turn the circus business into an industry. These men were a force to be reckoned with, and every circus in America felt the pressure of their growing empire.

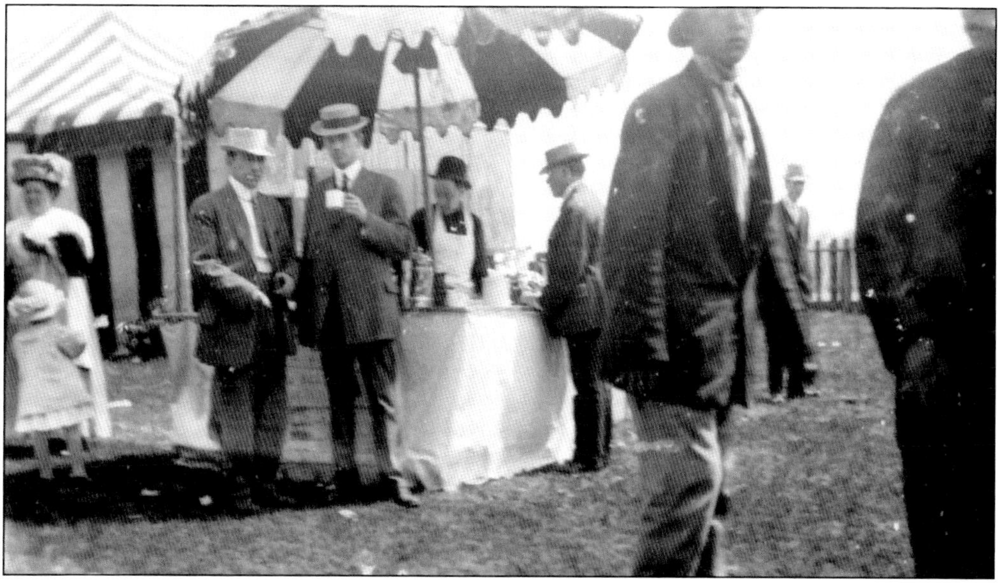

In the spring of 1921, Mugivan, Bowers, and Ballard organized the American Circus Corporation. The trio now owned more titles than any circus in history. It was the beginning of the Roaring Twenties, the economy was good, and the company knew there was a fortune to be made for those who dared to take the chance.

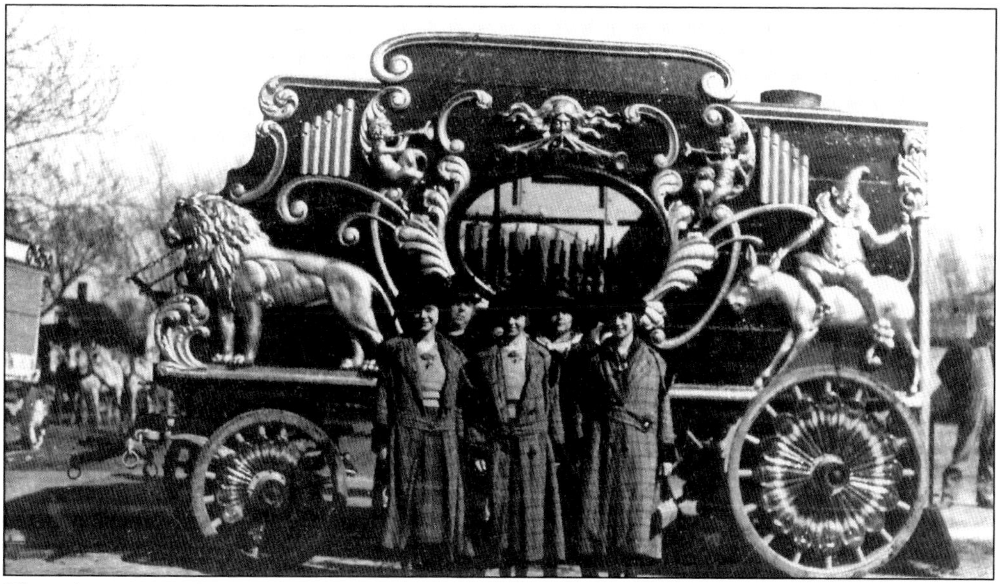

The American Circus Corporation opened the 1921 season with four circuses: the Hagenbeck-Wallace Circus, Sells-Floto Circus, John Robinson's Circus, and Howe's Great London and Van Amburg's Trained Wild Animals. The Howe's Great London Circus and Great Van Amburg Shows were combined this season and toured on 25 railcars freshly painted orange and trimmed in white with brown lettering. The corporation's plan was to send the Howe's and Van Amburg show west to put pressure on the Al G. Barnes Circus.

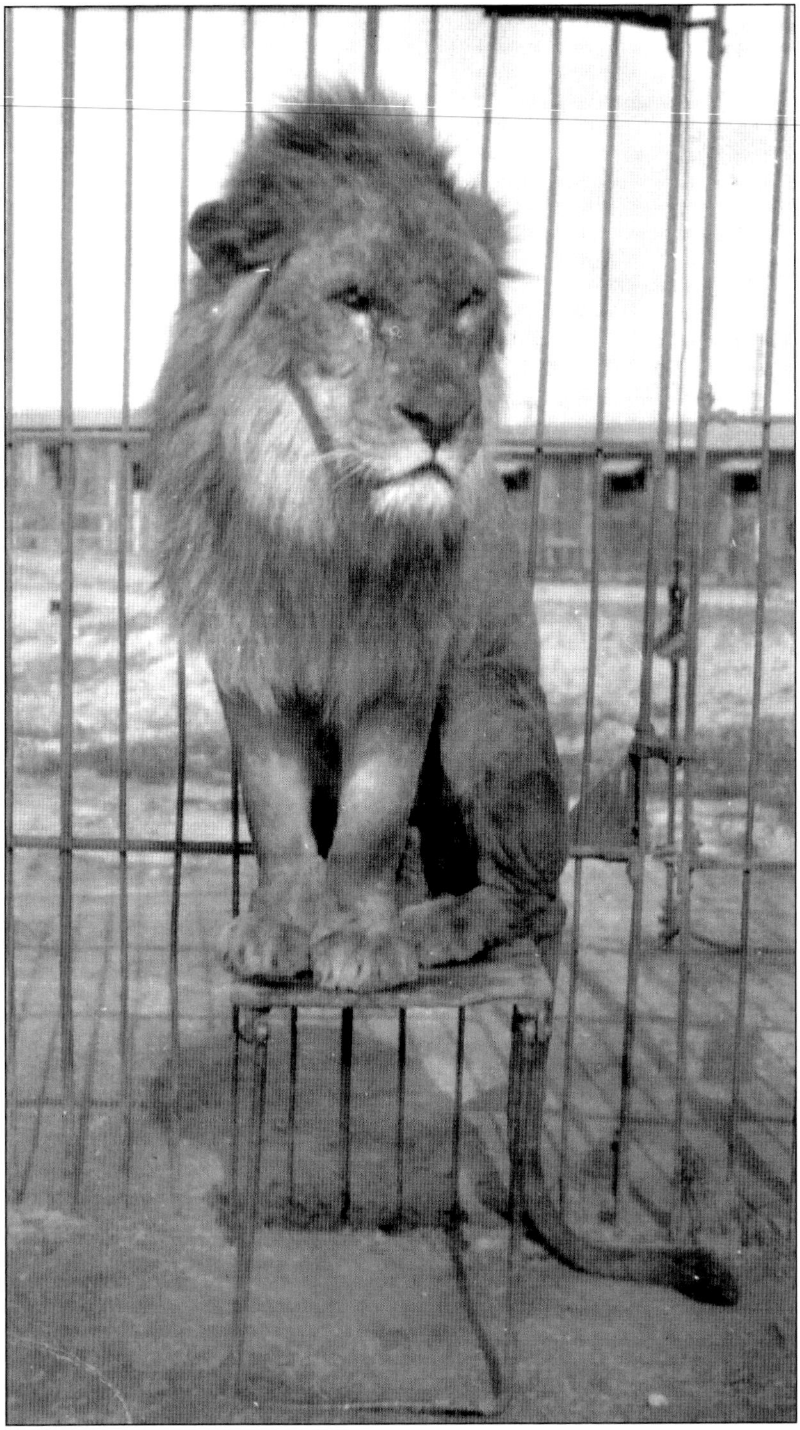

The Howe's–Van Amburg show suffered a setback early in the season after it "red-lighted" (tossed from the train) a troubling employee. Later the employee snuck into the show and poisoned the lions. The big cats were always a feature act, and losing them would be a catastrophe for even the biggest show.

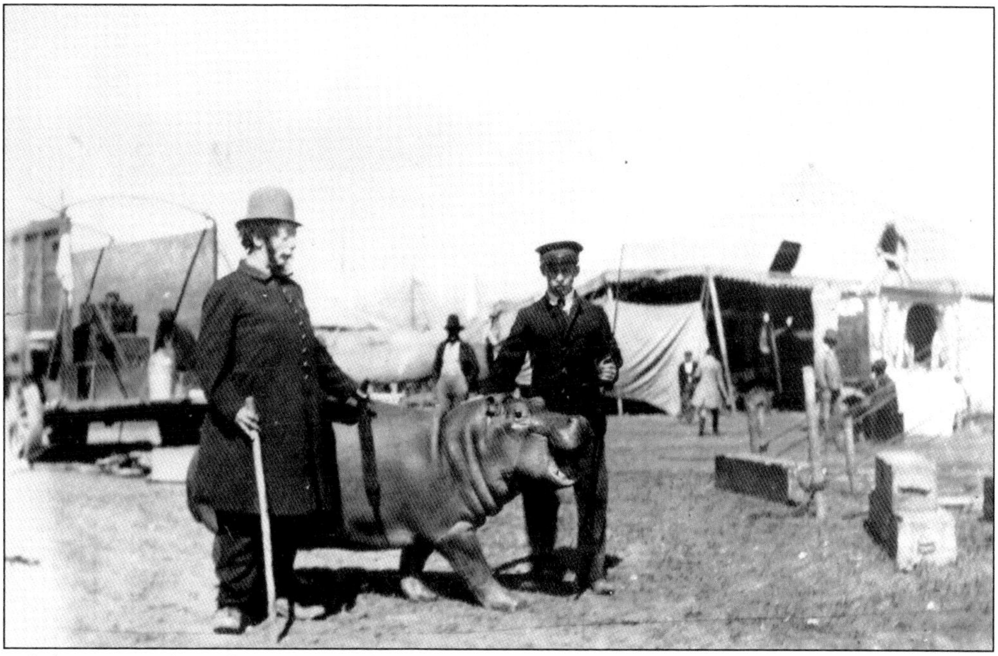

While touring through southern Ohio in August 1921, the menagerie boss of the Howe's Great London Circus hired an 18-year-old boy from Bainbridge, Ohio, named Clyde Beatty. Beatty's first job with the circus was cleaning cages. Little did anyone know that this cage boy would soon become a circus legend.

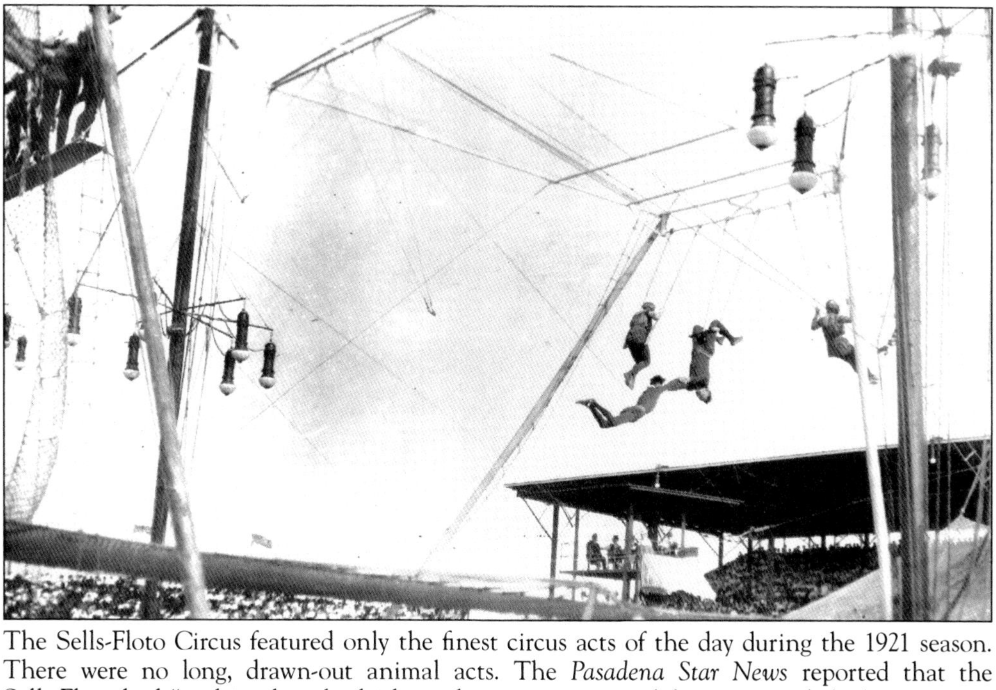

The Sells-Floto Circus featured only the finest circus acts of the day during the 1921 season. There were no long, drawn-out animal acts. The *Pasadena Star News* reported that the Sells-Floto had "nothing but the highest class circus acts and features worth looking at were on display and the big audience thoroughly enjoyed itself." The Sells-Floto was dubbed the "Circus Beautiful."

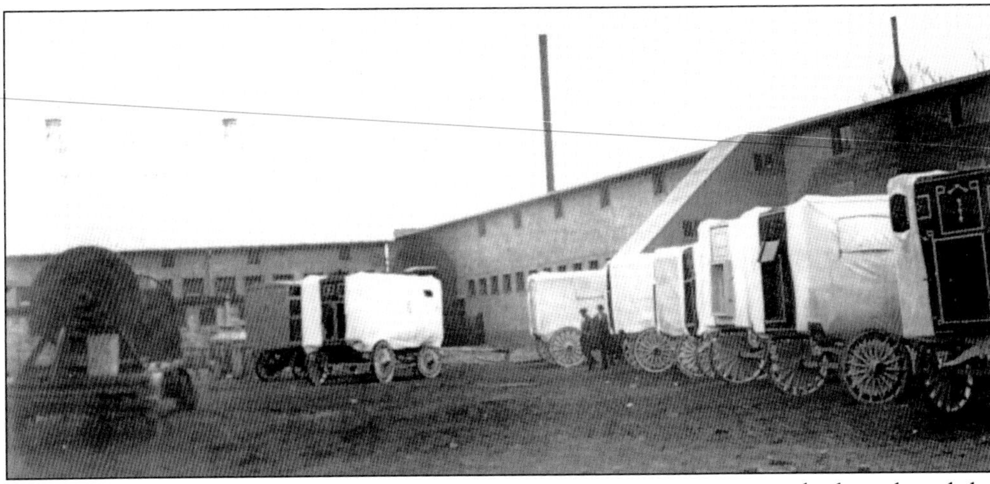

It was announced in the fall of 1921 that the American Circus Corporation had purchased the Wallace winter quarters for $500,000. The sale included all the miscellaneous circus equipment on the property as well as the circus railroad cars, shop, and yards at Washington Street in Peru. Benjamin E. Wallace had always said that he would never sell his holdings as long as he was alive, and he held true to his word.

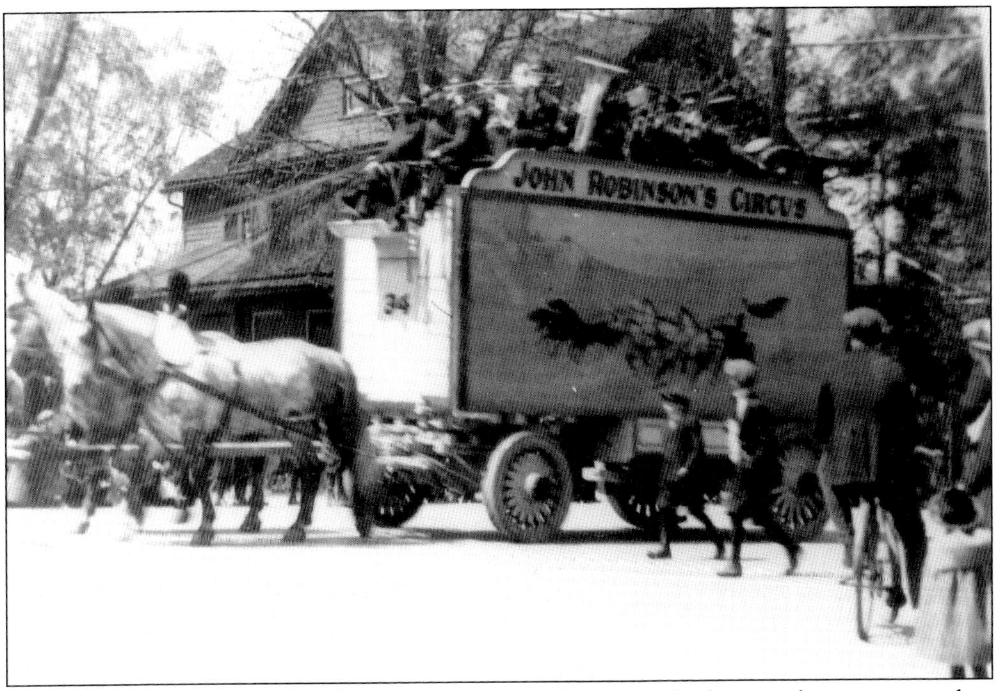


At the end of the 1921 season, the winter quarters in Peru were far from ready to accommodate all of the American Circus Corporation's shows. The John Robinson's Circus wintered in Peru; the Hagenbeck-Wallace Circus stayed in West Baden; Howe's Great London Circus went to Montgomery, Alabama; and the Sells-Floto Circus wintered in Denver, Colorado. All four shows enjoyed a profitable season, and now the partners were busy planning the routes and strategies for the 1922 season.

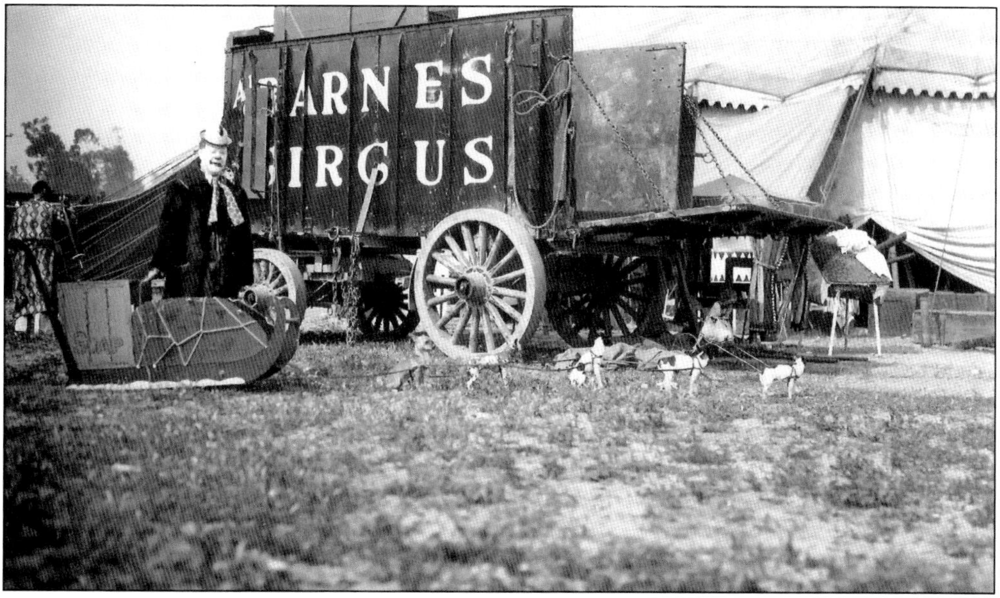

During the 1921 season, the American Circus Corporation had tested its competition's territory. Early in the season it had put the Howe's Great London in Al G. Barnes's territory in the West. Later in 1921, the Sells-Floto challenged the Al G. Barnes Circus. Jeremiah Mugivan, Bert Bowers, and Edward M. Ballard planned the 1922 routes of their circuses as if it were a game of chess.

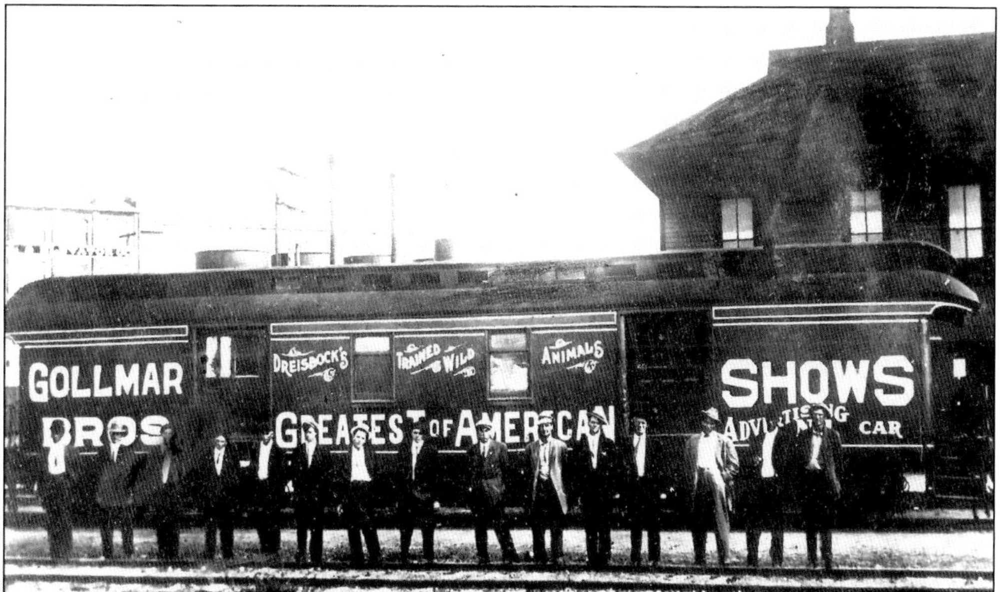


The American Circus Corporation made few changes to the Howe's Great London and Van Amburg Trained Wild Animal Circus in 1922. However, this season it would troupe under the title of Gollmar Brothers. The Gollmar family of Baraboo, Wisconsin, who were cousins to the Ringling brothers, had leased the title. The Howe's Great London title was leased to Mike Golden to be used on the Palmer Brothers Circus that had recently been purchased at a sheriff's sale in California.

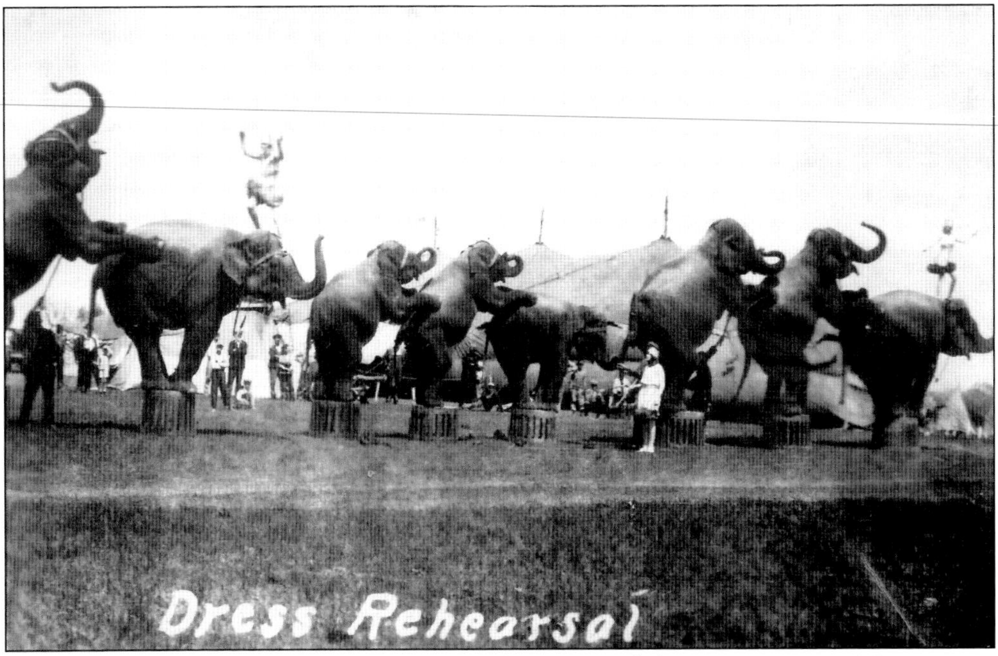


Gollmar Brothers Circus: America's Greatest Shows opened the 1922 season in Montgomery, Alabama, and moved north into Tennessee, Kentucky, and Indiana before turning west to Illinois and Missouri. At one point during the season, management thought it beneficial to add the Yankee Robinson Circus title to the show. The title that appeared in the official route book published was Gollmar Brothers and Yankee Robinson's Combined Circus.

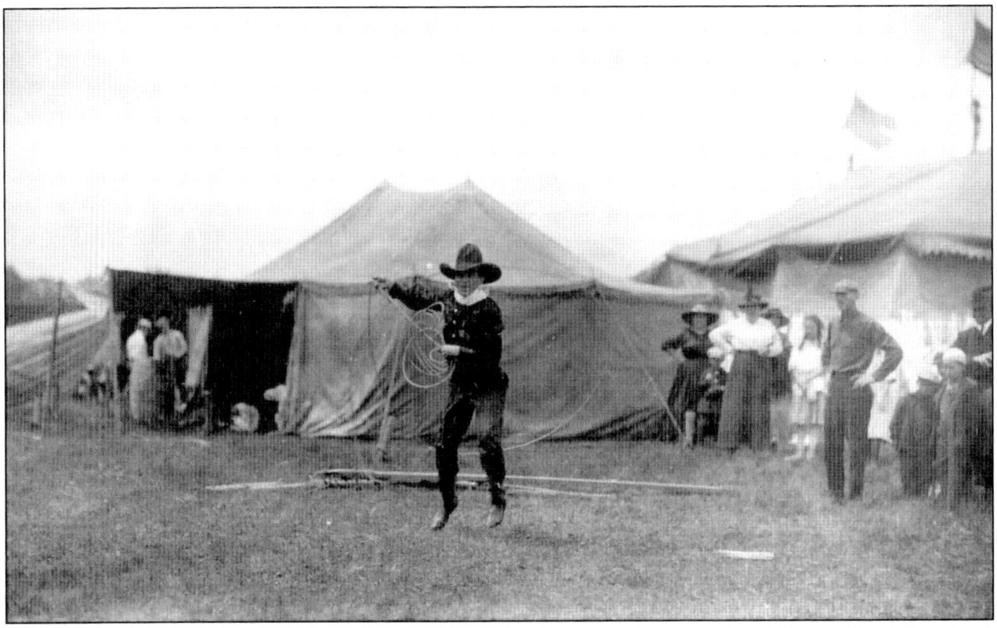

The Gollmar Brothers 1922 show featured seven wild animal acts trained by head wild animal trainer John Guilfoyle. The circus also featured many traditional ground and aerial performances. It was popular for circuses to feature a Wild West pageant in shows, and Gollmar Brothers had some of the best roping and trick riders in the world.

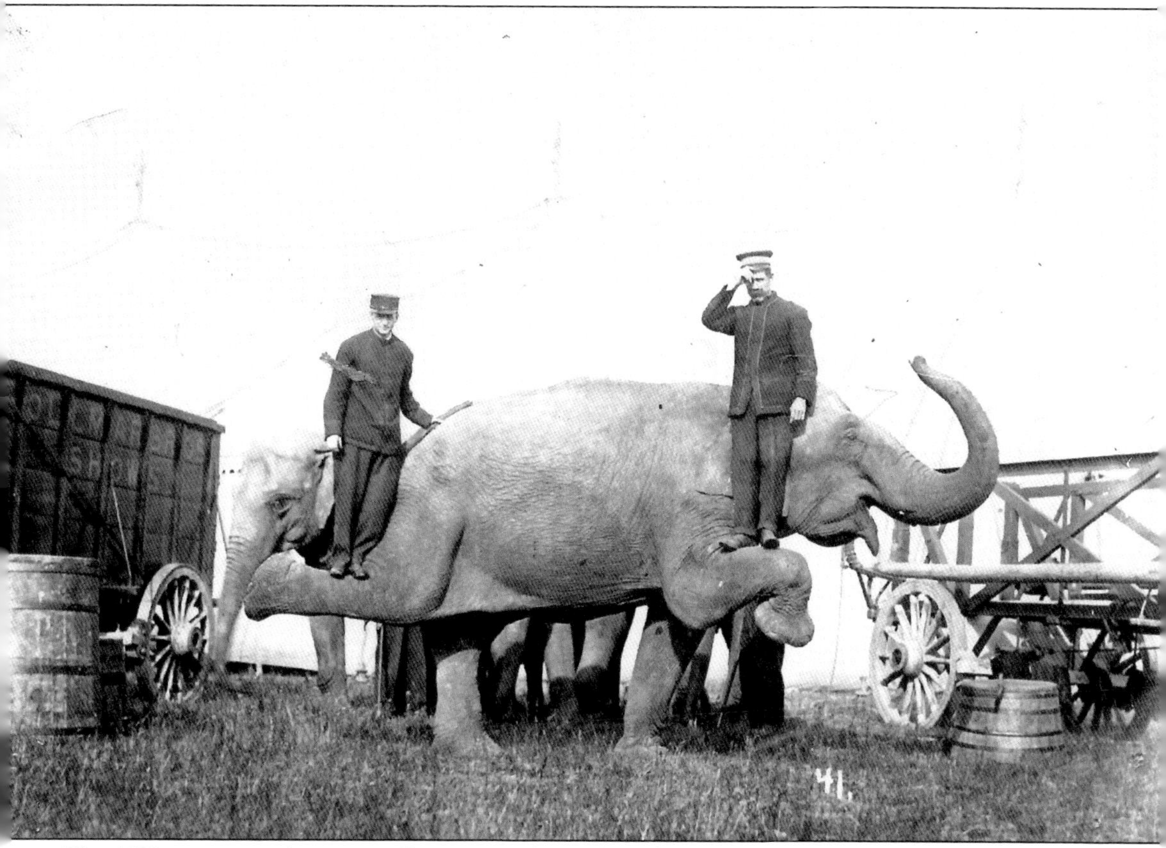

The 1922 street parades were still very popular and used to entice the public to come and see the show. Ringling Brothers and Barnum and Bailey Circus had given up the practice in 1921. The Gollmar Brothers Circus featured a spectacular street parade led by the finest horse teams. The baggage wagons were painted orange with white trim and brown letters, the same as the Howe's theme in 1921. The steam calliope was pulled by a Mack truck and, as remembered by one spectator, played "Dardenella" and "Last Night on the Back Porch" during the march.

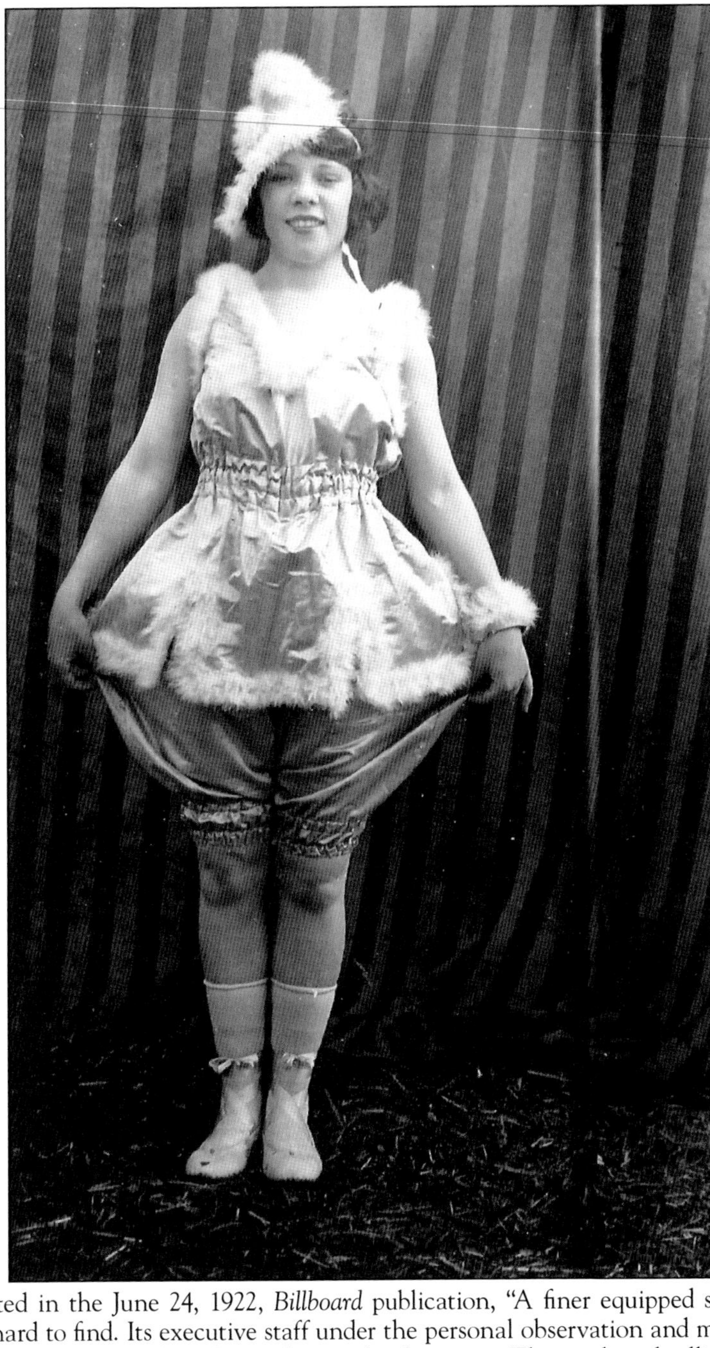

It was reported in the June 24, 1922, *Billboard* publication, "A finer equipped show in all its branches is hard to find. Its executive staff under the personal observation and management of Danny Odom, is most complete, fast and in perfect harmony. The stock and rolling stock bring forth the most flattering comment, the parade is excellent and the show's appearance on the lot cannot be surpassed for cleanliness. The program offers two hours of novelty animal acts and high class circus acts combined that bring forth remarks of approval for all that is claimed and that accounts for the remarkable good business and grand record the Gollmar show enjoys. Also wish to add that the treatment and comfort enjoyed cannot be surpassed. At this writing Columbus, Neb. is giving the show a turn away afternoon house."

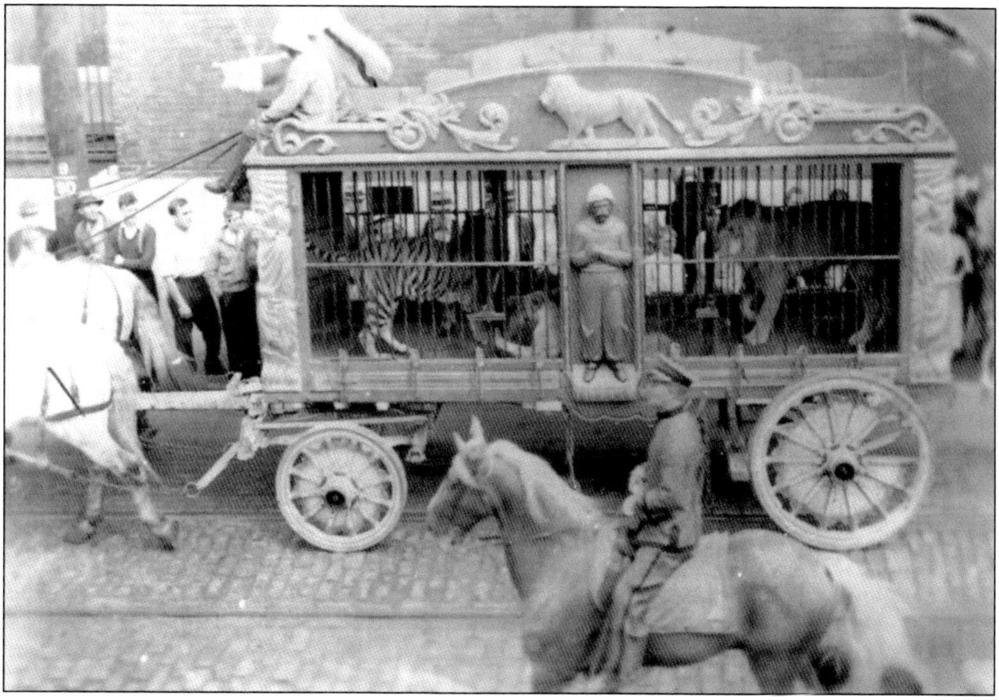

During the July 8, 1922, stand at Devils Lake, North Dakota, the passing of the Gollmar Brothers Circus street parade interrupted the morning court proceedings. The courtroom cleared to watch the passing spectacle. The good-humored judge adjourned the session until 2:00 p.m. The circus reported a great turnout for the matinee and evening performances.

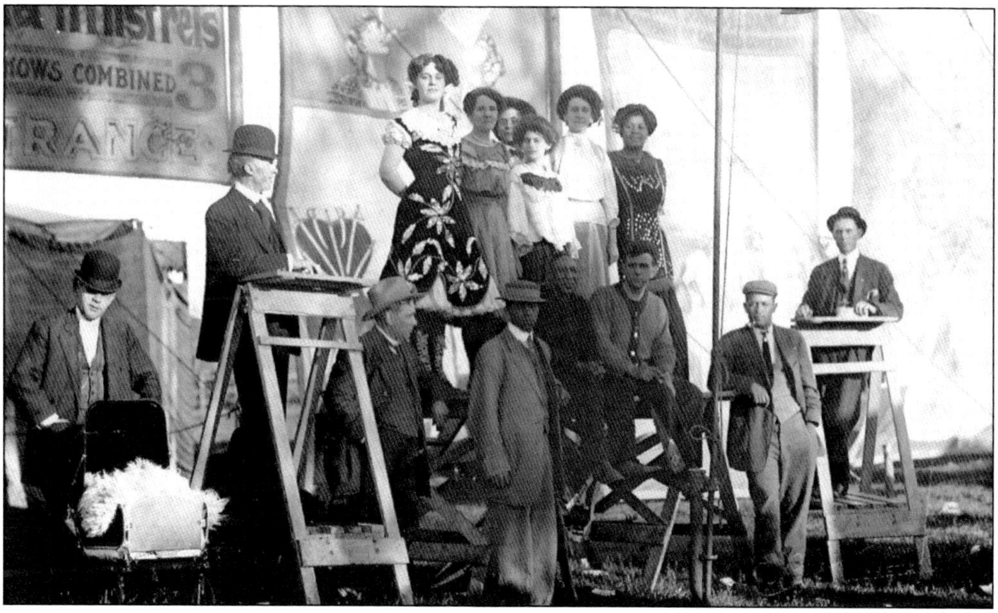


In late summer and early fall, there was a push led by Charles Ringling and others that all circuses in the country should operate free of grift during the 1923 season. *Grift* was a term used by showmen for games of chance, cooch dancers, and shortchanging customers. These activities usually took place in the sideshow and were common practices with American circuses.

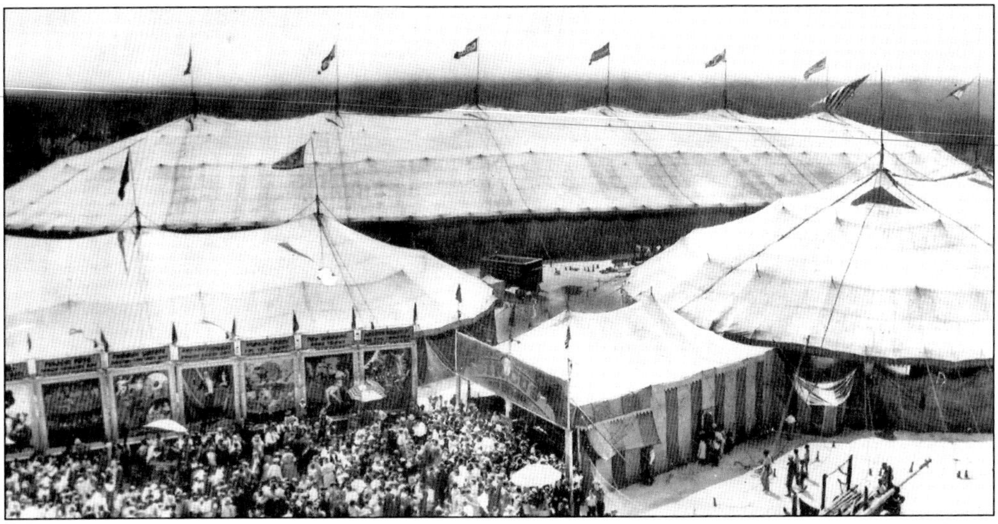

Jeremiah Mugivan and Bert Bowers, being seasoned showmen, felt that grift had always been practiced, and payoffs to local authorities in forms of cash or free tickets was just part of doing business. Without the payoffs they ran the risk of being shut down on a misdemeanor charge and cost the show thousands of dollars in revenue.

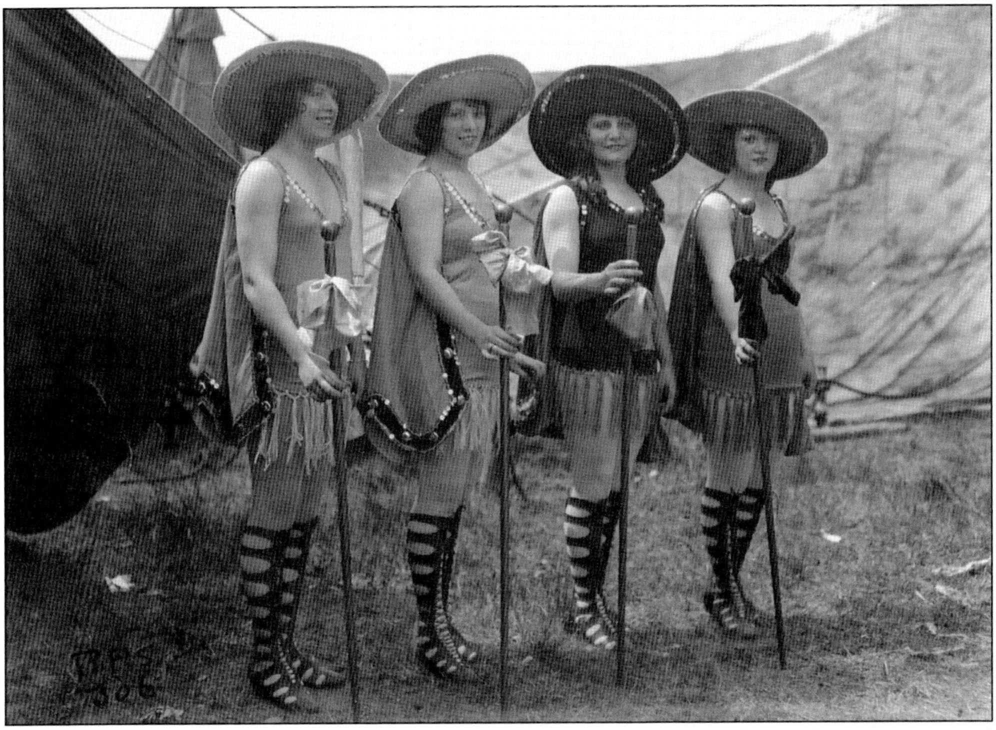

The American Circus Corporation showed very little interest in the do-gooders' request until October 23, 1922. While the Gollmar Brothers Circus was playing Earle, Arkansas, a deputy sheriff objected to the activities in the sideshow tent. Billy Miles, the show's legal adjustor, stepped in and argued with the officer that his superiors approved the activities. During the confrontation, the officer pulled his pistol and fatally wounded Miles. Miles passed away the following night, and the officer was later acquitted of all charges.

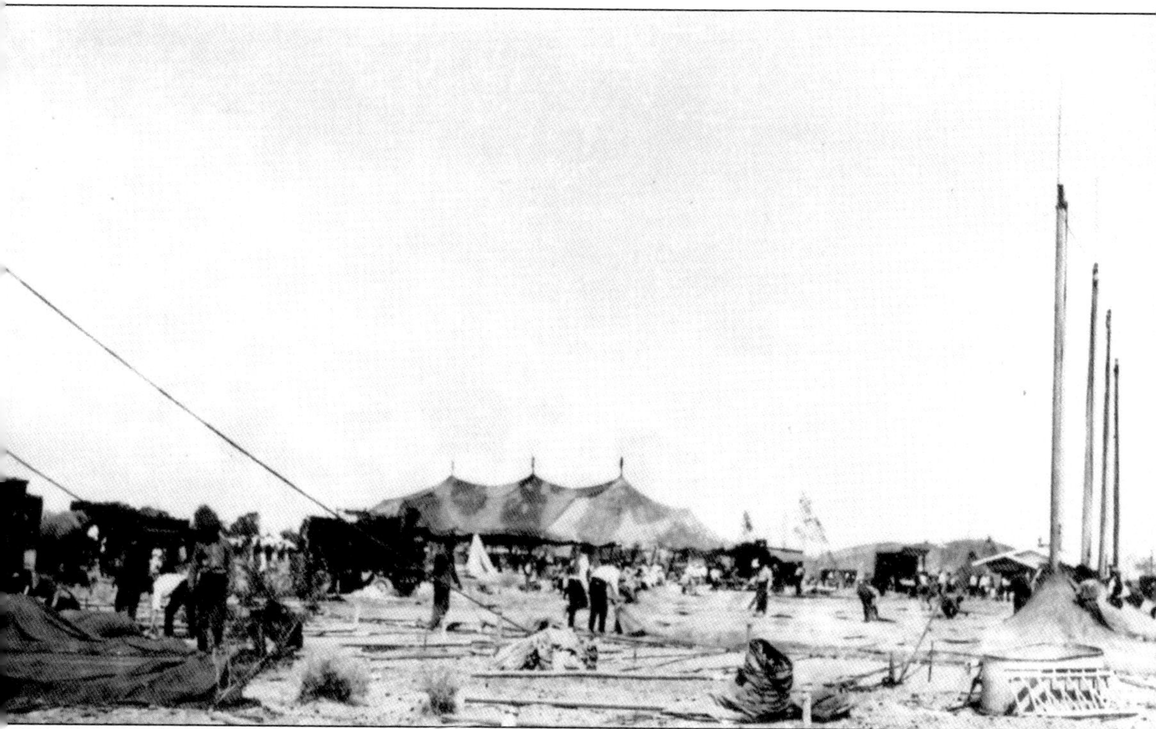

At the end of the 1922 season, the Gollmar Brothers Circus: America's Greatest Shows arrived at the Montgomery, Alabama, winter quarters. The show weathered railroad strikes, miner strikes, and the death of a manager but still finished the season profitably. In the spring of 1923, management decided that the Gollmar Brothers Circus would not go out. Some of the equipment and animals were sold to the Christy Brothers Circus, and the rest was transferred to the John Robinson's Circus. The 1922 Gollmar Brothers route book featured a tribute to Gollmar manager Danny Odom that read, "To 'Danny Odom:—Soon the members of your huge circus family will scatter to the four corners of the earth. Some will return to serve you once more, others will not. Nevertheless, we want you to know that the kindness and generosity, which you have manifested towards each and every one of us, will always be remembered with deep appreciation. With watching eyes and hoping hearts we shall watch your progress in the years to come and whether it is our good fortune to again be serving you, or though we are engaged elsewhere; you can rest assured that to each and every member of the Gollmar Circus Family of 1922 you will always be 'Danny' of whom no more fitting phrase can be found than 'A Prince There Was', Au Revoir, and Good Luck, Frank Davis."

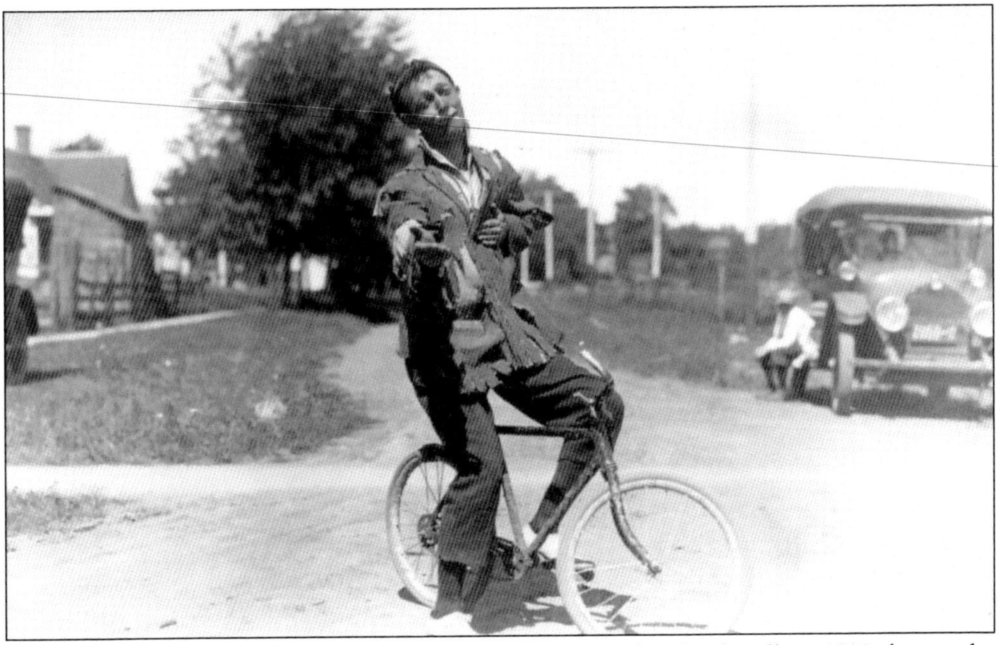

The American Circus Corporation's other three circuses also fared well in 1922 due to the masterful strategies of the corporation's management. The Sells-Floto Circus opened at the Chicago Coliseum before heading east into Ringling Brothers territory. For weeks the Sells-Floto played towns and cities just a few days before the Ringling Brothers and Barnum and Bailey Circus arrived.

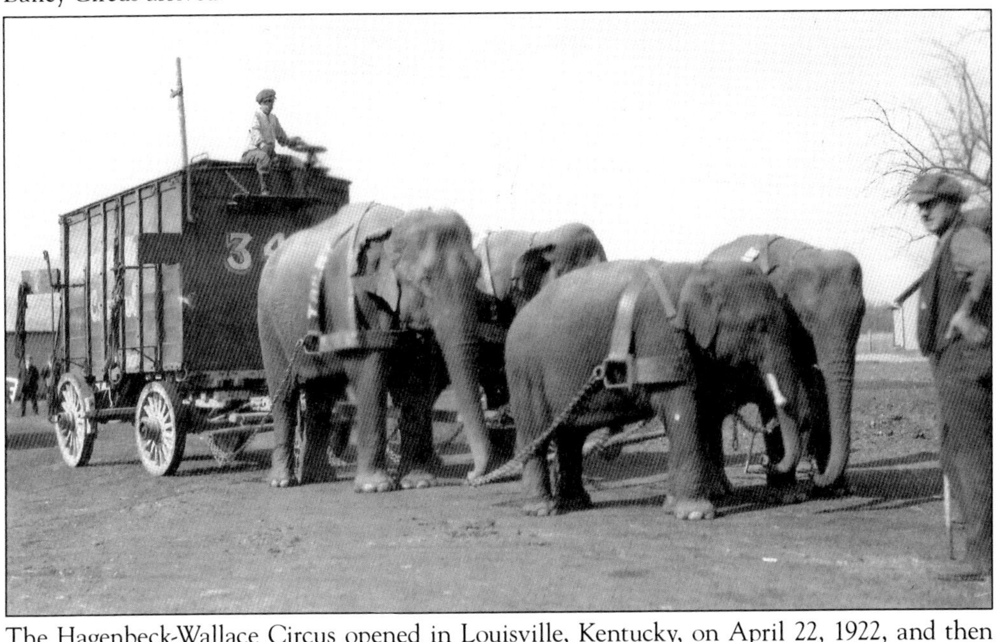

The Hagenbeck-Wallace Circus opened in Louisville, Kentucky, on April 22, 1922, and then spent the next few weeks in Ohio and Pennsylvania. The John Robinson's Circus opened in Peru on April 26 and also trouped east into Ohio and Pennsylvania. Now the American Circus Corporation had all three of its big shows in Ringling Brothers territory. Adding fuel to the fire, the Sparks Circus and the Walter L. Main Circus were playing the same area.

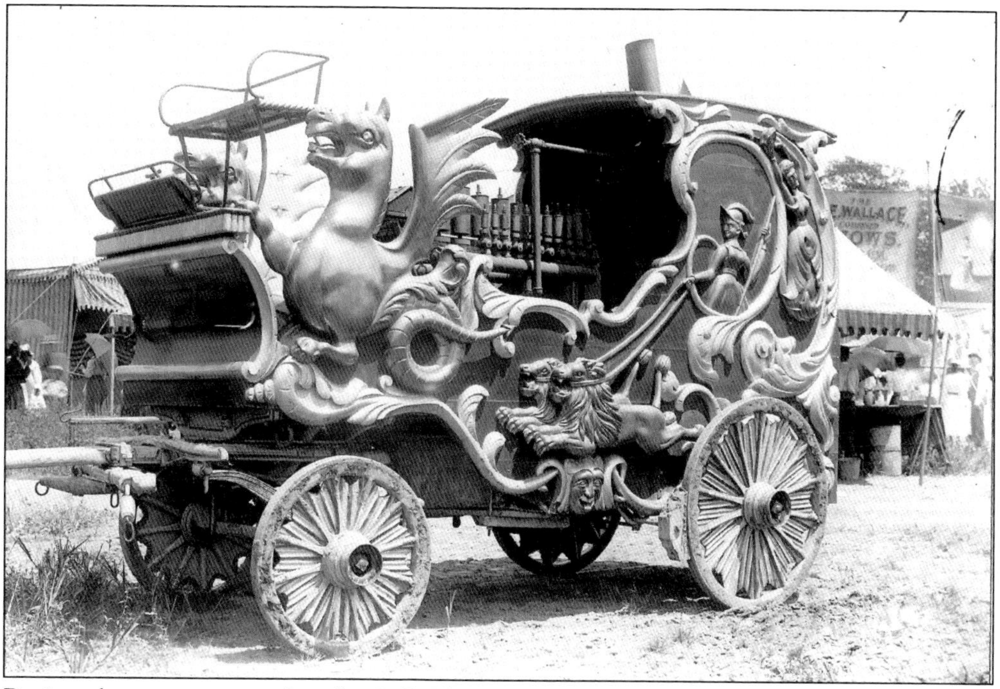

During the summer months, the Sells-Floto moved west of the Mississippi River and the Hagenbeck-Wallace moved through the New England states and on into Canada with the Ringling Brothers and Barnum and Bailey Circus following behind them. By the time the Ringling show arrived in Michigan, it found itself sharing the territory with the John Robinson's Circus. With the season half gone, a frustrated Ringling was still playing stands already made by the circuses of the American Circus Corporation.

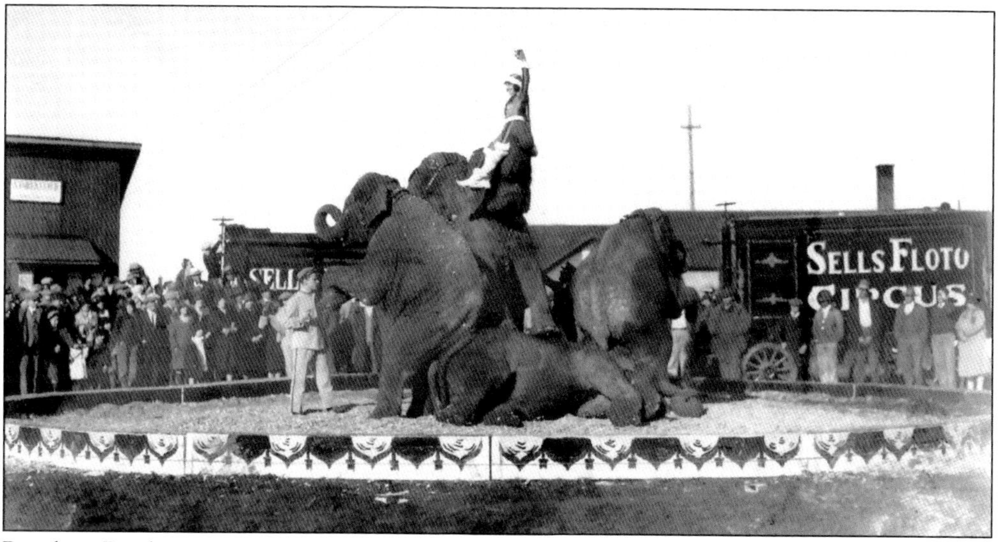


Ringling Brothers saw an opportunity to take a western route through Canada that had not been played by other shows. Upon arriving in Washington State, the Ringling show was once again following the Sells-Floto down the West Coast and through the South. On September 18, the Ringling show caught up to the Sells-Floto in Phoenix, Arizona, and played the city at the same time.

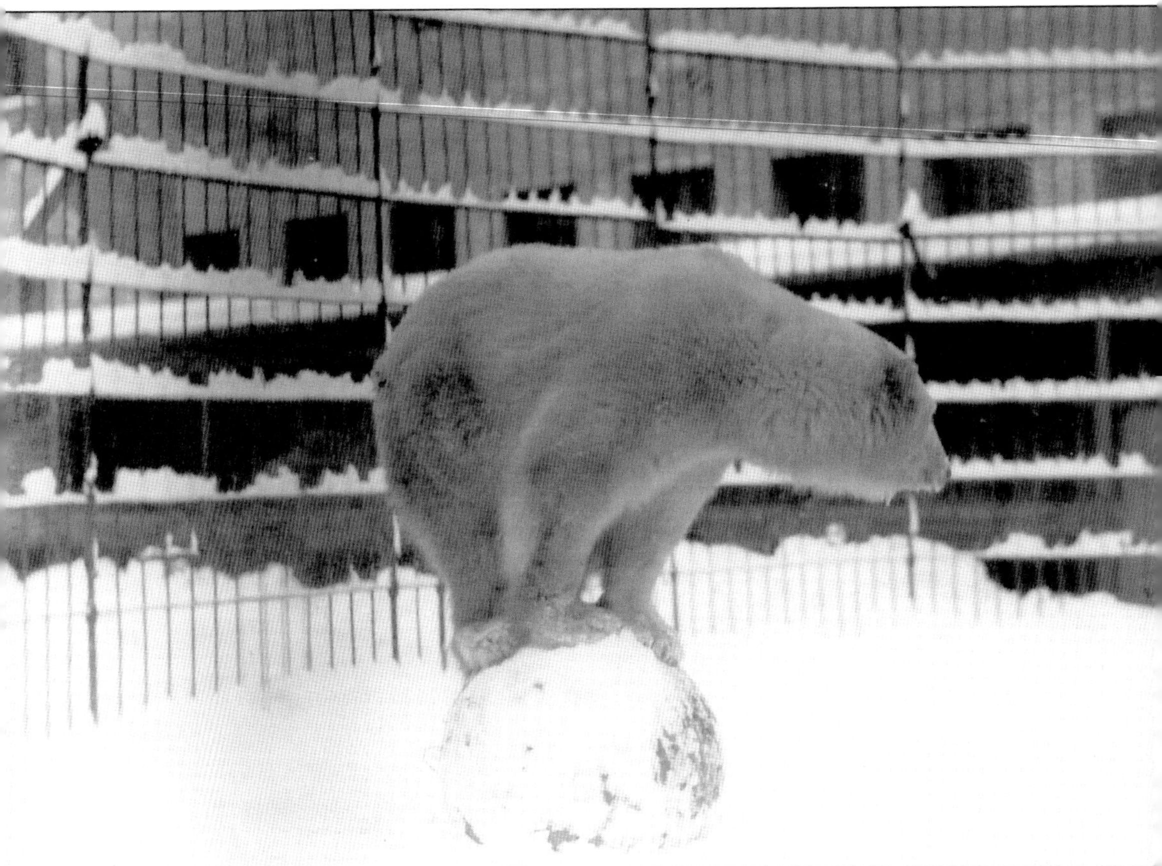

The John Robinson's Circus closed the 1922 season on October 12 and wintered in Peru. The Hagenbeck-Wallace Circus closed November 2 and wintered in West Baden. The Sells-Floto Circus closed on November 8 and, for the first time, wintered in Peru as the Sells-Floto winter quarters in Denver, Colorado, were closed. Until the winter of 1922–1923, the American Circus Corporation maintained four winter quarters: the Sells-Floto in Denver; the Howe's Great London–Gollmar Brothers Circus in Montgomery, Alabama; the Hagenbeck-Wallace in West Baden; and the John Robinson's at the Peru winter quarters. Maintaining four winter quarters and four circuses required the labor of more than 4,000 employees.

*Five*

# "How's the Crowd in the Big Show?"

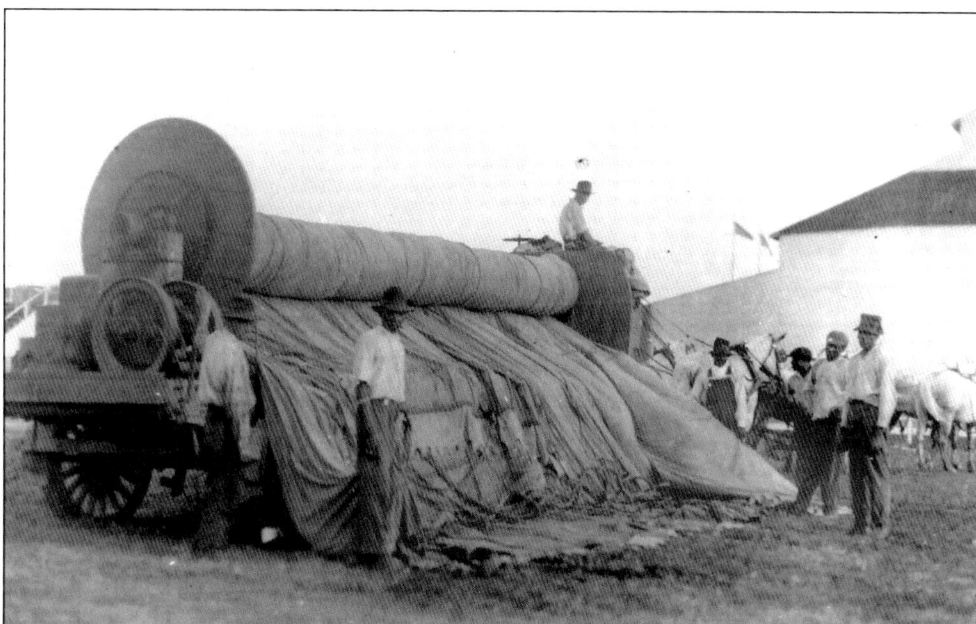

The American Circus Corporation put out three circuses in 1923: The John Robinson's Circus, Sells-Floto Circus, and Hagenbeck-Wallace Circus. The Hagenbeck-Wallace was the same show as in 1922 with a few minor changes. The Hagenbeck-Wallace was a moneymaker and changes were not necessary. The show opened in Louisville, Kentucky, on April 28.

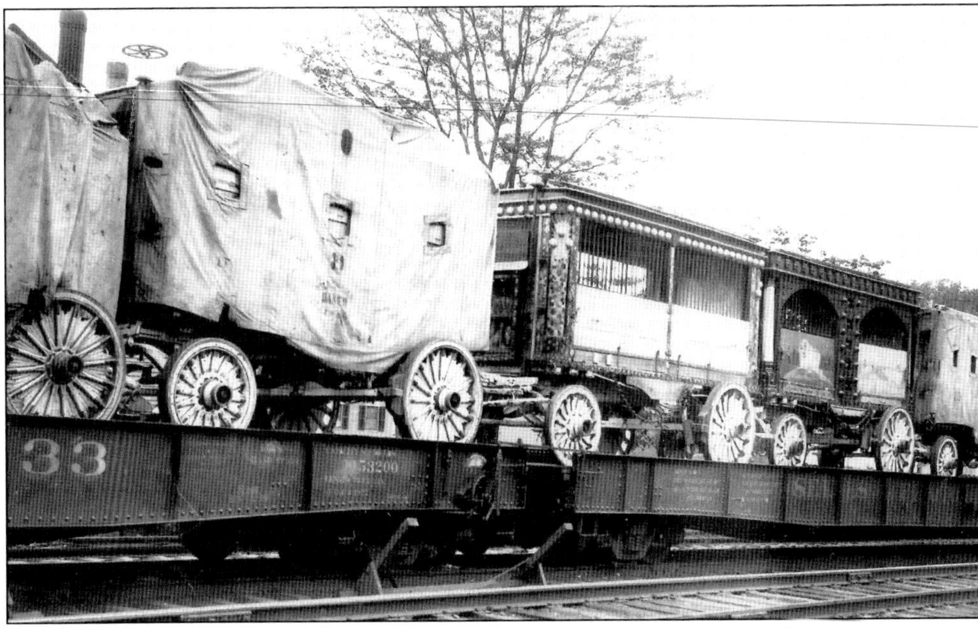

The 1923 Sells-Floto Circus featured a complete circus performance with only one animal act. It was scheduled to open the season on Saturday, April 7, at the Chicago Coliseum. The Sells-Floto left Peru by rail on April 3 for Chicago. The Peru winter quarters was now focused on rolling out the 100th annual tour of the John Robinson's Circus.

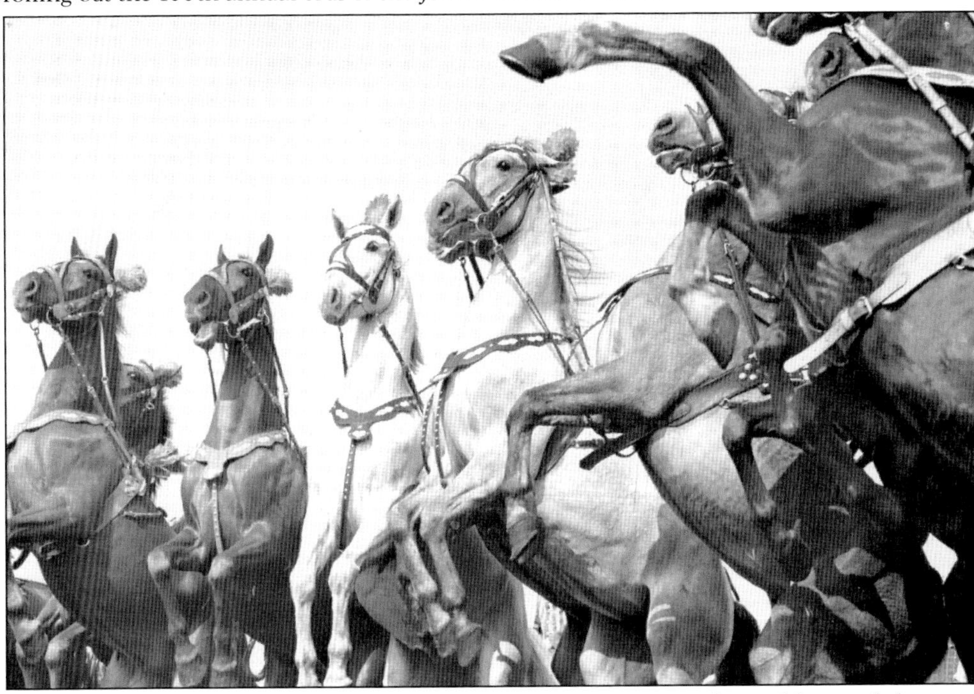

The 100th anniversary tour of the John Robinson's Circus was strictly a wild animal show and touted as "the largest of all such entertainments now before the public." The show would use some of the equipment and staff from the 1922 Gollmar Brothers Circus. The rest of the Gollmar Brothers equipment and animals were sold off.

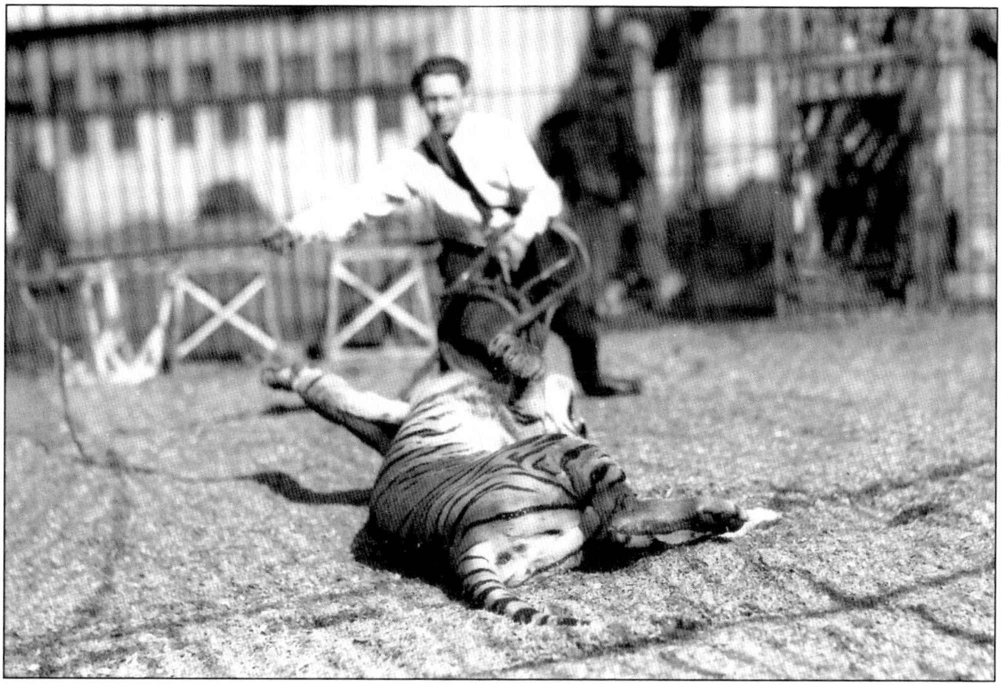

LaVerne Hauser was a well-known wild animal trainer and, during the 1923 season, worked leopards in the big cage of the John Robinson's. Also featuring wild animal acts were husband-and-wife team John "Chubby" and Harriet Guilfoyle, Peter Taylor, and Clyde Beatty.

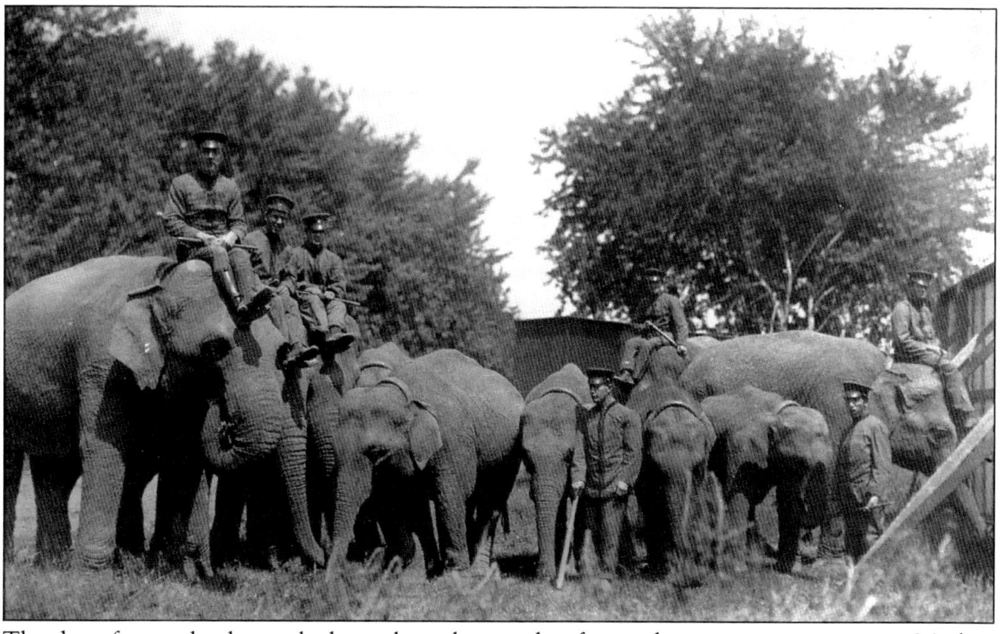

The show featured a dozen elephants brought together from other corporation circuses. Modoc, Jewel, Pearl, Judy, Lizzie, Mary, Dutch, Betty, Blanche, and the two punks Jenny and Ruth were added to the lineup in Peru. Before leaving Peru, one of the Sells-Floto elephants, Major, took a swing at the show's general manager Zack Terrell and was left in Peru. Cheerful Gardner, the John Robinson's head elephant trainer, took Major with him to make an even dozen.

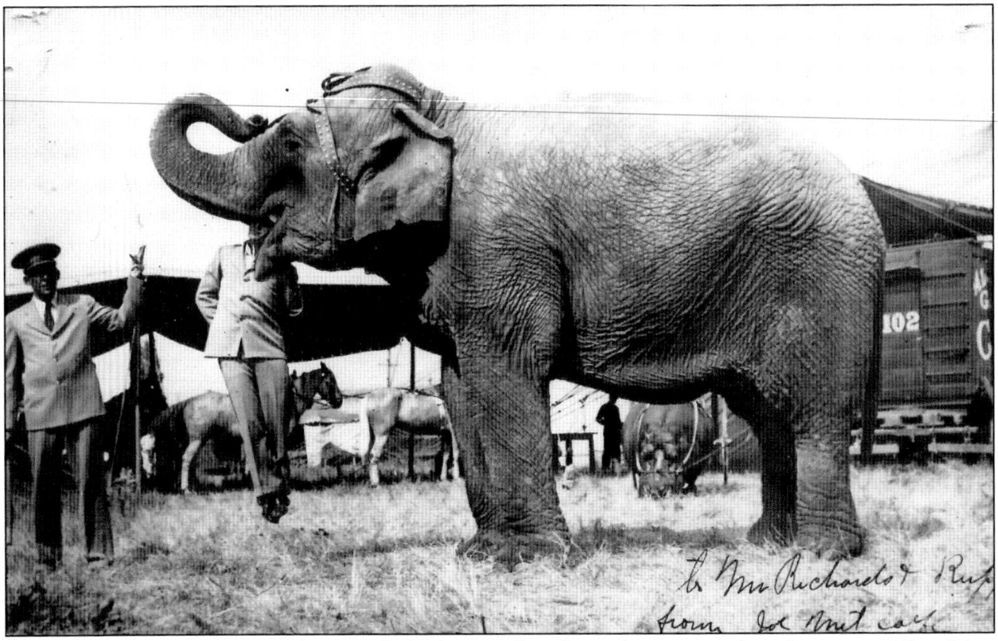


Most elephant acts are made up of elephants that have been together for years. The John Robinson's Circus had three bulls, plus one from the Yankee Robinson Circus, four from the Gollmar Brothers Circus, one from the Howe's Great London Circus, and Major and the two punks from Peru. Under the skillful hands of master handler Cheerful Gardner, "the Human Pendulum," these bulls worked the 1923 season with hardly a mishap.

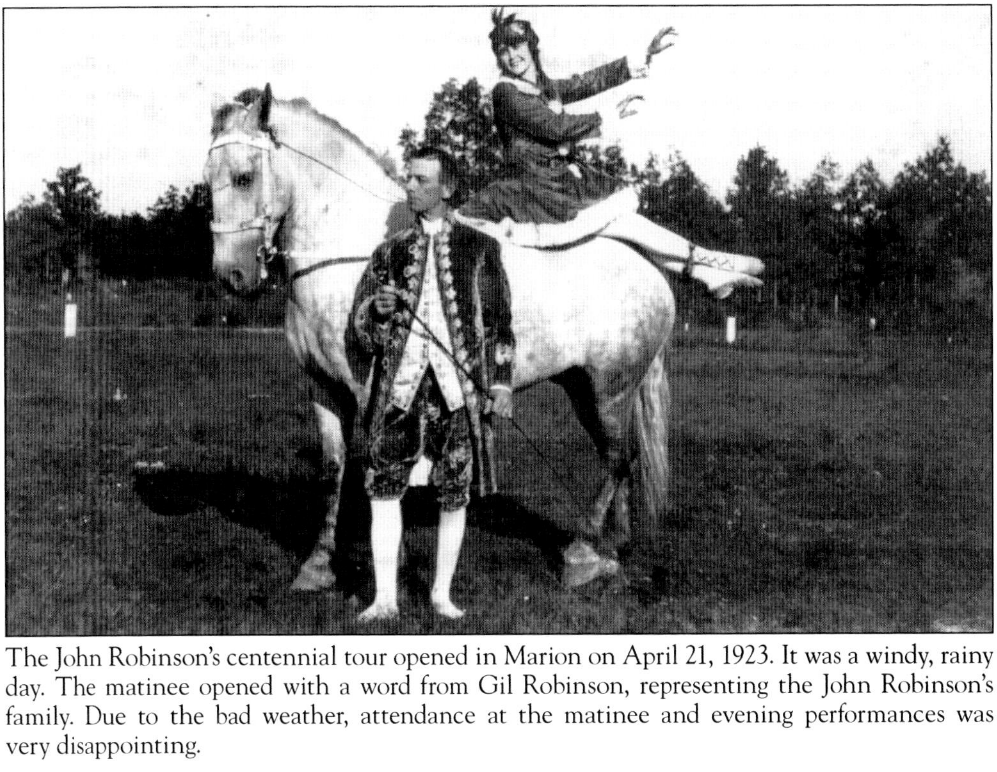

The John Robinson's centennial tour opened in Marion on April 21, 1923. It was a windy, rainy day. The matinee opened with a word from Gil Robinson, representing the John Robinson's family. Due to the bad weather, attendance at the matinee and evening performances was very disappointing.

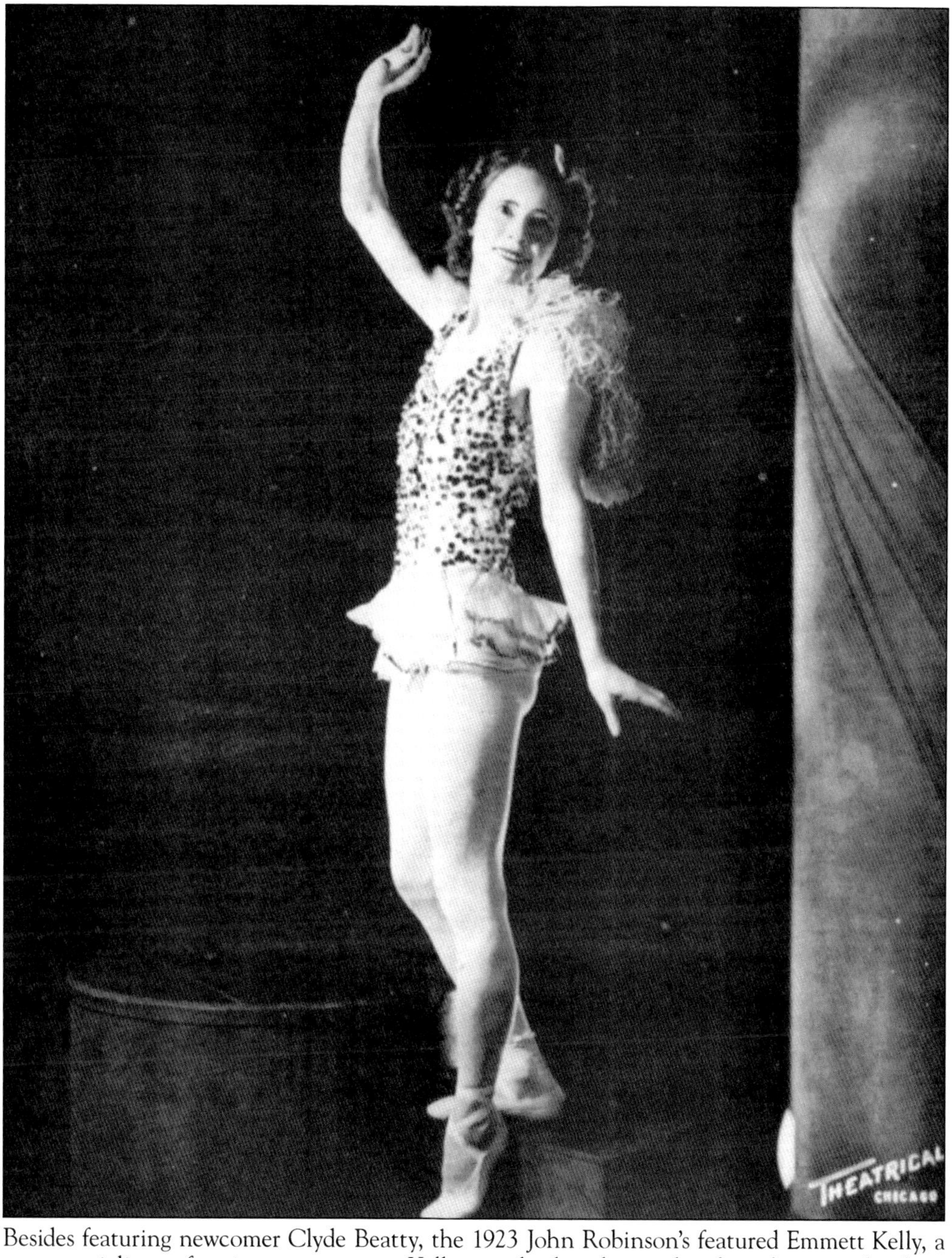

Besides featuring newcomer Clyde Beatty, the 1923 John Robinson's featured Emmett Kelly, a young aerialist performing a trapeze act. Kelly was also listed as a whiteface clown on the show but not as the famous Weary Willie. Tramp clowns were considered dirty and vulgar at the time. In 1923, Kelly married Eva Moore, an aerialist who performed with the Moore sisters in the show.

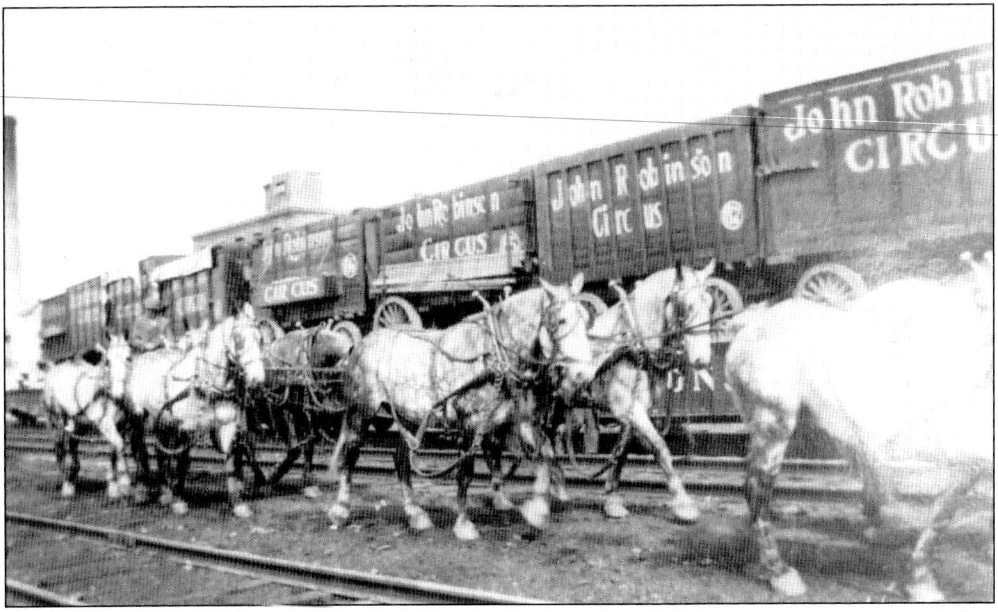


The advance car, the advertising department for the John Robinson's Circus, reported that competitors had beaten it to many of its planned destinations. They would post Sparks Circus, Walter L. Main Circus, and Ringling Brothers and Barnum and Bailey Circus lithographs all over the towns days or weeks ahead of the circus—even in towns that the John Robinson's was going to play a month before the competition.

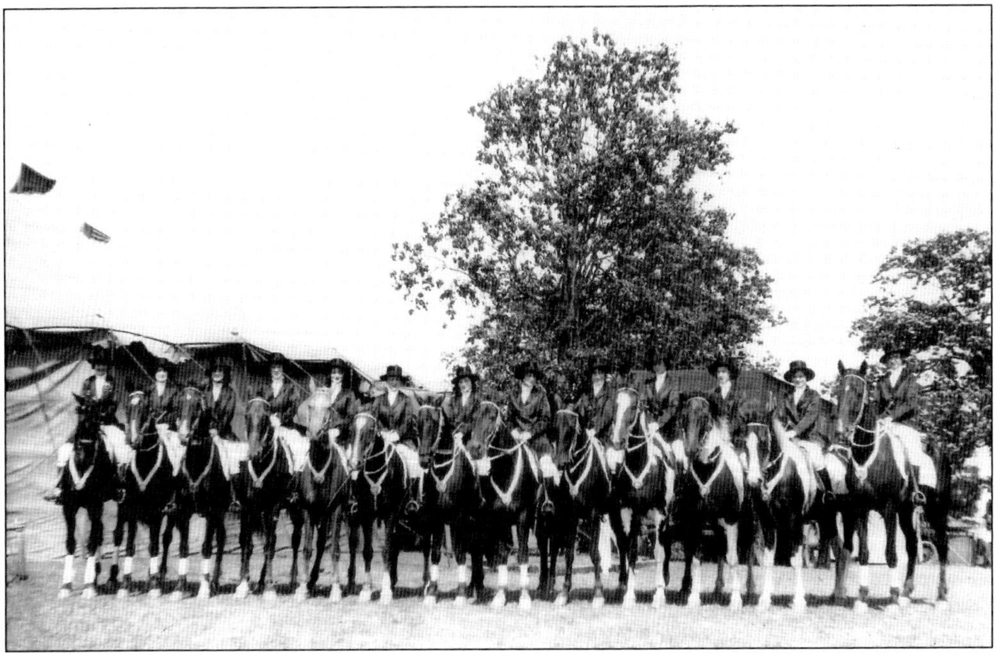

For the next month, the John Robinson's World of Wonders trouped through Indiana, Ohio, West Virginia, and Pennsylvania. Stand after stand it was met with rain, snow, and mud. In some instances, the parade or even the show had to be canceled. However, the show enjoyed great ticket sales when the big top went up.

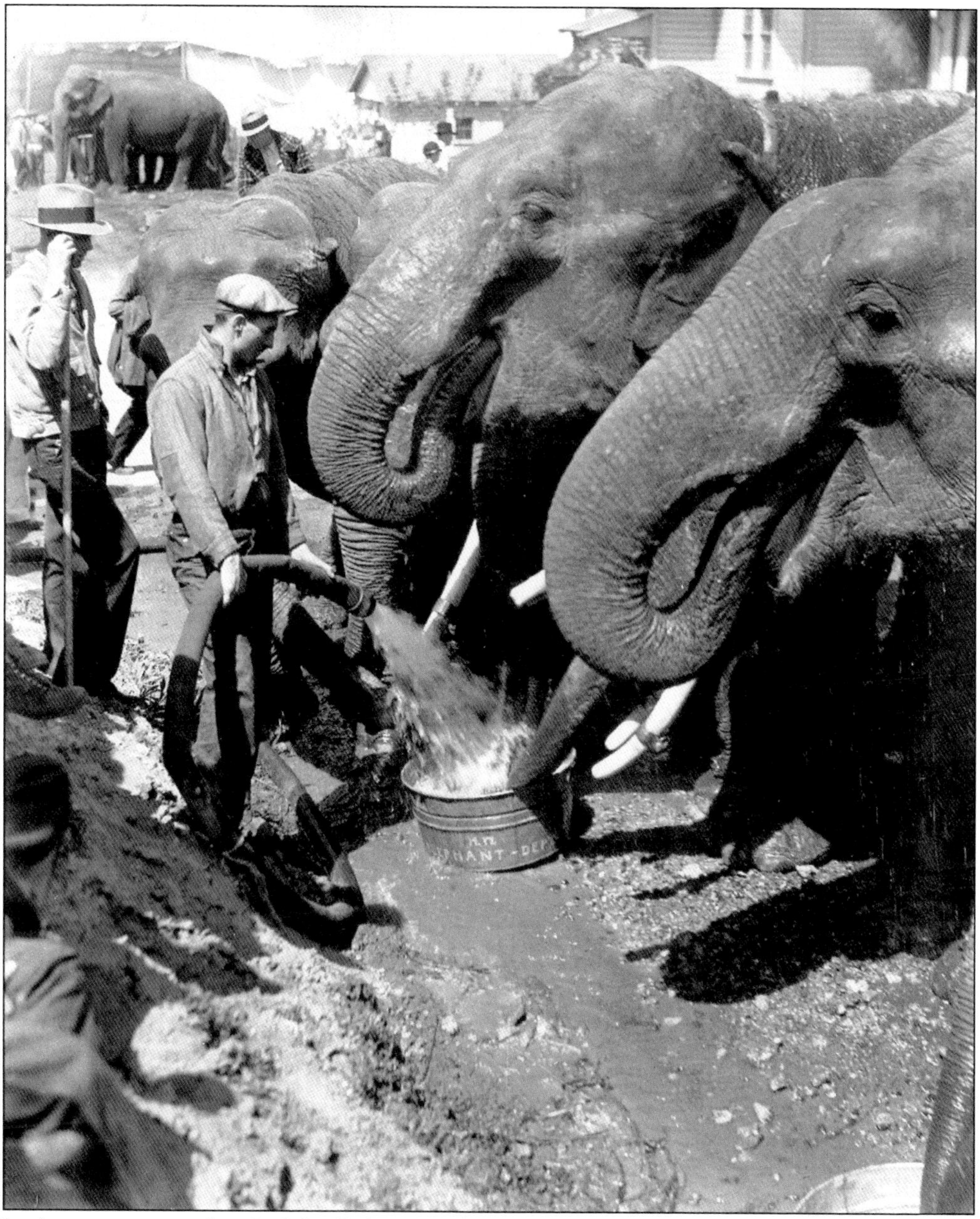

In the summer months, the John Robinson's show was prosperous and without incident until late summer in Frankfort. An express wagon passed and spooked 8 of the 12 elephants. Attendant John Guilfoyle tried to calm the beasts when two elephants chained together knocked him to the ground and passed over him. The elephants ran a city block before they could be persuaded to stop. Guilfoyle received only minor injuries and was released from the hospital for the evening performance.

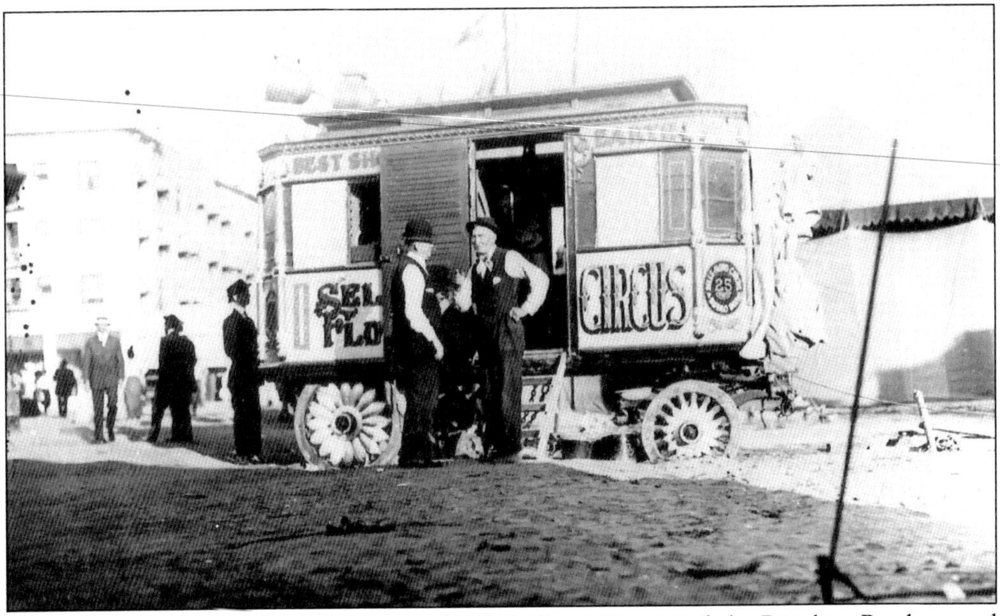


During the first half of the 1923 season, the Sells-Floto Circus and the Ringling Brothers and Barnum and Bailey Circus were focusing on the eastern half of the country. As in 1922, the Sells-Floto played ahead of Ringling Brothers as its goal was to get to the money first. Since the railroad and miner strikes of 1922 were over, the shows were reporting good attendance.

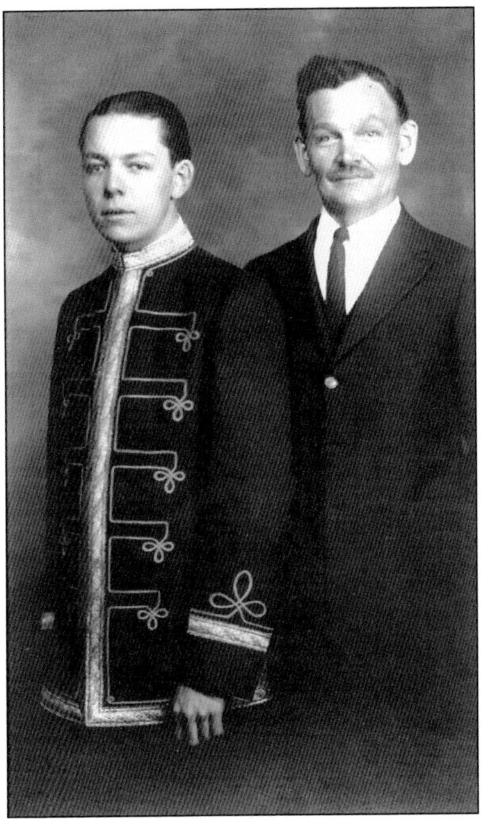

In 1923, a young animal trainer, Terrell Jacobs, was working with the Sells-Floto. As a boy, Jacobs always dreamed of working with the big cats in a circus. Jacobs landed a job at the Peru winter quarters and his dream soon came true. He was billed as "Capt. Terrell Jacobs, world's youngest and most fearless animal tamer." While working a lion in the sideshow tent, Jacobs had a chance encounter with a young girl that changed her life forever.

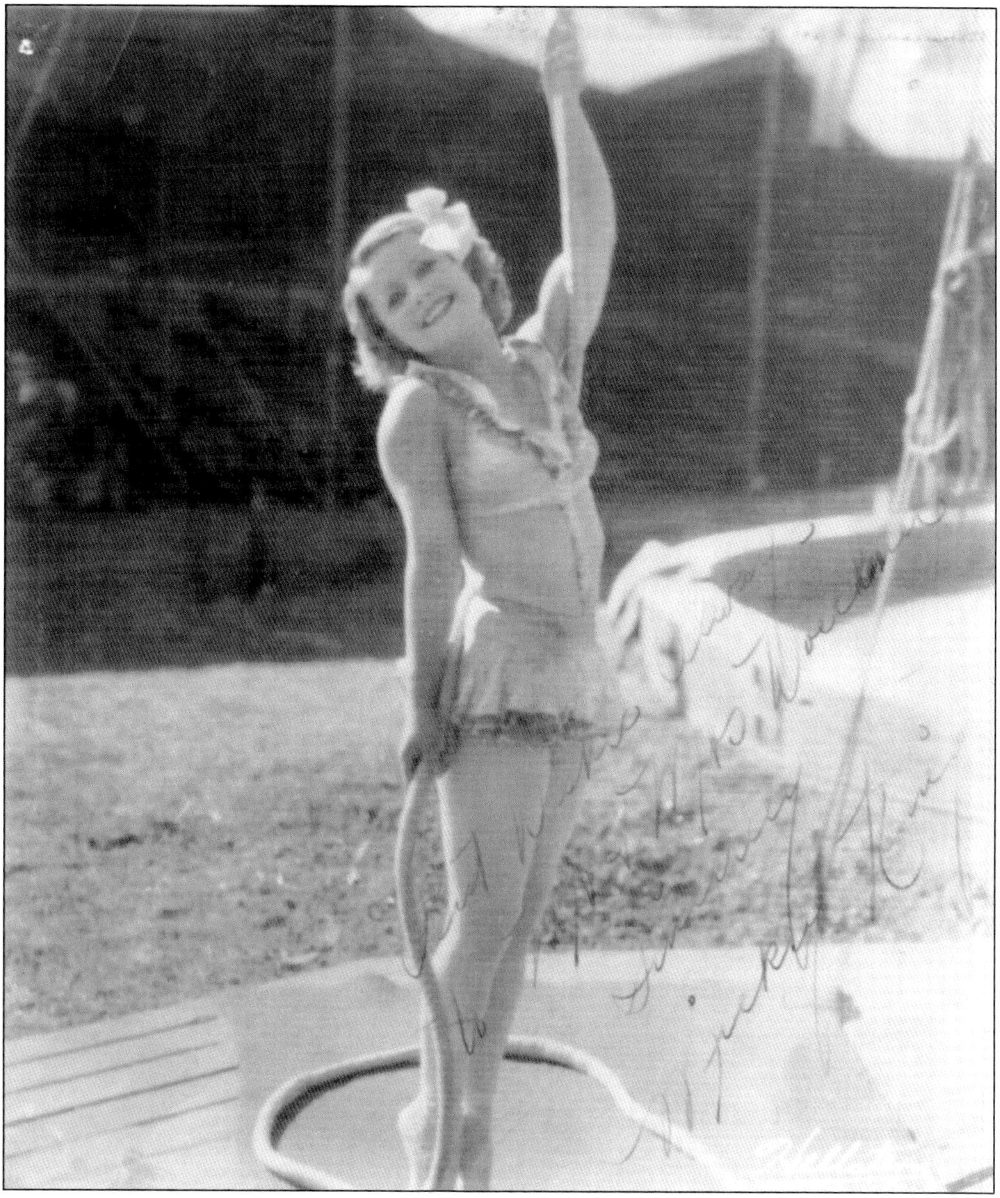

On July 2, 1923, the Sells-Floto was in Holyoke, Massachusetts. Seventeen-year-old Mickey Comeau (later King) was awed by Terrell Jacobs's performance. Upon leaving the cage, Jacobs said to Comeau, "How's the crowd in the big show?" She replied, "I don't know." After asking a few more questions and getting the same answer, Jacobs said, "Aren't you with the big show?" Comeau answered, "No." Jacobs then told her they needed girls like her and told her whom to contact. After securing a job, Comeau ran home, packed a bag, and forged a letter of consent. Comeau ran away from home the next morning and joined the circus.

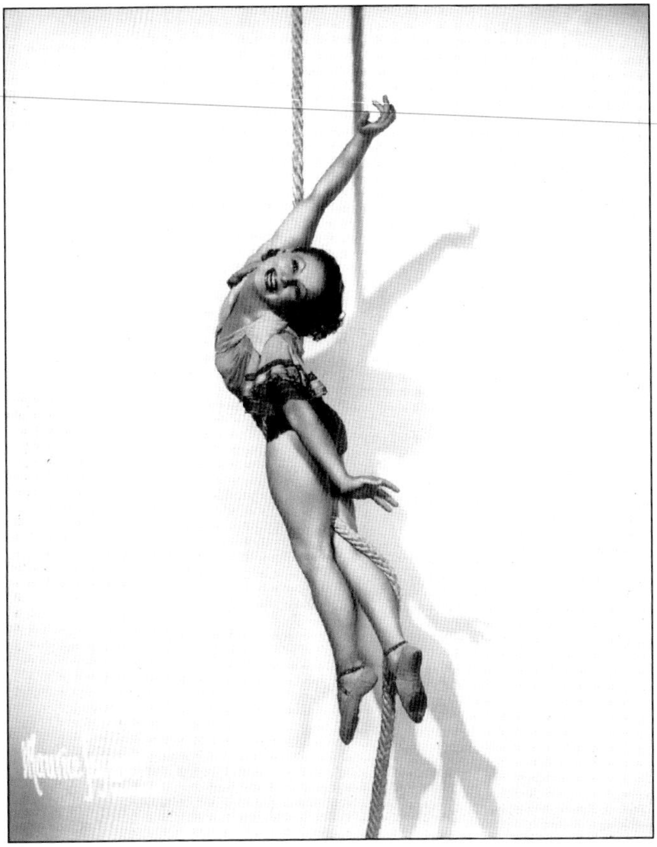

Mickey Comeau's first job was doing ballet in the show. Later that season, Comeau joined the Flying Wards trapeze act. In 1924, she met and married wild animal trainer Allen King, who performed a cat and a polar bear act in the show. Even though her marriage only lasted six years, Comeau went on to perform with circuses and travel the world until she retired to Peru in 1968. She said the circus was a fool's paradise and she loved every minute of it. (Courtesy of the International Circus Hall of Fame.)

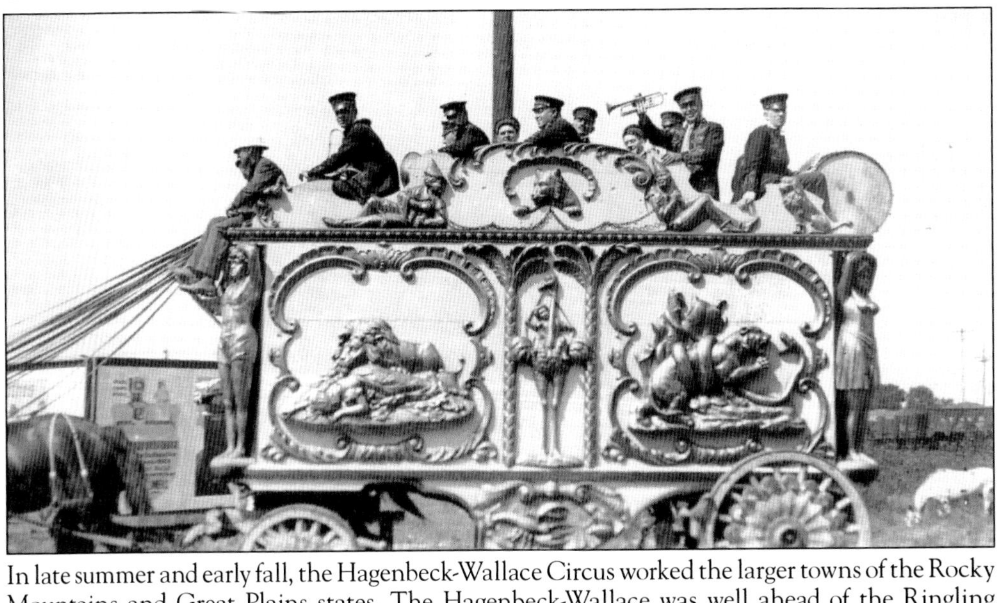

In late summer and early fall, the Hagenbeck-Wallace Circus worked the larger towns of the Rocky Mountains and Great Plains states. The Hagenbeck-Wallace was well ahead of the Ringling Brothers and Barnum and Bailey Circus and pretty much unchallenged. By late September, the show was playing in Texas and went on to play the southern states before heading for the winter quarters in early November.

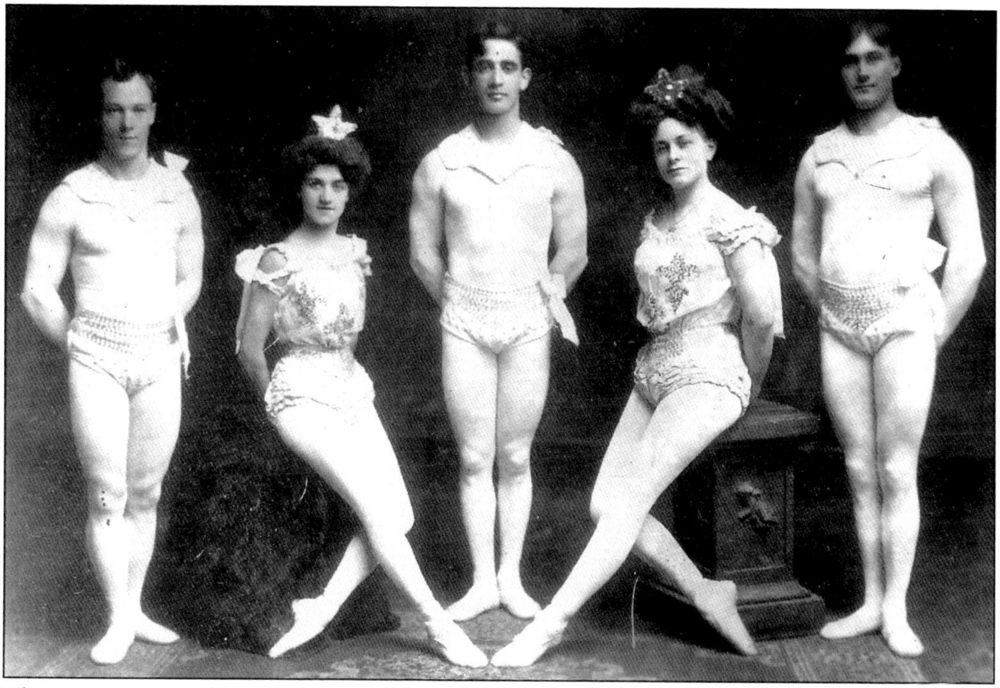

The Hagenbeck-Wallace Circus toured for 27 weeks and 1 day in 1923. It had 169 actual show days, trouped over 28 states, and covered 13,994 miles. The circus was only in the winter quarters at West Baden a short time before leaving for a winter tour. The winter tour was basically the same show as the summer tour but performed inside large coliseums.

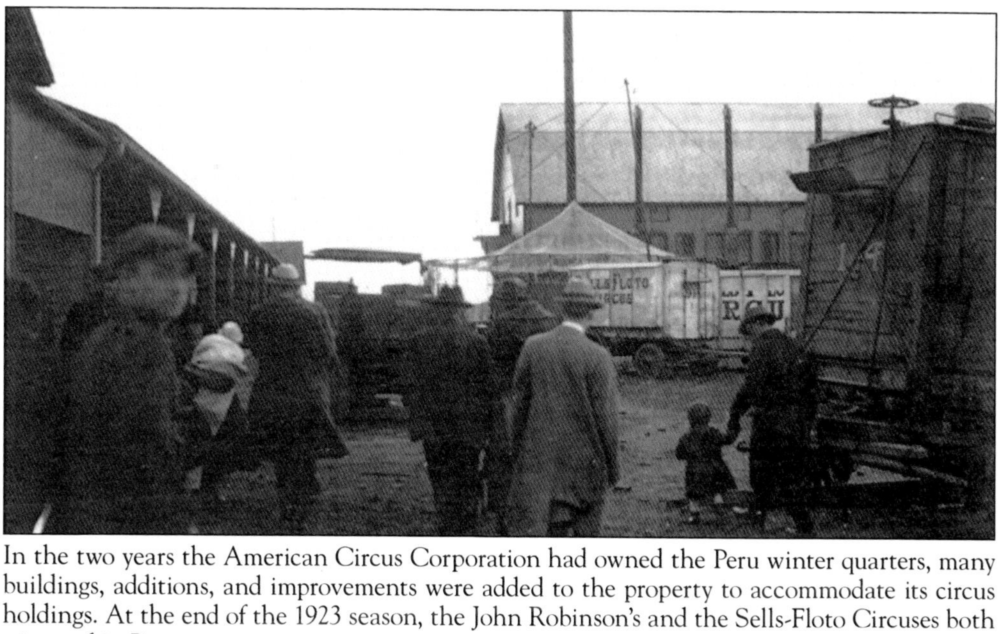

In the two years the American Circus Corporation had owned the Peru winter quarters, many buildings, additions, and improvements were added to the property to accommodate its circus holdings. At the end of the 1923 season, the John Robinson's and the Sells-Floto Circuses both wintered in Peru.

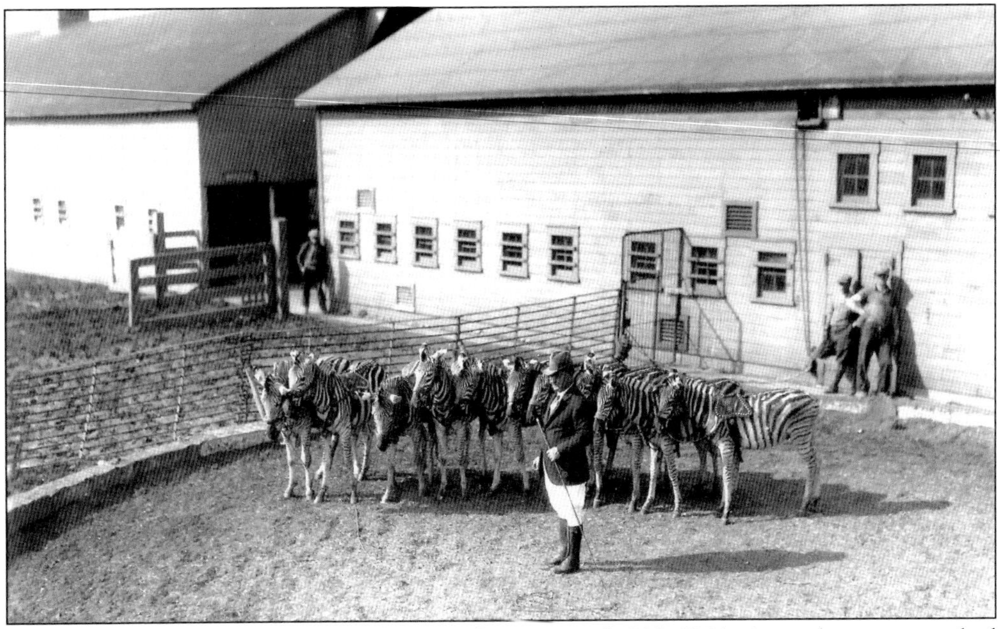

The Peru winter quarters was very busy in the winter of 1923–1924. Animal trainers worked relentlessly to polish their acts for the upcoming season. The four-ring barns and three-arena buildings were occupied 24 hours a day. Trainers for the John Robinson's Circus would use the barns during the day and the Sells-Floto Circus trainers would work in the barns at night. Shifts were alternated each week throughout the winter.

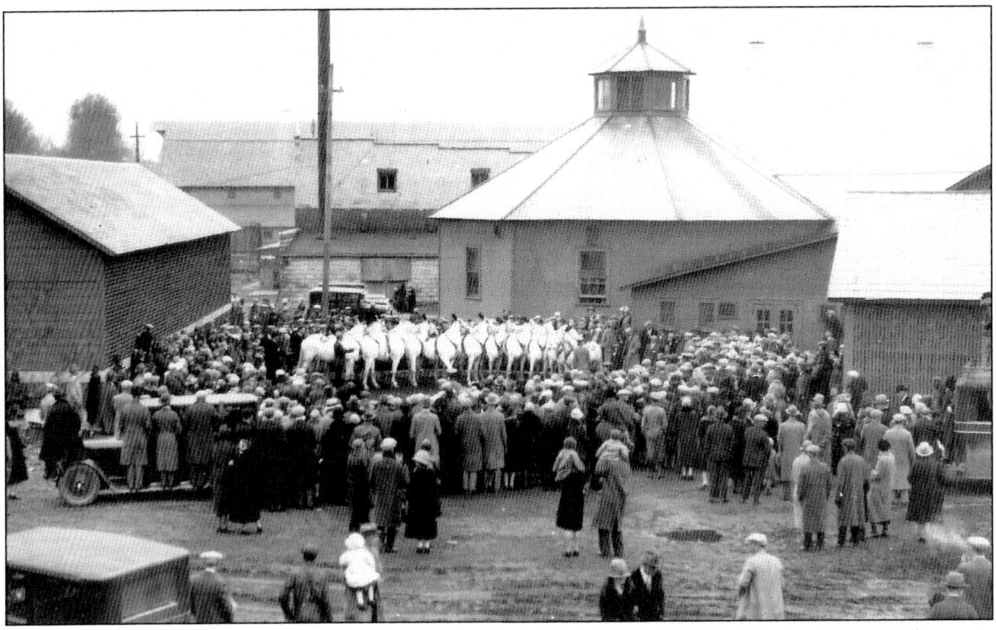

Animal trainers for the John Robinson's were Peter Taylor, Charles Guilfoyle, Ernest Schuman, Clyde Beatty, Robert Thornton, W. W. Weaver, Bernie Griggs, Fred Nelson, and Cheerful Gardner. The Sells-Floto trainers were Louis Reed, Aage Christensen, Joe Miller, Jules Jacot, Allen King, Fred Collier, R. M. LeDantes, Grover McCabe, Frank R. Kelso, George Allen, Terrell Jacobs, and John Smith.

# *Six*

# WELCOME HOME

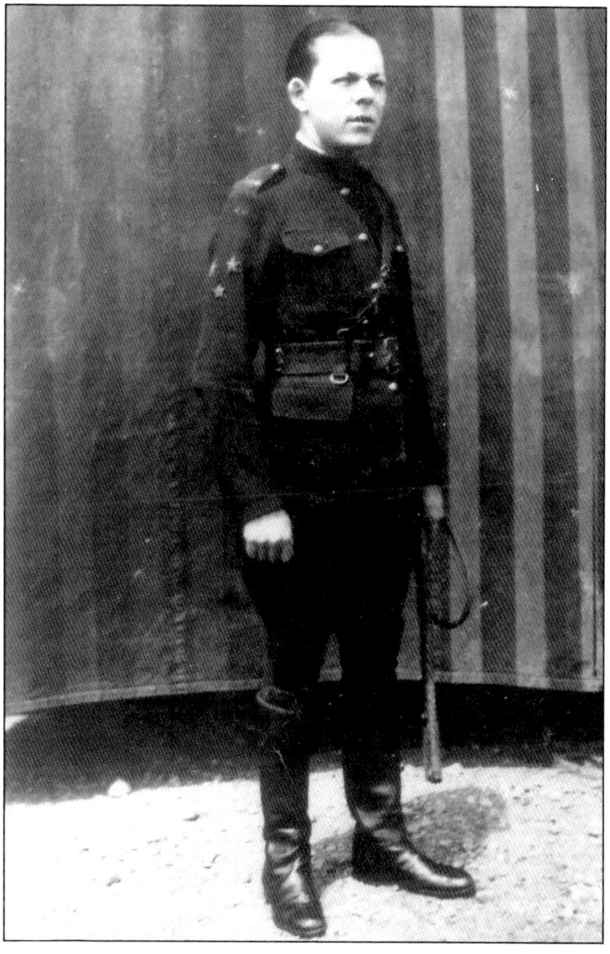

In the spring of 1924, the American Circus Corporation sent three circuses on tour: the Hagenbeck-Wallace, John Robinson's, and Sells-Floto Circuses. The Gollmar Brothers title was subleased to Chester Monahan of Wabash, who was planning a five-car show of his own. The Howe's Great London, Van Amburg's Trained Wild Animals, Yankee Robinson, Famous Robinson, and Buffalo Bill's Wild West titles were owned by the American Circus Corporation but not used in 1924. This photograph is of animal trainer Terrell Jacobs with the Sells-Floto Circus.

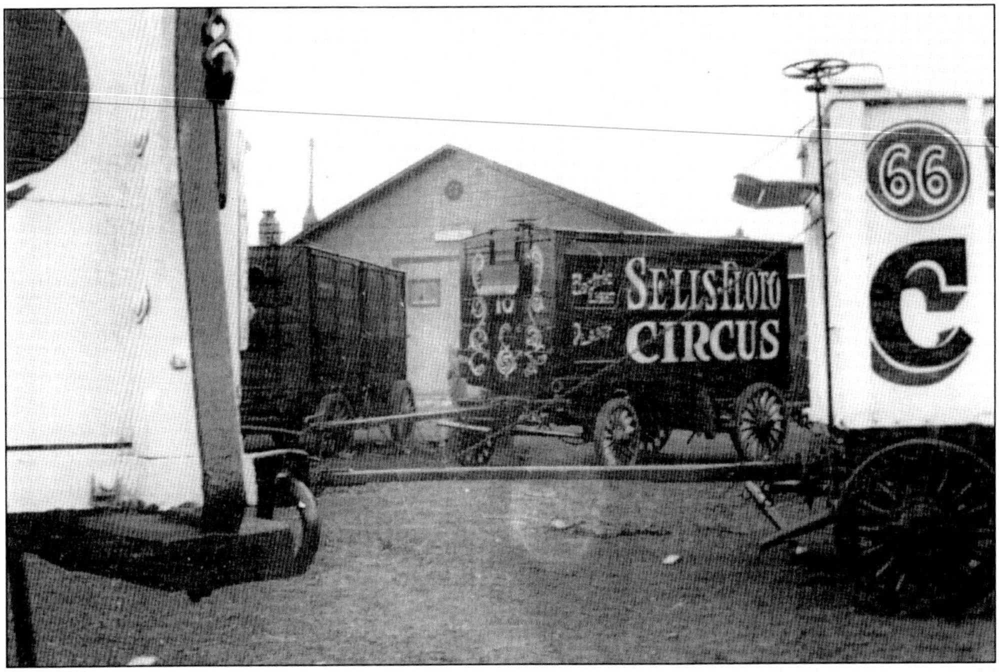


The American Circus Corporation management decided that the 1924 Sells-Floto Circus would feature animal acts along with the usual circus acts. The Sells-Floto was scheduled to open the season in April at the Chicago Coliseum. While the final touches were being made to the acts and equipment, general manager Zack Terrell left Peru ahead of the show to make changes at the coliseum to accommodate the new animal acts.

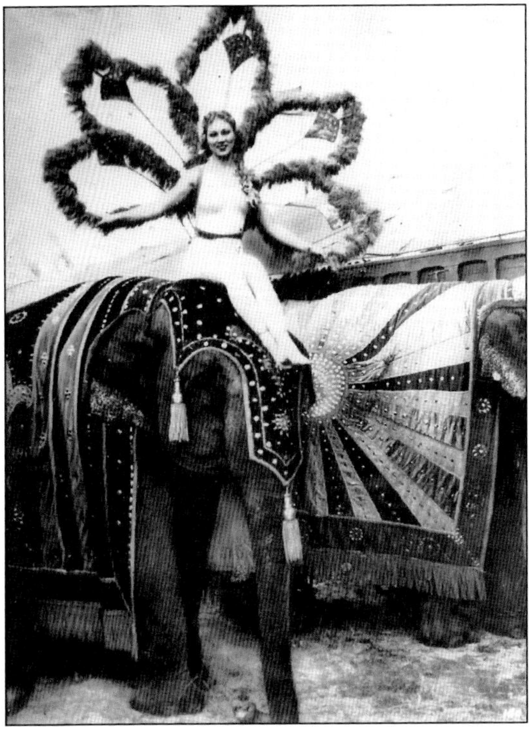

The new animal acts included Jules Jacot, with a mixed group of pumas, lions, and leopards. Jacot also had an act of 15 female lions. Allen King's acts consisted of 10 male lions and a polar bear. Fourteen elephants were trained by Louis Reed and worked in three rings featuring Kathryn Thompson, Irene Ledgett, and Madge Fuller. A tiger riding an elephant in a steel arena was also featured.

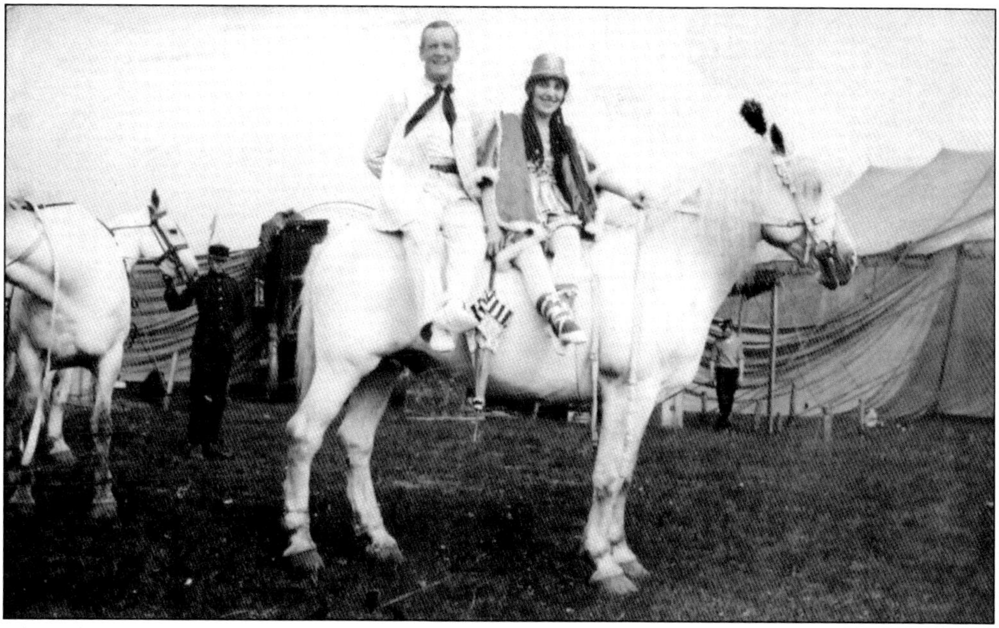

The Sells-Floto opened in the Chicago Coliseum on April 5, 1924. The strategy of adding animal acts paid off for the American Circus Corporation. During the opening engagement, the show played before several sold-out crowds and was more profitable than any past Sells-Floto openings. The show left Chicago for a stand in its hometown of Peru on April 28.

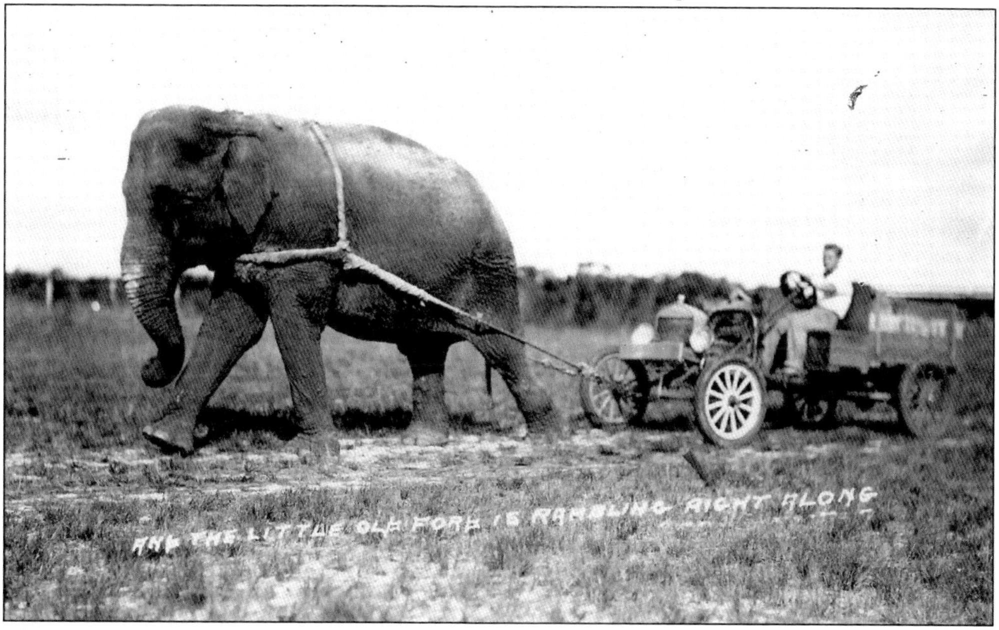


The Hagenbeck-Wallace Circus opened the 1924 season in Louisville, Kentucky, on April 26, and the John Robinson's Circus opened in the Cleveland Auditorium on April 16. The American Circus Corporation planned to send the Hagenbeck-Wallace and the Sells-Floto east after their opening engagements and to send the John Robinson's west. The competition had caught on to its first-to-the-money strategies, and some planned to turn the tables on the corporation circuses.

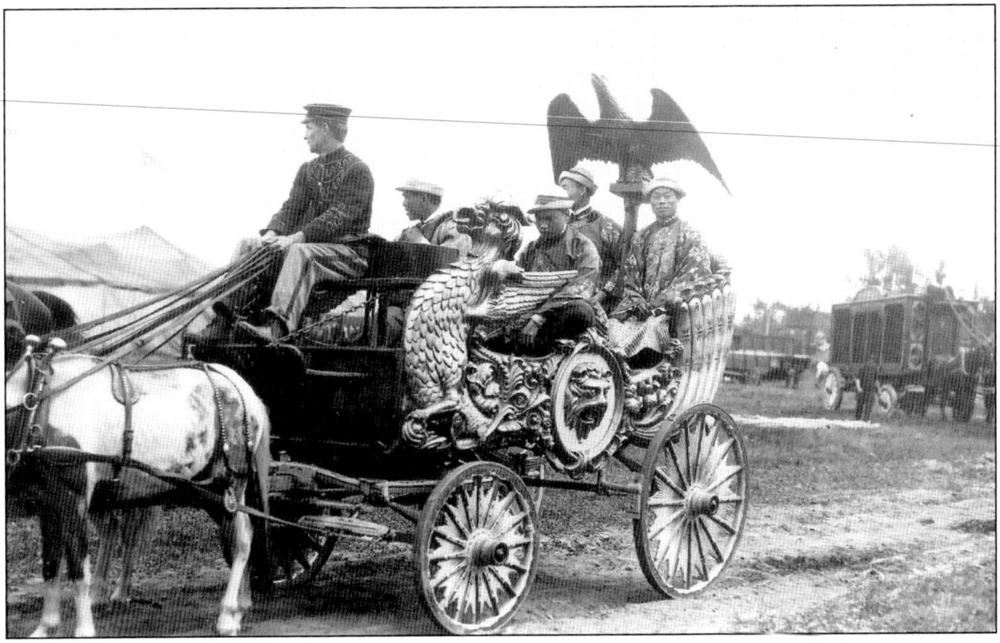

On May 5, 1924, the Sparks Circus played Akron, Ohio, and the Hagenbeck-Wallace Circus was due to play Akron on May 8. However, before the Hagenbeck-Wallace advance crew could reach town, the Ringling Brothers and Barnum and Bailey Circus advance crew arrived on May 5 and covered up all the Sparks advertising. The Hagenbeck-Wallace crew then arrived in Akron and papered over Ringling's advertising.

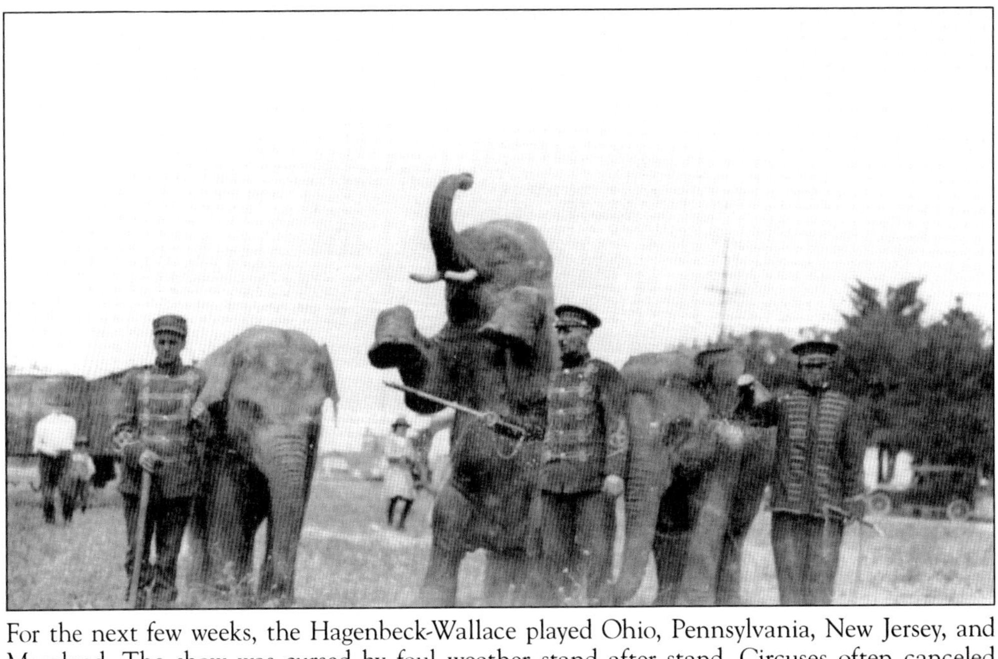

For the next few weeks, the Hagenbeck-Wallace played Ohio, Pennsylvania, New Jersey, and Maryland. The show was cursed by foul weather stand after stand. Circuses often canceled parades and even engagements due to rain and mud. Bert Bowers told a reporter that the Hagenbeck-Wallace Circus had only experienced four nice days in the last several weeks.

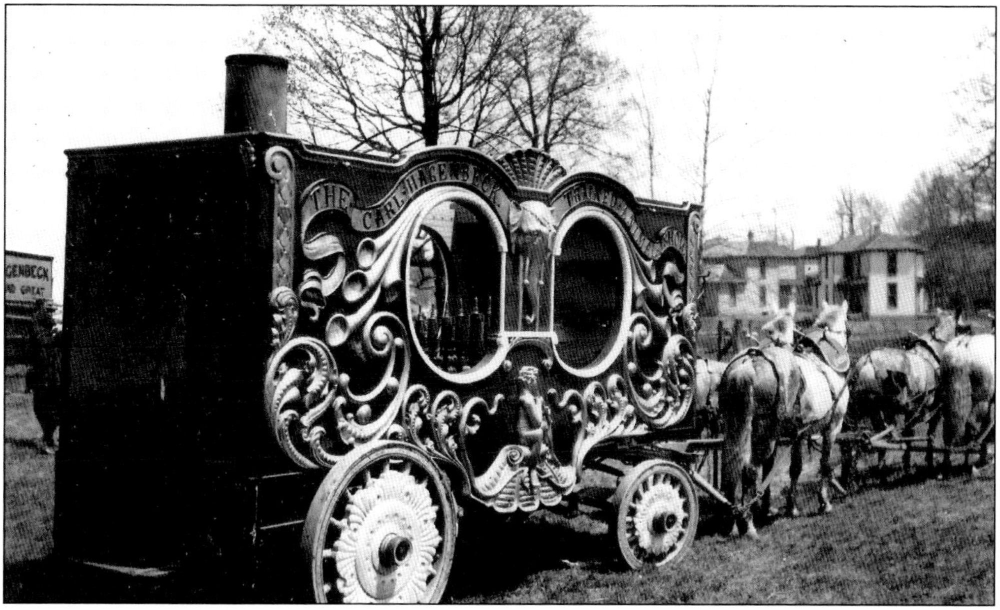


On June 16, 1924, the Hagenbeck-Wallace was in Watertown, New York. The show was finally seeing favorable weather and hoping for a turn-away crowd. The townspeople lined the streets watching the parade when, without warning, a team pulling a calliope was spooked and ran wildly down the street. One of the horses fell during the sprint and stopped the team. Luckily no one was hurt, but the fallen horse was missing a little hide.

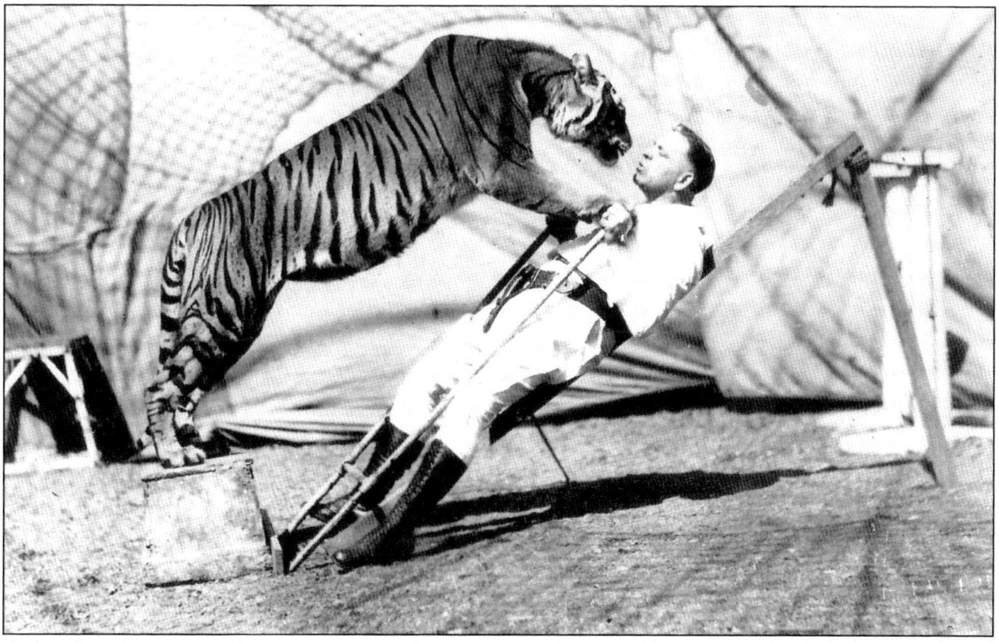

A few days later at Lock Haven, Pennsylvania, animal trainer Robert McPherson (pictured) was in the middle of his big cat act when one of his tigers attacked and badly injured him. A week later McPherson was back performing his tiger act when a storm came up and knocked the lights out in the big top. When the lights came on, the audience was amazed that McPherson was still in control of the nine tigers and had escaped death for the second time in a week.

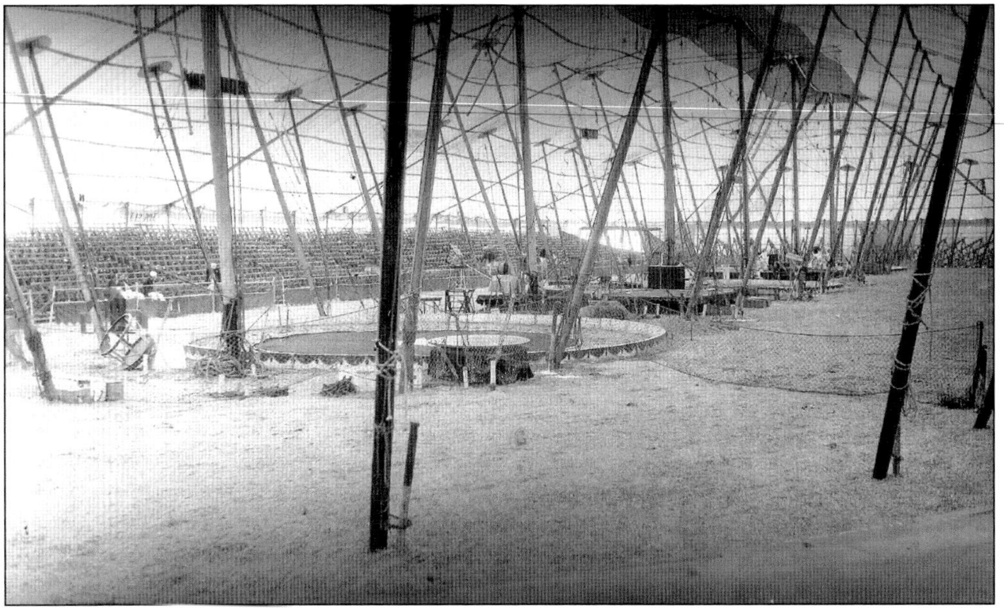

One summer evening while playing Bedford, John Helliott was attacked by one of his performing lions, Caesar. He was in the hospital for several days. The show finished its tour through Indiana and began playing Michigan. It was here that Jeremiah Mugivan replaced his partner Bert Bowers as manager of the show while Bowers and Edward M. Ballard visited Europe.

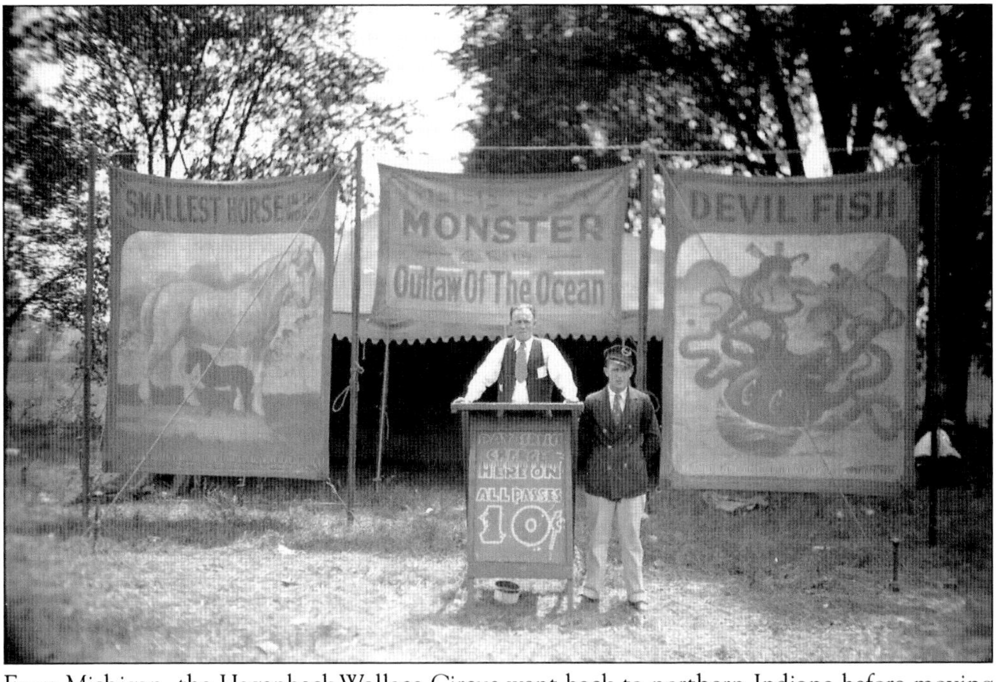


From Michigan, the Hagenbeck-Wallace Circus went back to northern Indiana before moving into Illinois. Foul weather once again plagued the show for a few weeks. While in Illinois, an aerialist fell during the show and was out for a few weeks. During this time, "Albino Girl" Lillian Maloney and "Snake Enchantress" May Gilmore joined the show.

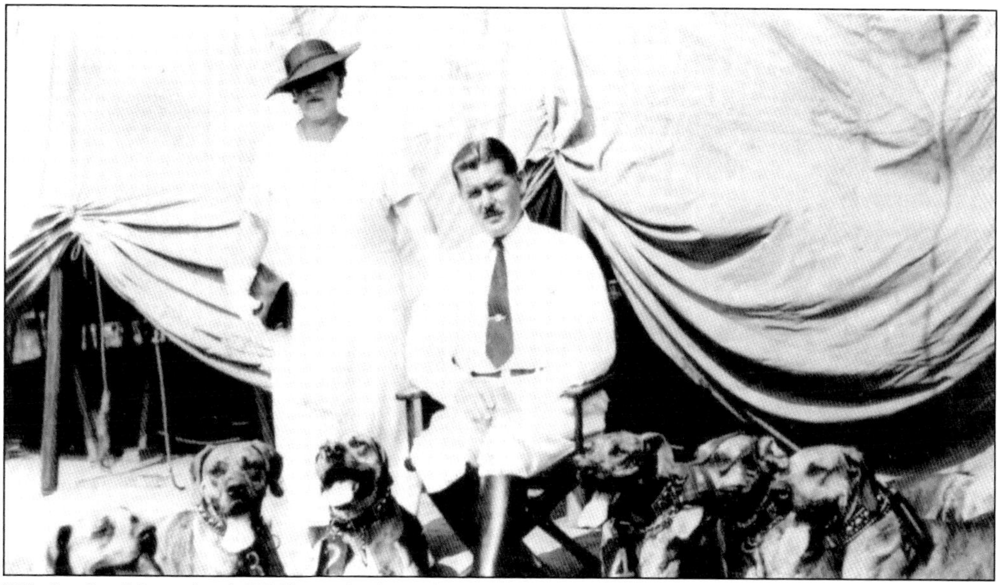

While the Hagenbeck-Wallace dealt with its shortcomings over the summer, the Sells-Floto Circus was battling weather and fierce competition from the Sparks Circus and the Ringling Brothers and Barnum and Bailey Circus. The show was still reporting good crowds thanks to the newspapers' and radio stations' reviews. Some radio stations such as WNAC Boston broadcast the entire show.

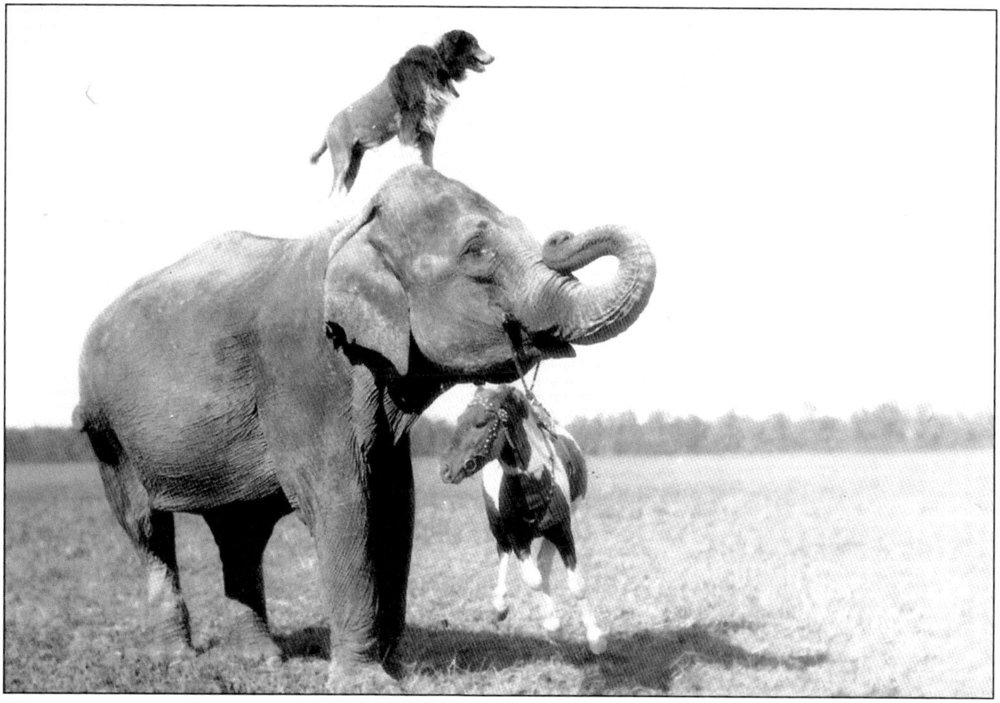

The competition between the Sells-Floto, Sparks, and Ringling Brothers shows got so tough that the Ringlings dropped Boston's show dates and switched other dates around to avoid the Sells-Floto and the Sparks shows. The advance cars of theses circuses were still papering over one another's billing posters. It had become a never-ending battle.

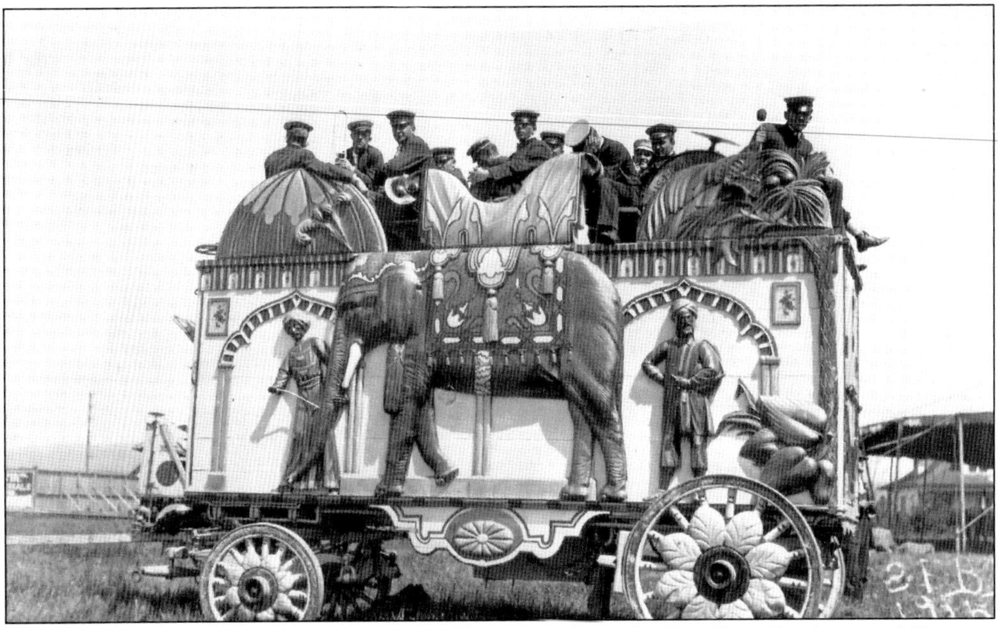

Although the Sells-Floto Circus was a smaller circus than the Ringling Brothers and Barnum and Bailey Circus, "the Circus Beautiful" featured some of the finest circus and animal acts in the world. Unlike Ringling Brothers, it still featured a street parade. The elephant bandwagon was the lead wagon in 1924. It was built at the old Sells-Floto winter quarters in Denver, Colorado, in 1905.

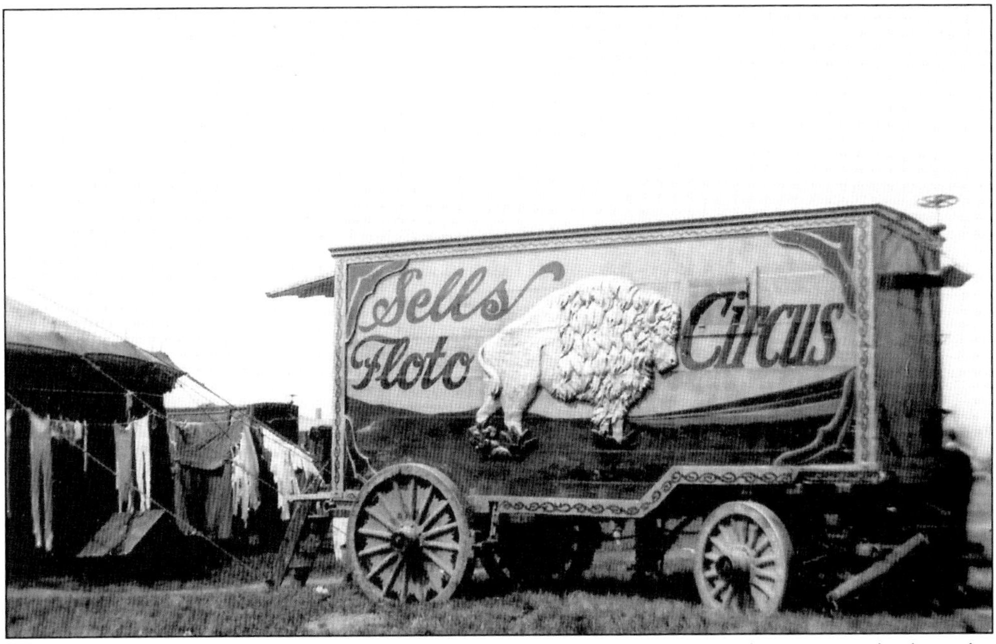


The Sells-Floto parade also featured a big wagon called the "Buffalo Tableau." It was built in the 1890s for the Buffalo Bill's Wild West Show. It later appeared on the Buffalo Bill–Pawnee Bill Show from 1909 to 1913 and on the Sells Floto–Buffalo Bill Show from 1914 to 1915. It originally had many carvings on the wagon, but by 1924, the buffalo was the only carving left.

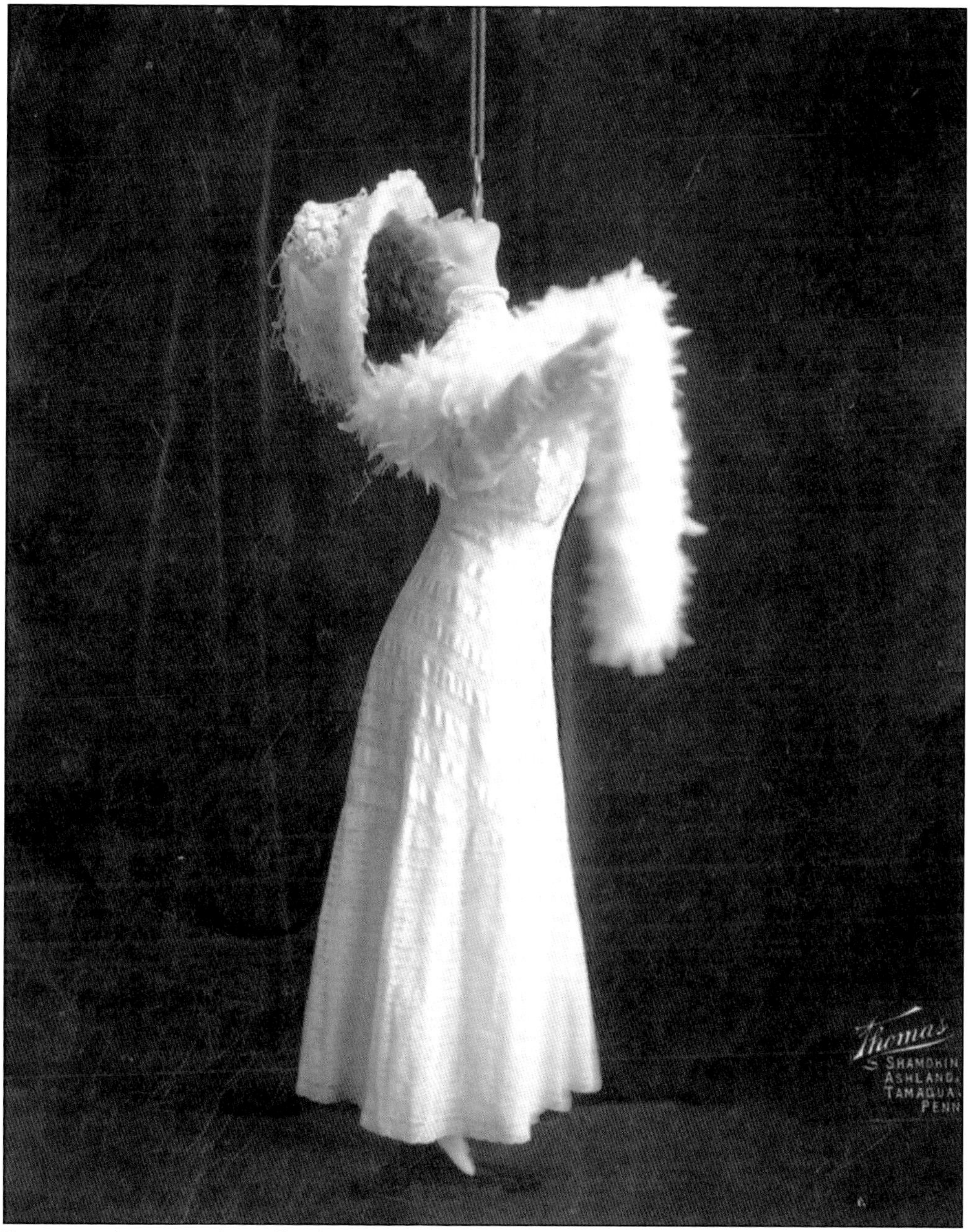


During midsummer, the Sells-Floto ran into a hurdle when its advertising crew was arrested and jailed for posting circus advertising around Norfolk, Virginia, prior to a county fair. Virginia state law prohibited a circus from billing a town within 30 days of a county fair. The crew was billing two weeks ahead of the show date, and the show date was a week before the fair. The American Circus Corporation hired local Norfolk attorneys to argue that the law should not apply to its circus because it was playing before the fair. An agreement was met with the county attorney and the crew was released. The Sells-Floto played Norfolk on August 18 with great attendance.

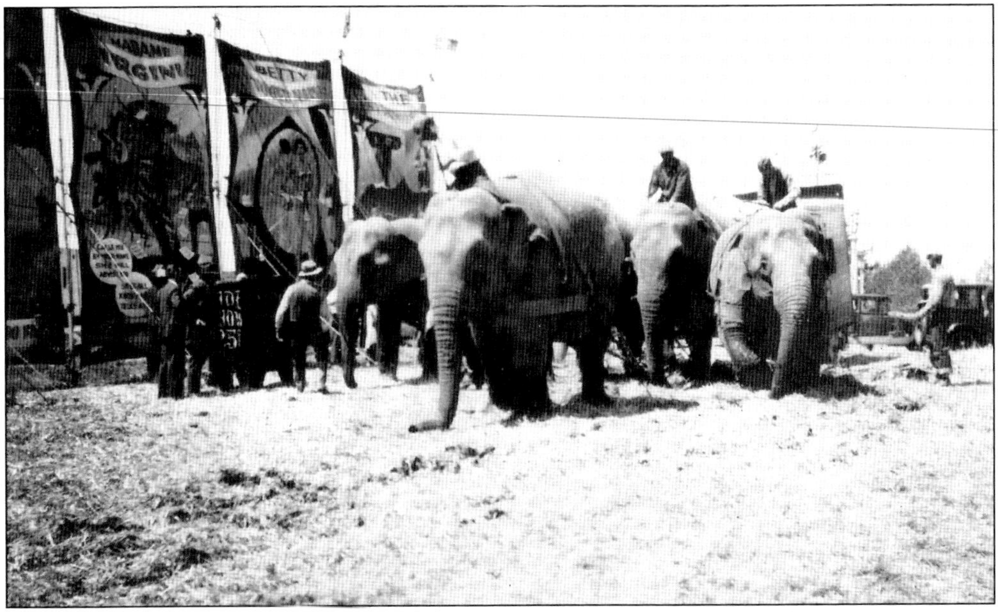

In September, the Sells-Floto Circus advance crew was once again jailed. This time it was in Statesville, North Carolina, for tearing down the Sparks Circus billing posters and replacing them with its own. When brought to court, both sides accused each other of the wrongdoing. The judge ordered that neither show could interfere with the advertising of the other's show and both parties had to pay half the court cost.

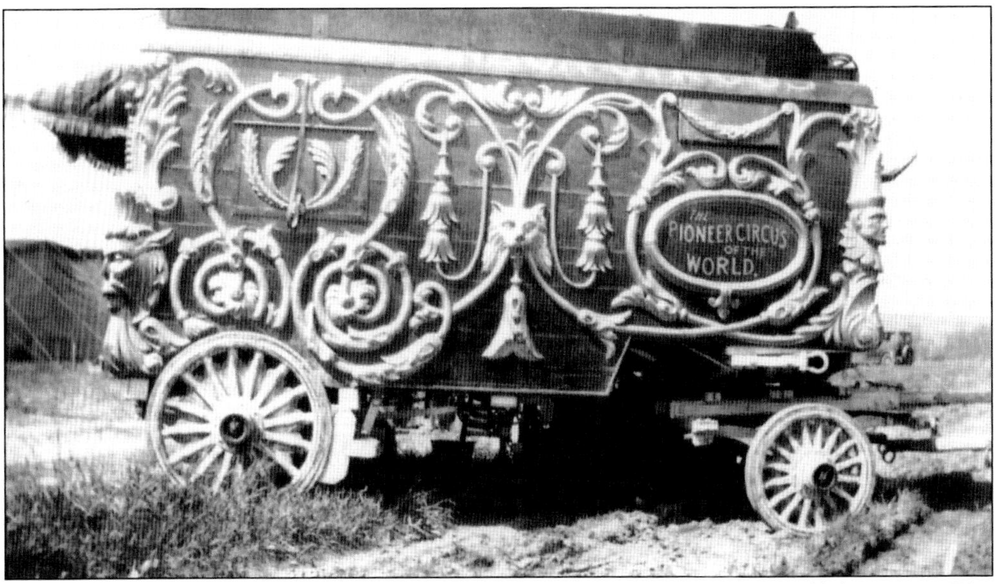


In the fall of 1924, the South was a boiling pot full of opposing circuses in all directions. The Sparks Circus, the Christy Brothers Circus, the Sells-Floto, and the John Robinson's Circus were all trying to finish their seasons with good weather and big crowds. The Ringling Brothers and Barnum and Bailey Circus was quarantined in Texas with hoof-and-mouth disease but entered the mix upon release.

The Hagenbeck-Wallace Circus was playing Texas in October when it hired Jess H. Adkins as assistant manager. Adkins had just resigned his post at the Gentry Brothers–James Patterson Circus. He had previously worked for Jeremiah Mugivan and Bert Bowers on the 1922 Gollmar Brothers Circus. Adkins played a major role in the management of the Hagenbeck-Wallace Circus for the next 10 years.

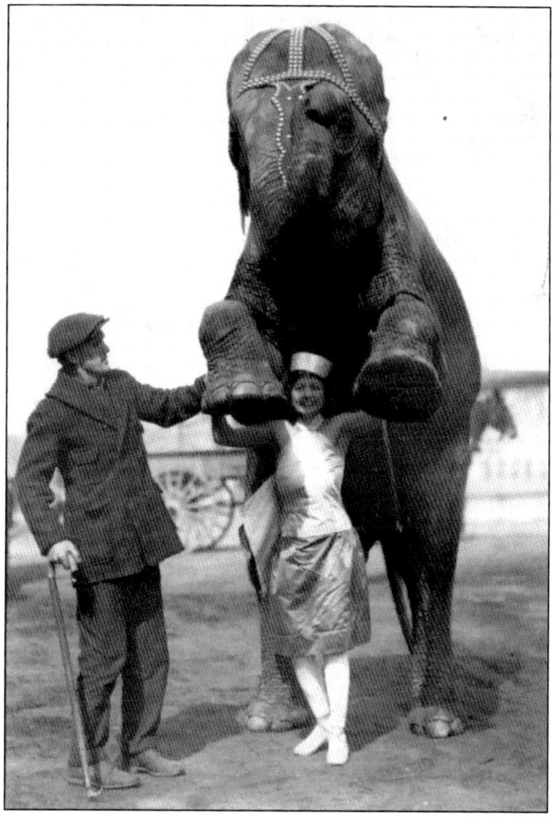

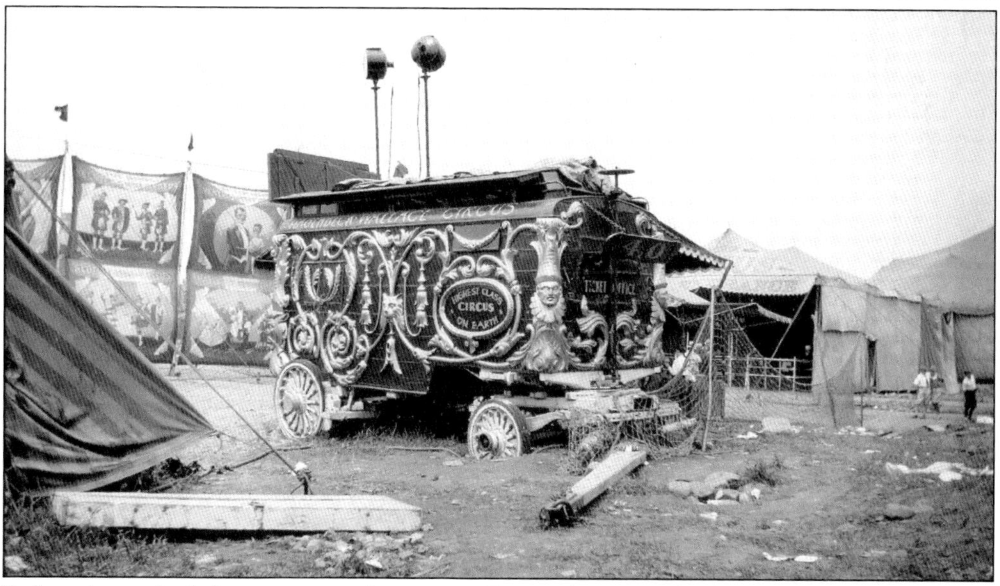

Before the end of the season, in Longview, Texas, the Hagenbeck-Wallace suffered another loss when two sleeper cars were damaged by fire. During the 1924 season, the show braved a tornado, countless days of rain, a snowstorm, a train car fire, and five general managers. The Hagenbeck-Wallace closed the 1924 season in Little Rock, Arkansas, on November 19. The show traveled 14,558 miles and played in 177 engagements in 20 states.

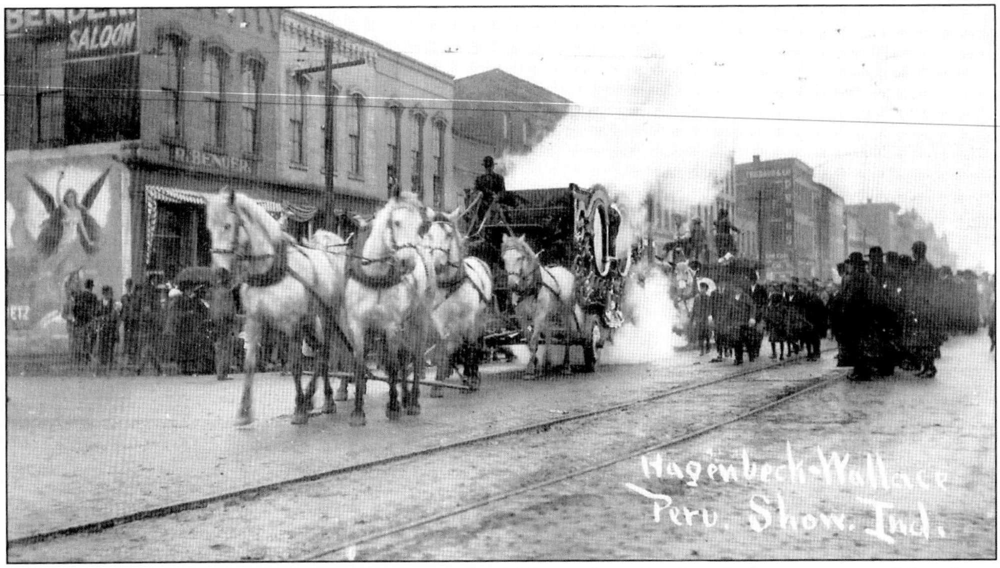


The Sells-Floto Circus toured until the end of November. It closed the season at Meridian, Mississippi, then headed for the Peru winter quarters. The John Robinson's Circus closed at Dyersburg, Tennessee, on November 13, during the evening performance, Emmett and Eva Kelly rushed to the hospital for the delivery of their first-born, Emmett Kelly Jr. From Dyersburg, the John Robinson's was sent to West Baden to winter, and the Hagenbeck-Wallace Circus was sent to Peru.

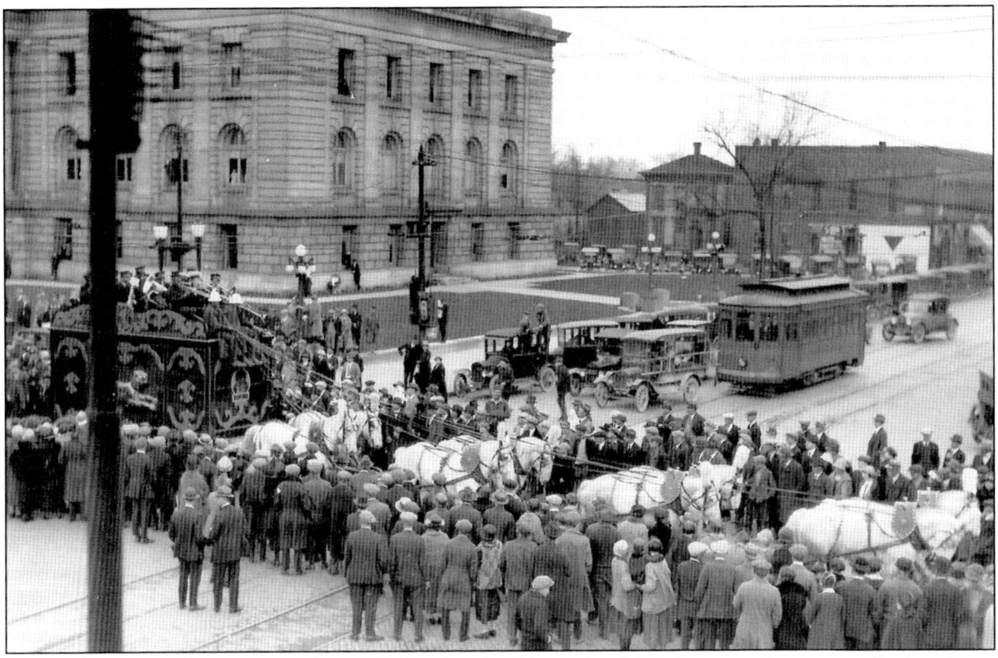

The American Circus Corporation brought the Hagenbeck-Wallace to Peru to refit the show with animals recently bought from Ringling Brothers. It would also switch elephant herds with the John Robinson's show. For the first time in 10 years, the beloved Hagenbeck-Wallace Circus returned home and paraded through Peru on its way to the winter quarters. It was said that the whole town lined Broadway to witness the homecoming.

*Seven*

# THE END OF THE STREET PARADES

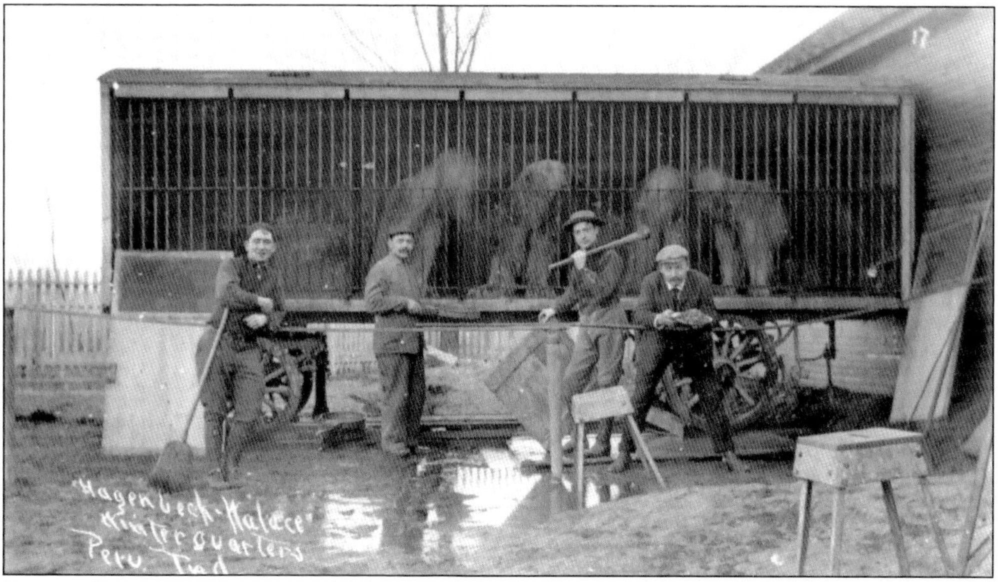


During the winter of 1924–1925, the Hagenbeck-Wallace Circus was reworked to be the jewel of the American Circus Corporation. At this time Jeremiah Mugivan, Bert Bowers, and Edward M. Ballard decided that the corporation circuses would discontinue the tradition of street parades. However, each show would leave their winter quarters with everything needed for a parade except for their steam calliopes. It had always been thought that the street parades helped excite the townspeople and increase ticket sales.

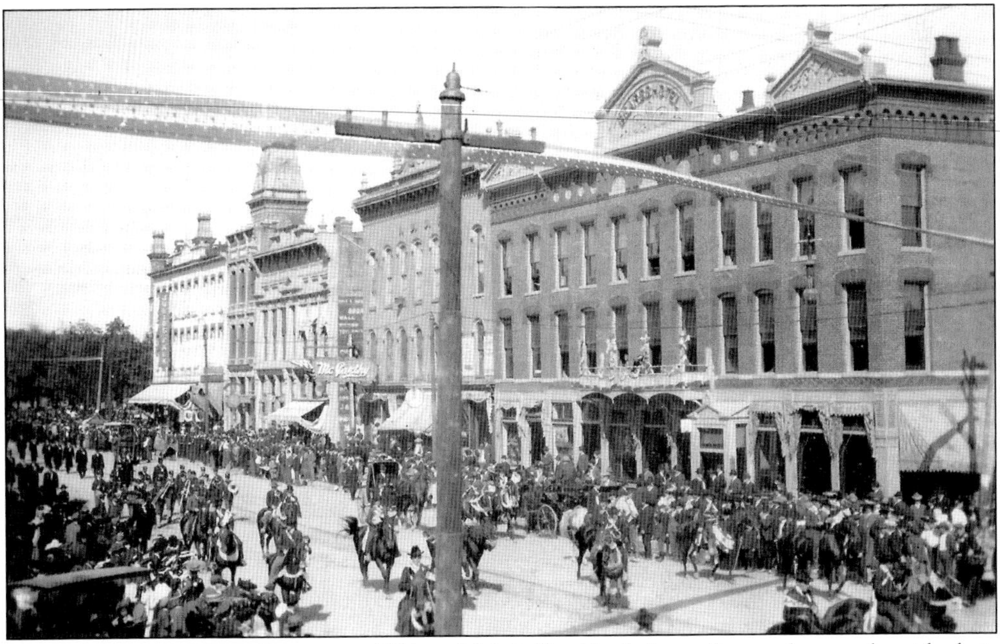

Jeremiah Mugivan, Bert Bowers, and Edward M. Ballard had always featured a parade with their circuses unless burdened by rain or mud or arriving late to an engagement. The corporation may have gotten the idea from John Ringling, who abolished street parades on the Ringling Brothers Barnum and Bailey Circus schedule in 1921. Ringling's policy had little effect on ticket sales. In fact, John Ringling was listed as one of the wealthiest men in the world and was featured on the cover of the April 6, 1925, *Time* magazine.

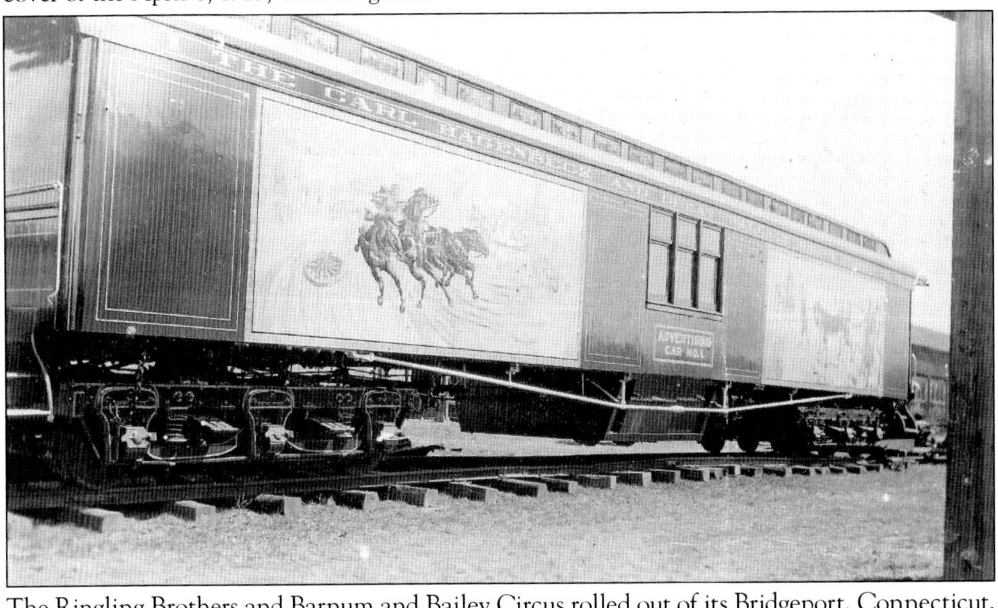


The Ringling Brothers and Barnum and Bailey Circus rolled out of its Bridgeport, Connecticut, winter quarters on 100 railcars in the spring of 1925. The Hagenbeck-Wallace, Sells-Floto, and John Robinson's Circuses left their winter quarters on 30 railcars each. The Ringling Brothers show was the largest in the country and was called the "Big One." The corporation shows were the second largest.

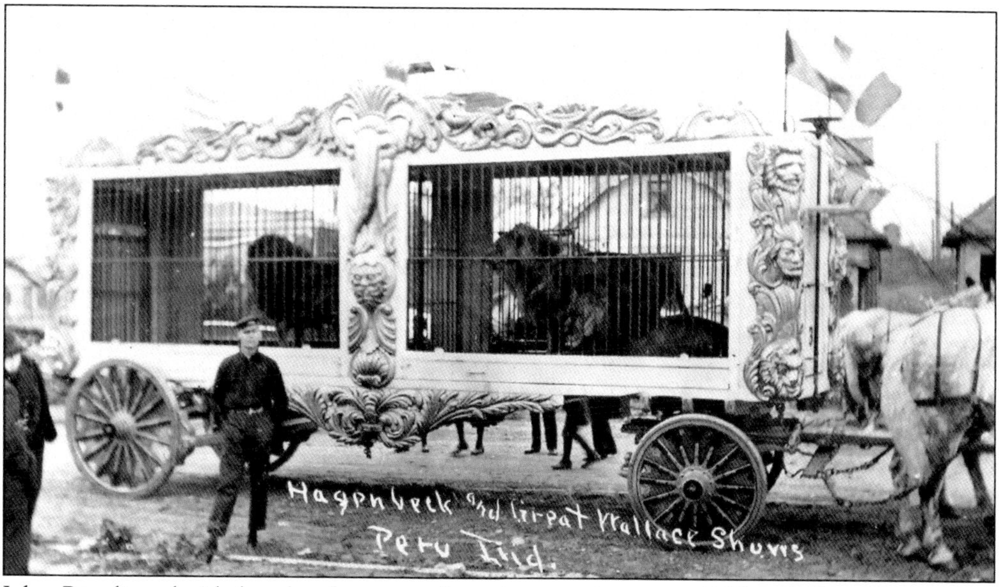


John Ringling decided to break yet another circus tradition in 1925 and abandon the wild animal acts in his show. Ringling commented that the wild animals were dangerous and a pain to transport. The American Circus Corporation jumped on the opportunity to buy some of the Ringling animals to add to the Hagenbeck-Wallace Circus. With the aid of newspapers and posters, the corporation sensationalized the wild animal acts in its three circuses.

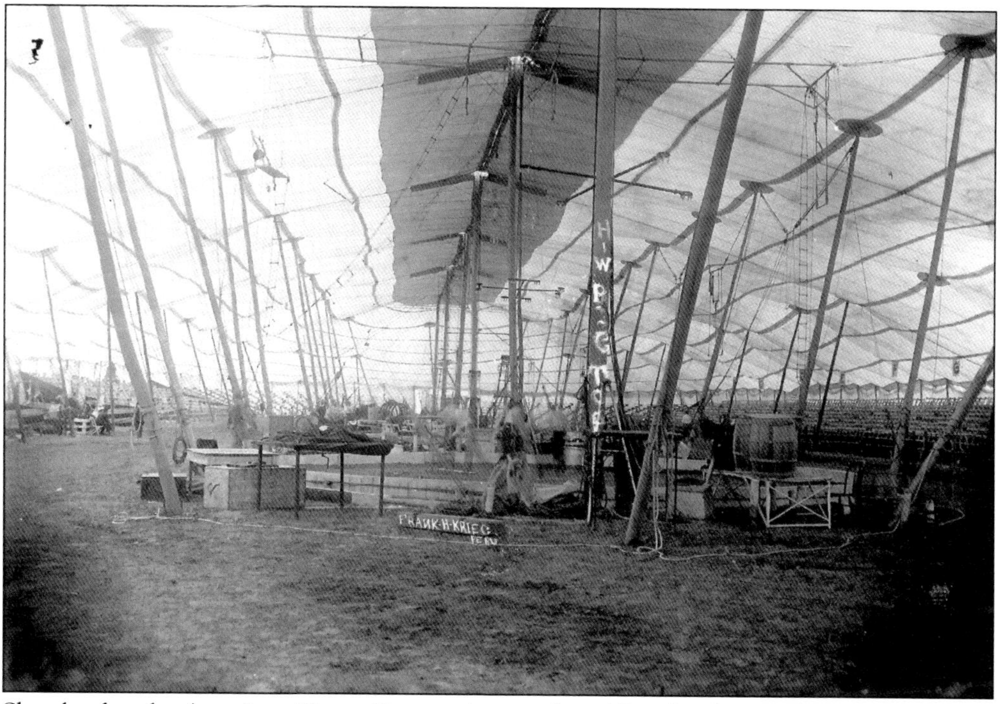


Shortly after the American Circus Corporation purchased Ringling's animals, it announced to *Billboard* magazine its plans for the additional animal acts in the Hagenbeck-Wallace show. The magazine stated, "The steel arena will be left in place during the entire performance and animal acts will be on view for the major part of the time."

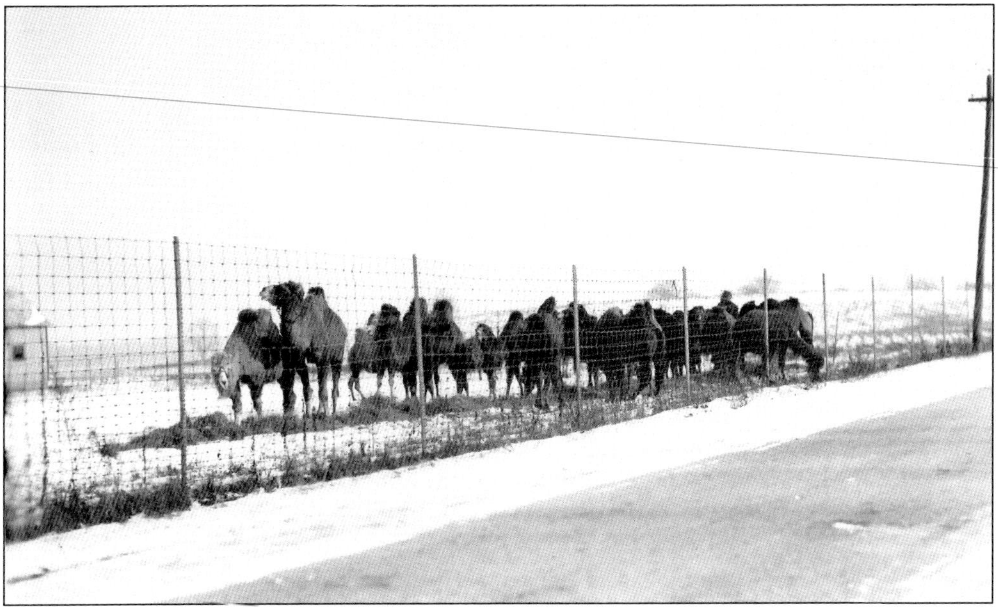

The menageries of the Hagenbeck-Wallace, Sells-Floto, and John Robinson's Circuses consisted of animals from all over the world. Some of the most popular were camels, zebras, hippopotamuses, lions, tigers, giraffes, bears, and monkeys. More than 2,000 animals were cared for at the winter quarters in Peru and West Baden. The American Circus Corporation owned the largest collection of animals in the world.

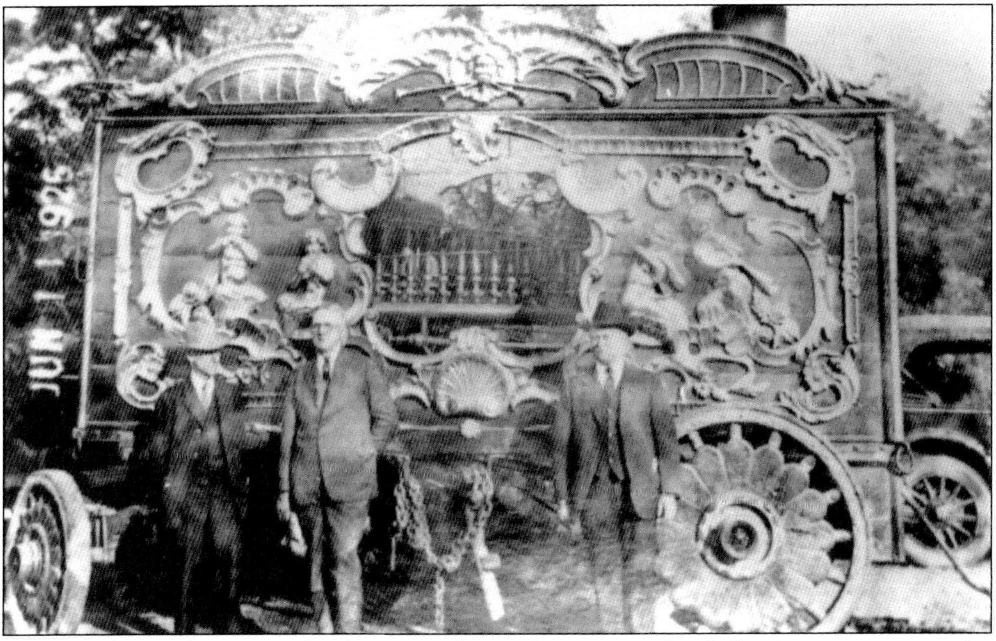

One month into the season, the American Circus Corporation decided to feature street parades with its circuses to boost the sluggish ticket sales. The steam calliopes for each show were immediately dispatched. All three shows paraded the remainder of the 1925 season. However, the American Circus Corporation then reinstated its no-parade policy for the 1926, 1927, and 1928 seasons.

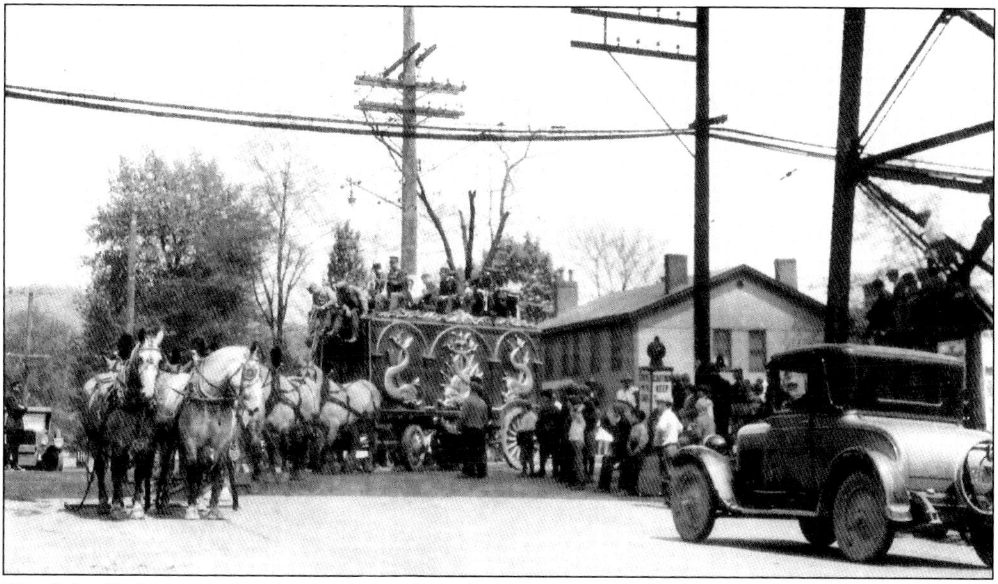

The John Robinson's Circus was not only without its steam calliope in the spring of 1925, but it was also missing the Aerial Kellys, featuring Emmett and Eva Kelly. Corporate policy prohibited acts to travel with small children. The Kellys trouped in 1925 with the Rogers and Harris and the Mighty Haag shows. The Rogers and Harris show went bust 15 weeks into the season. The Kellys finished the season with the Mighty Haag Circus, which was a truck show.

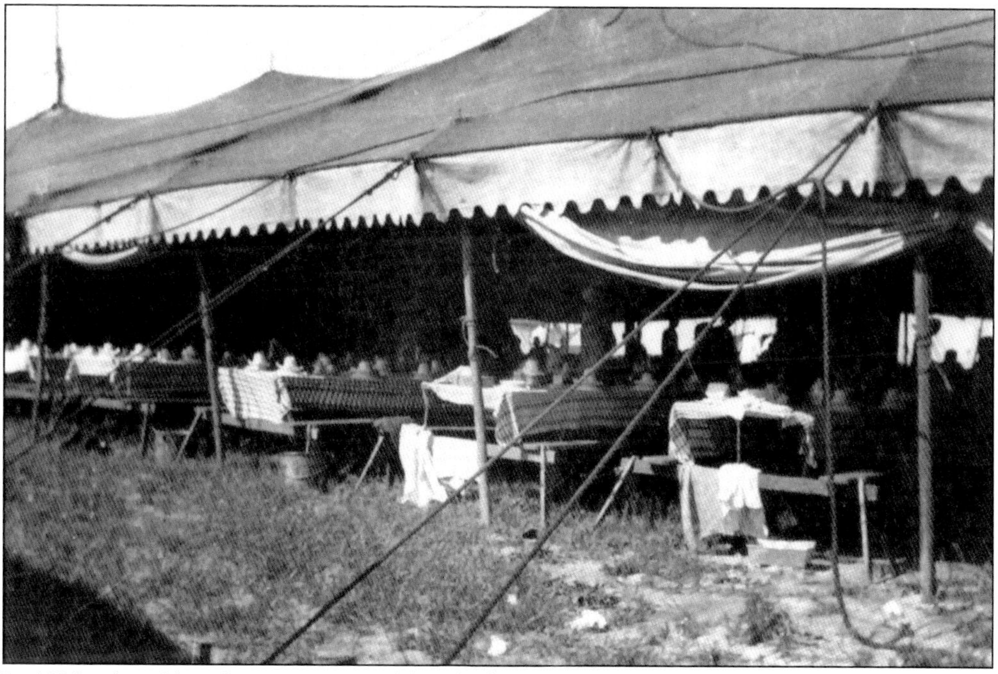

In 1925, a hired hand on a circus could make $20 a week, sleep under a wagon, and eat free in the cookhouse tent. A good skilled act could make $50 to $100 a week with a berth on the train and free meals. Even a cage boy like Clyde Beatty made $3 a day, which was good money for a young man. Good pay and benefits allowed the wise circus employees to save enough money to carry them through the off-season.

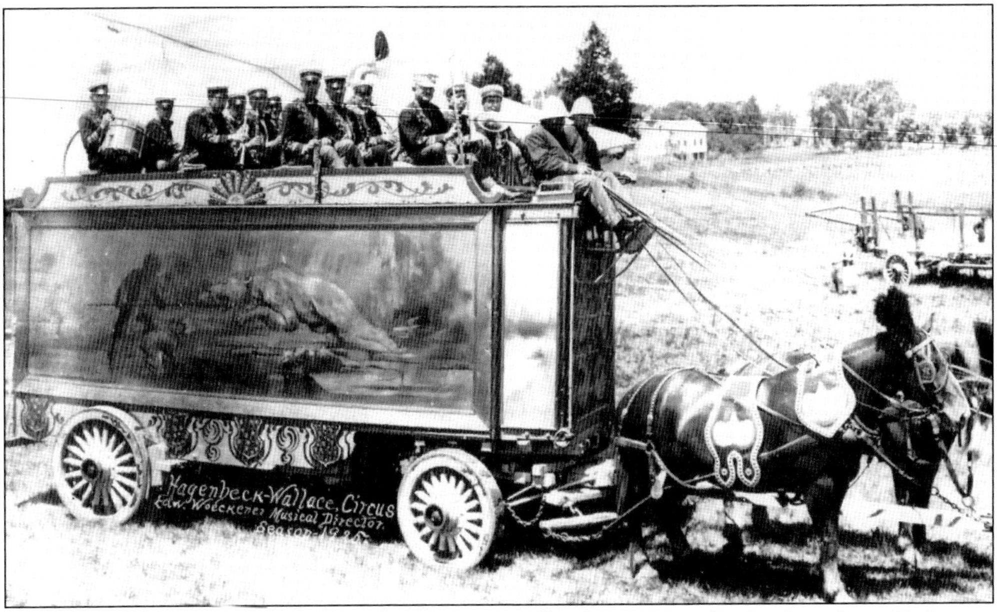


On July 2, 1925, the Hagenbeck-Wallace Circus suffered a major setback when Peter Taylor, its feature animal trainer, left the show. There are many stories concerning his departure. Some say he fell in love and ran off with a woman. Others say he suffered a head injury that prevented him from performing. Another rumor is that he suffered from "arena shock," which meant he lost his nerve to enter the steel arena. Whatever the reason, Taylor's vacancy left manager Danny Odom in a desperate situation.

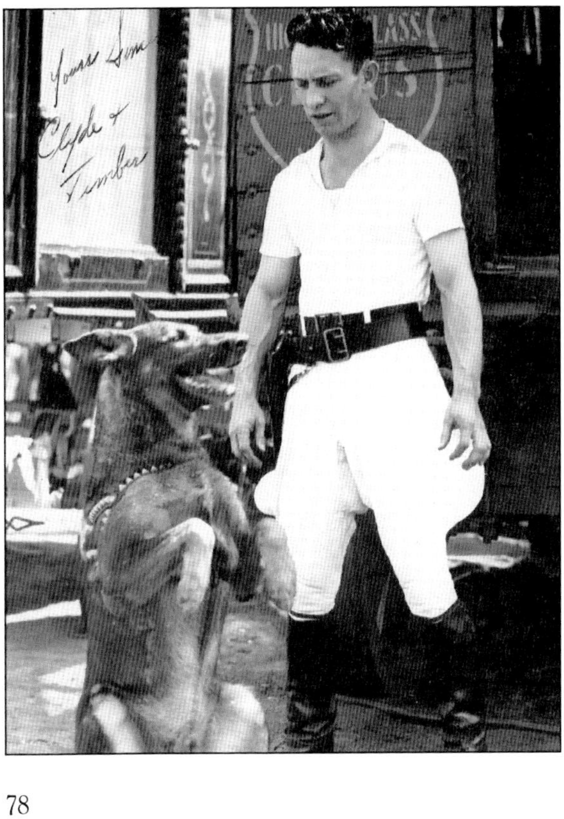

Twenty-three-year-old Clyde Beatty approached Odom and volunteered to work Taylor's 10 lions and 4 tigers. Beatty had assisted Taylor with the animals and remembered how to cue the beasts. Odom gave in reluctantly, and Clyde Beatty stepped into the steel arena on July 3, 1925, and became the youngest animal trainer in the world.

In just a few short years, Clyde Beatty had gone from a cage boy on the Howe's Great London Circus to working a polar bear act on the John Robinson's Circus. By the end of the 1925 season, Beatty and the 14 lions and tigers would be the star attraction of the Hagenbeck-Wallace Circus. Beatty's style and technique in the arena was similar to Peter Taylor's. Like his predecessor, Beatty wore a military-type costume but soon favored a safari hat like big-game hunter Frank Buck and made the look and act his own.

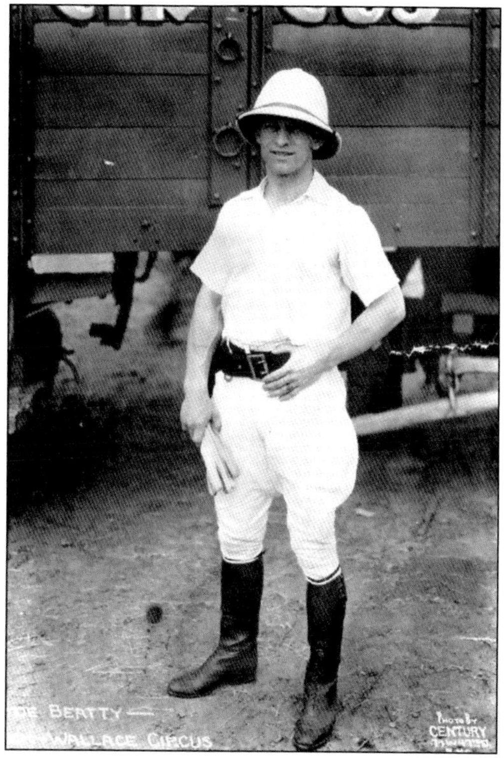

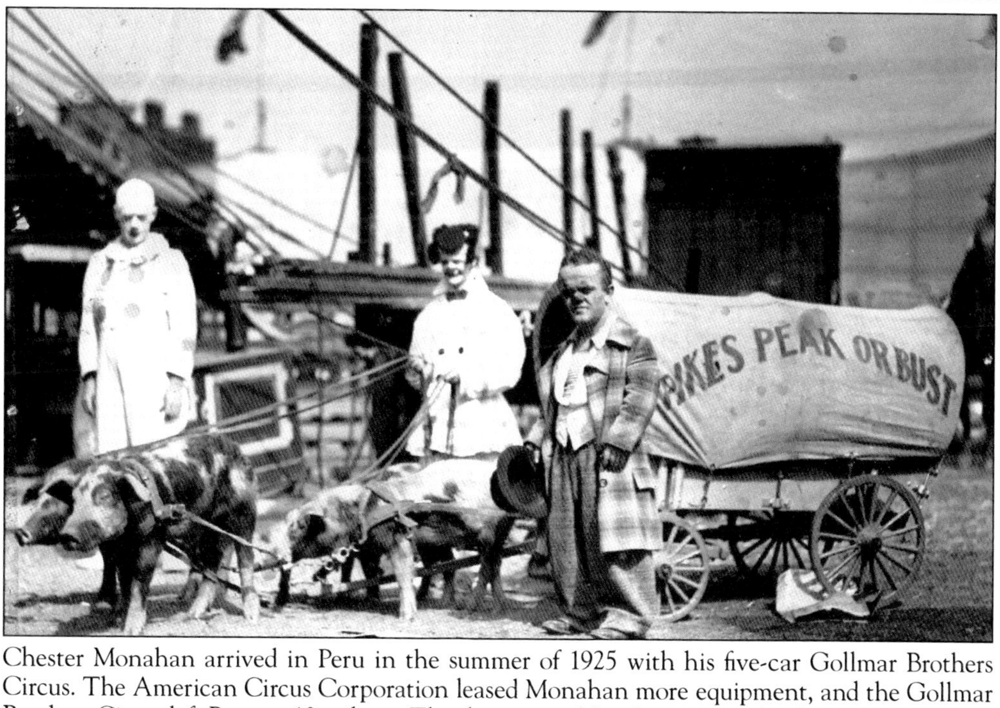

Chester Monahan arrived in Peru in the summer of 1925 with his five-car Gollmar Brothers Circus. The American Circus Corporation leased Monahan more equipment, and the Gollmar Brothers Circus left Peru on 10 railcars. The show toured for about a month when, unfortunately, the show experienced a lot of bad weather and went bust. The American Circus Corporation repossessed the circus and stored it at the West Baden winter quarters.

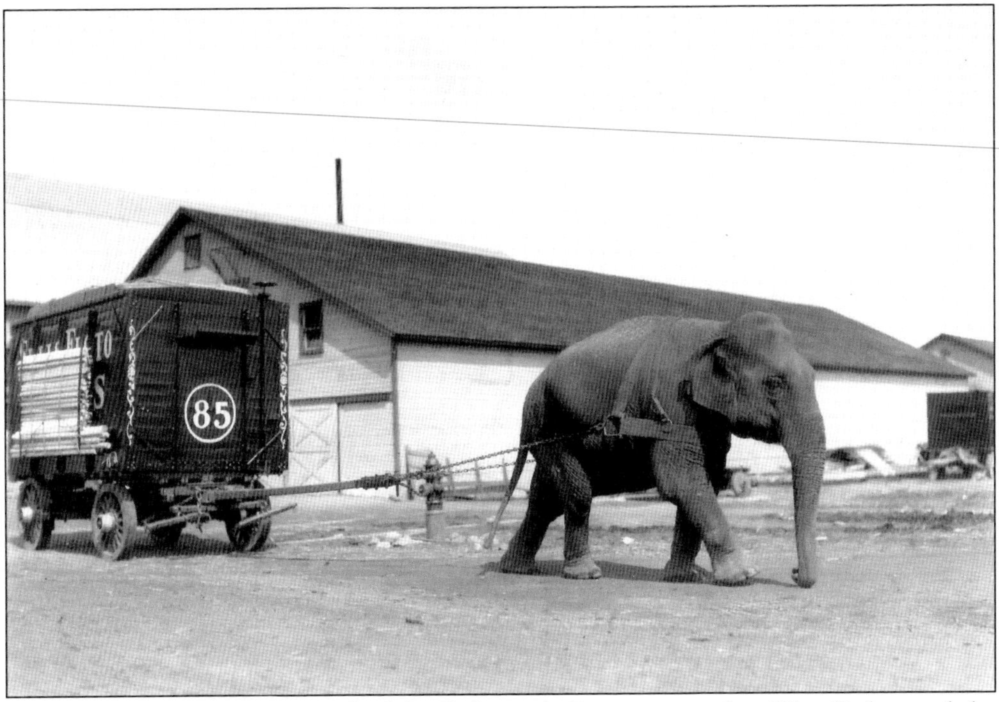

At the end of the 1925 season, the John Robinson's Circus wintered in West Baden, and the Sells-Floto and Hagenbeck-Wallace Circuses wintered in Peru. All the American Circus Corporation shows did well during the 1925 season. This season marked the beginning of what has been referred to as the "big money years."

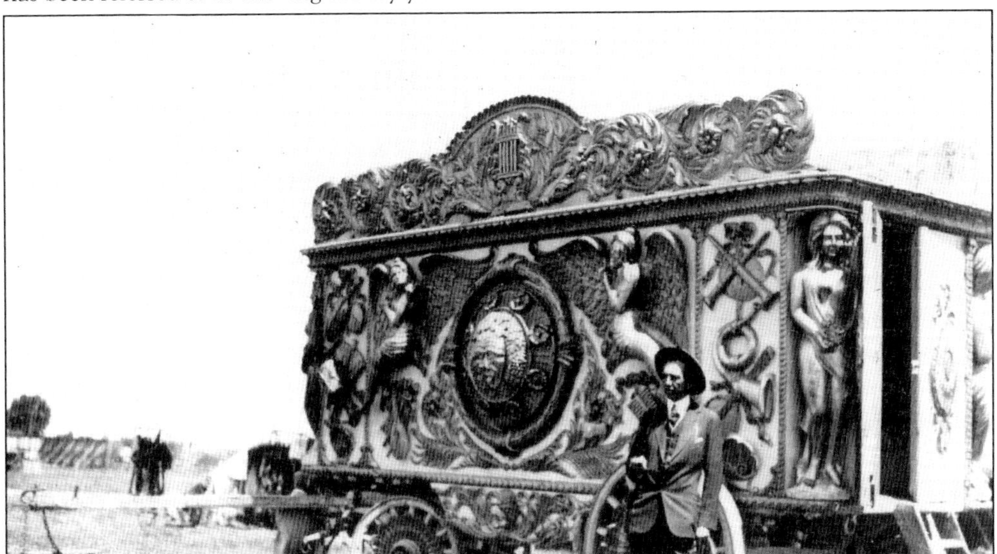

In the winter of 1925–1926, the 10-car Gollmar Brothers Circus stored at West Baden was sold to Arthur Hoffman, the former Hagenbeck-Wallace sideshow manager. Hoffman, whose real last name was Heritage, then moved it to Burlington, North Carolina. The show toured using the title of Heritage Brothers Circus. The Gollmar Brothers Circus title would never be used or leased again by the American Circus Corporation.

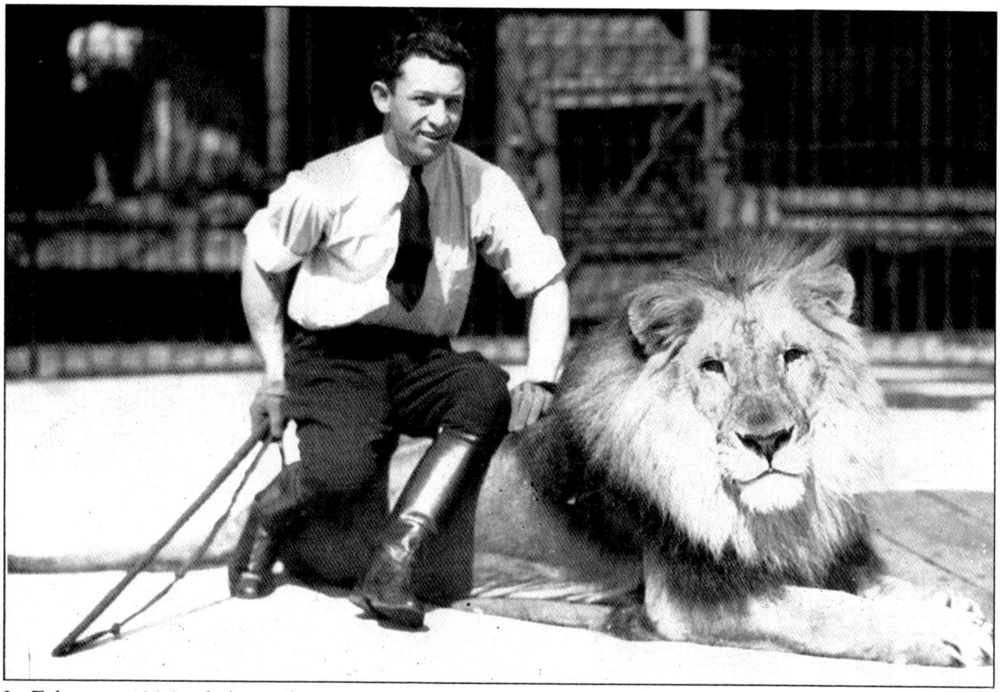

In February 1926, while performing in an indoor winter circus, Clyde Beatty received his first big newspaper headline and a full-page article in the February 16 edition of the *Detroit News*. The headline read, "He Enjoys Being in a Cage with 15 Lions and Three Tigers—Chewed Up Eight Times, but Trainer Who Thrilled Detroit Loves His Job."

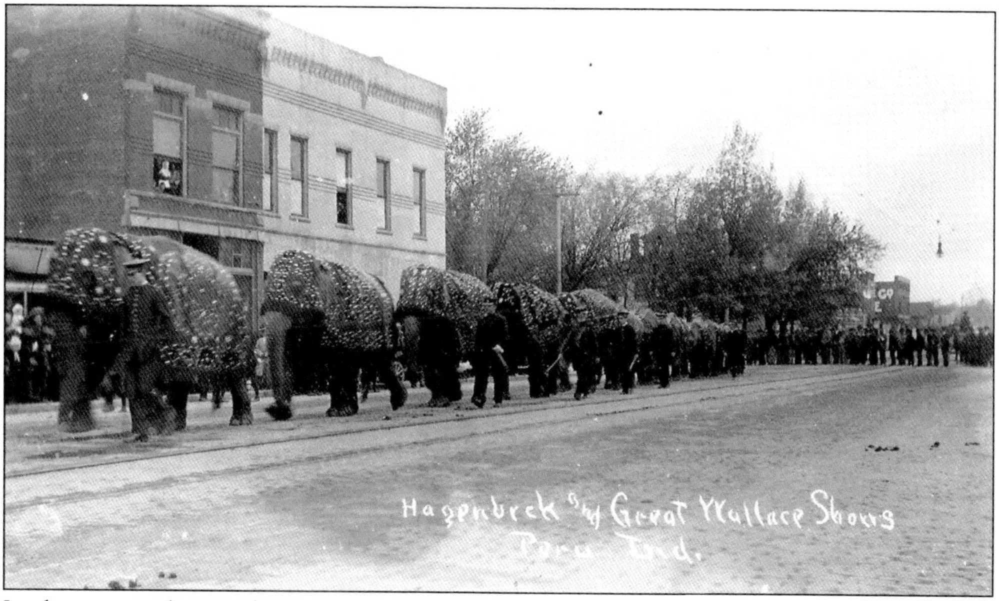


In the spring of 1926, the John Robinson's rolled out of West Baden and the Sells-Floto and Hagenbeck-Wallace rolled out of Peru without their steam calliopes. Since the American Circus Corporation had reinstated the no-parade policy, it was sticking to it this year. The steam calliopes were stored along with other parade equipment and costumes. For better or worse, the circus world was changing.

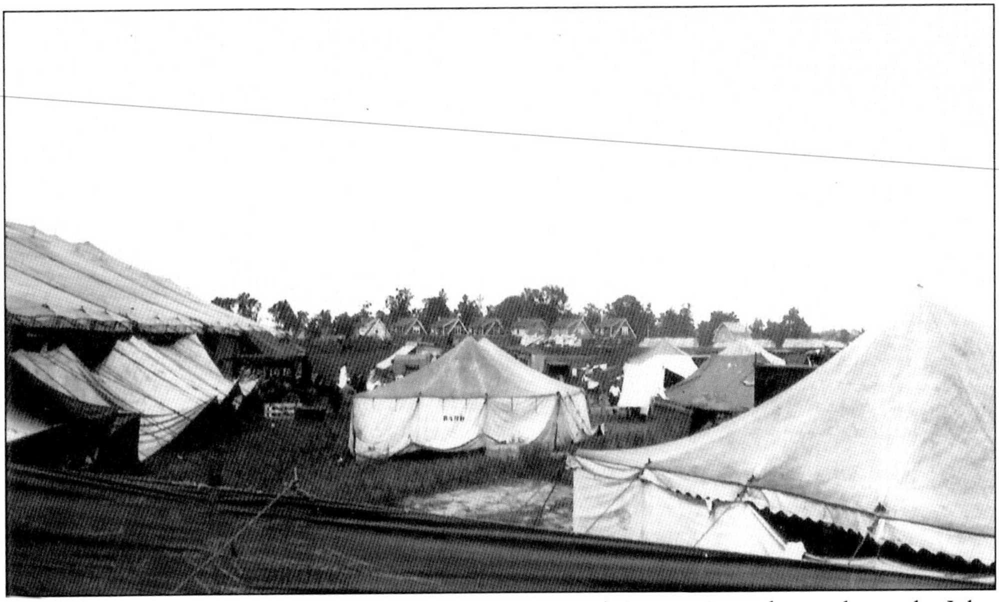

Emmett and Eva Kelly had planned to leave the baby with Emmett's mother and join the John Robinson's Circus in the spring of 1926. They received a letter from the John Robinson's show asking that Emmett double as a whiteface clown and asking Eva to work the swinging ladders while still performing their trapeze act. Emmett was furious; he wanted no part of clowning. He sent letters to other circuses and received a contract from the Gentry Brothers Circus for a trapeze act for only $55 a week. They took the job and raced to Fort Knox, Kentucky, to join the show.

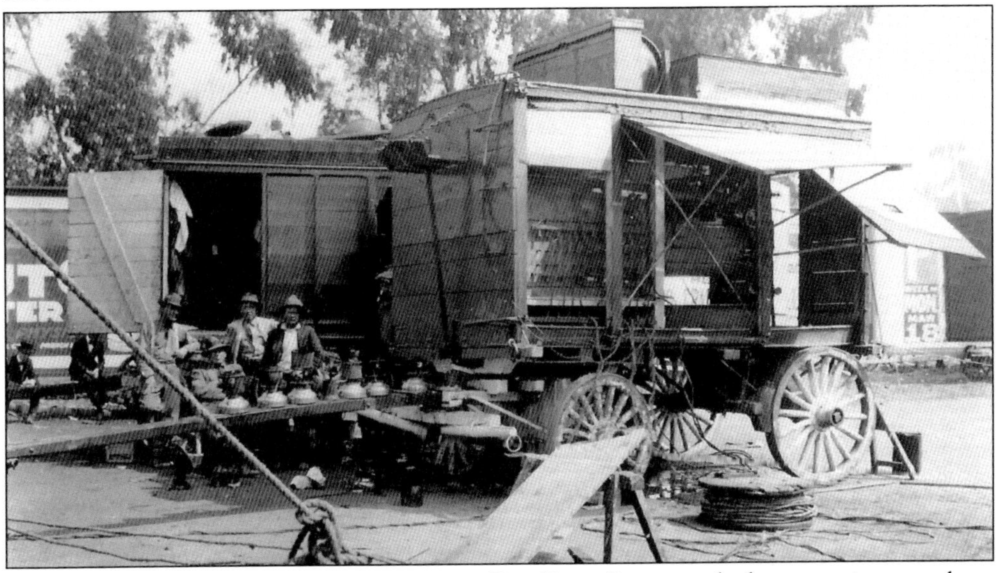

Arriving at Gentry Brothers' winter quarters in Fort Knox, Emmett asked an acquaintance about the show. He said, "You can see, it's a gypsy camp and it looks like we have half the Lucky Boys (grifters) in the business." Emmett and Eva thought that anything they would have to do on the John Robinson's show would beat touring a season on the Gentry Brothers show. Emmett and Eva toured the 1926 season with the John Robinson's show performing a single trapeze act while Emmett doubled as a whiteface clown and Eva performed in swinging ladders.

# *Eight*

# The Steel Arena

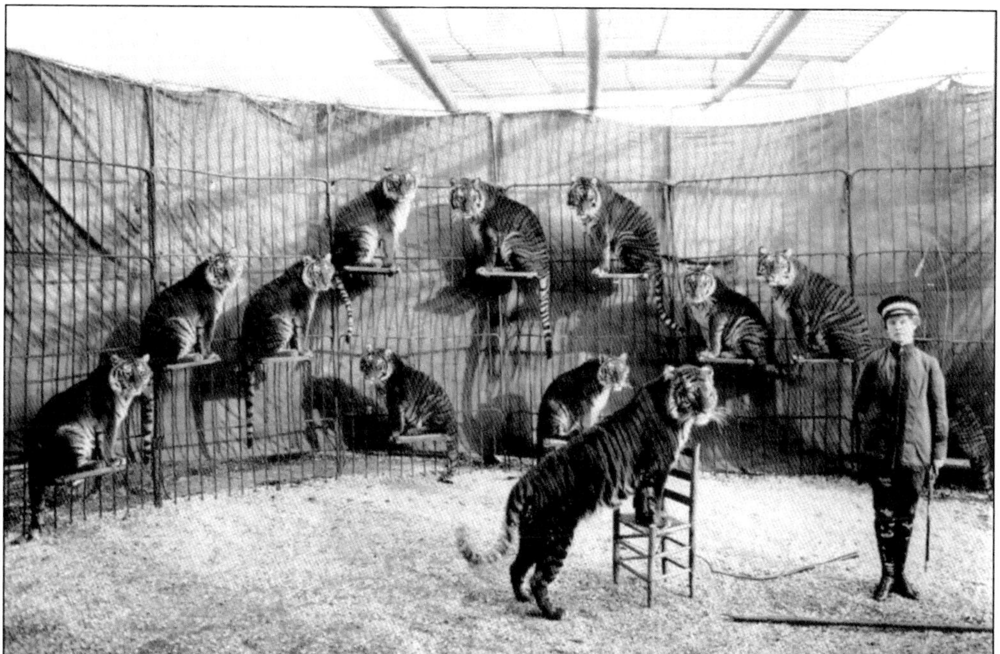

Also joining the John Robinson's Circus in 1926 was famed female cat trainer Mabel Stark. She had started as a cooch dancer and later had a goat act on the Al G. Barnes Circus. It was there she married cat trainer Louis Roth and began training cats. She had become a renowned cat trainer by 1920 and was working center ring in the Ringling Brothers and Barnum and Bailey Circus until John Ringling abolished the big wild animal acts. On the rainy, muddy day the John Robinson's Circus rolled into Bangor, Maine, the show was running behind. Stark's cats had laid in wet bedding all day and had not been fed. When Stark's act went on, she yelled, "Let them come," and the arena filled with 14 moody tigers. Stark immediately noticed the anger in the air and shouted, "Seat," to no response. Again she shouted, "Seat," and this time Belle settled on the seat of the meanest cat in the cage, Sheik. That was all it took to release Sheik's fury.

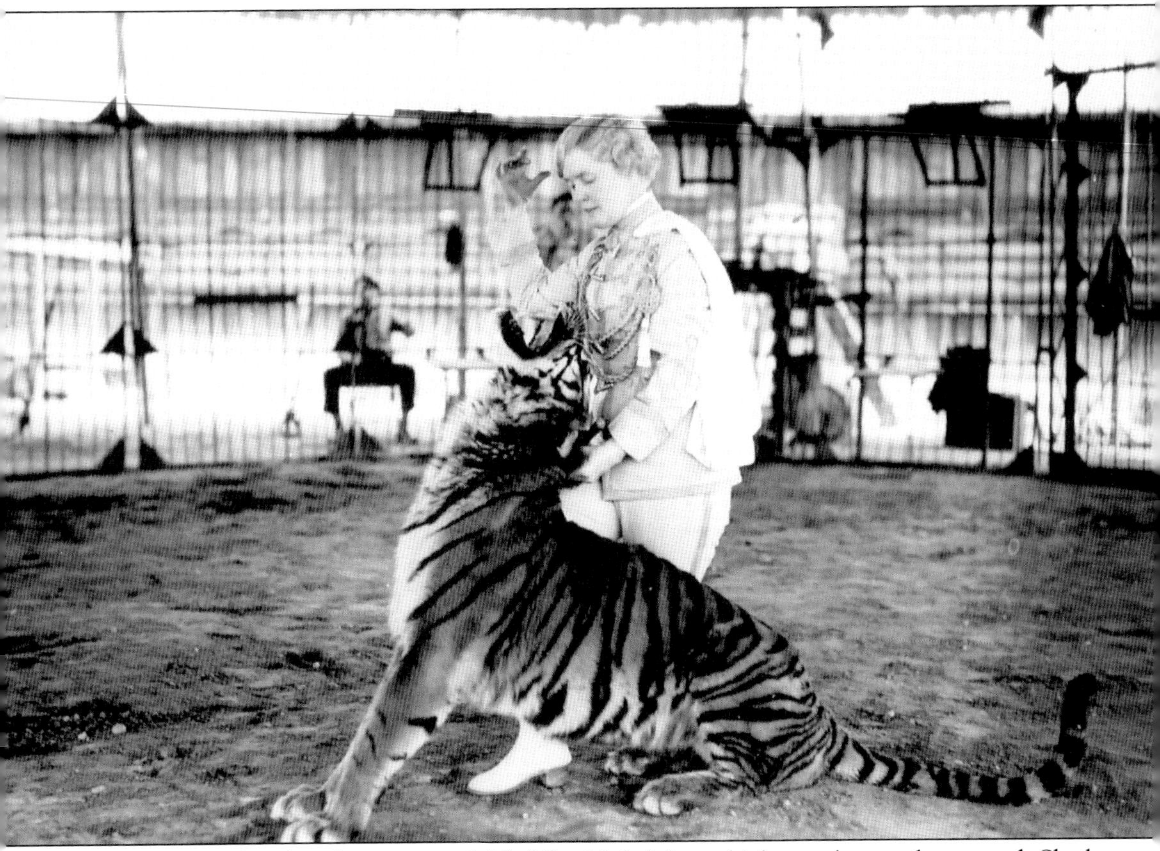

Sheik turned and took a swipe at Mabel Stark's left leg, which sent her to the ground. Sheik ran for the tunnel and ran into Zoo, another mean cat. He too charged Stark and bit her right leg. As she struggled to her feet, Stark shouted, "Seat," but Sheik attacked her again. Then Zoo joined the attack and bit her again on her right leg. Stark received several more blows before Bobby Thornton, the equestrian director, and Terrell Jacobs, the show's lion trainer, charged into the arena and fought the tigers back, saving Mabel Stark's life. In an armlock, Jacobs and Thornton pulled Stark from the arena and out of the big top. Emmett Kelly brought an army cot for her to lie on until the ambulance came. At the hospital, a still-conscious Stark instructed the doctors how to care for her wounds to avoid infection from her cat bites. It was touch-and-go for a few weeks, but Stark rejoined the show at Columbus, Ohio, and immediately began working her cats while wrapped in bandages and walking with a cane.

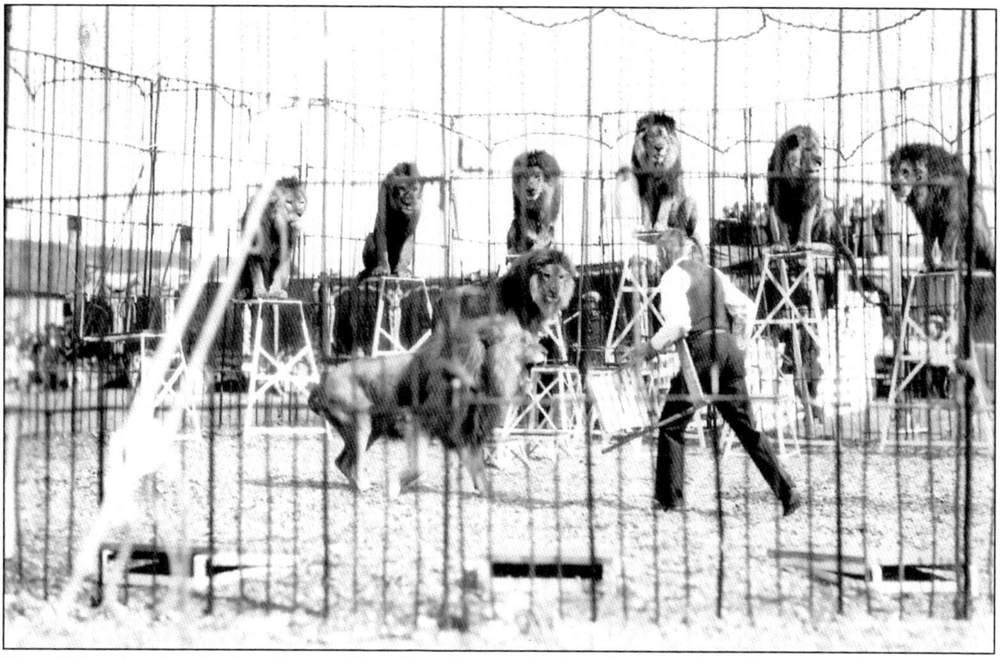

Terrell Jacobs also had a close call with a big cat during the season. While he was working his lion act one afternoon, a mean lion took a swipe at Jacobs and tore his shirt. Jacobs pulled his revolver and fired a blank round at the cat to drive him off. After the act, Jacobs was arrested for cruelty to animals. When Jacobs went before the judge and showed him his torn shirt and the claw marks on his chest, the judge let him go and fined the lion $10.

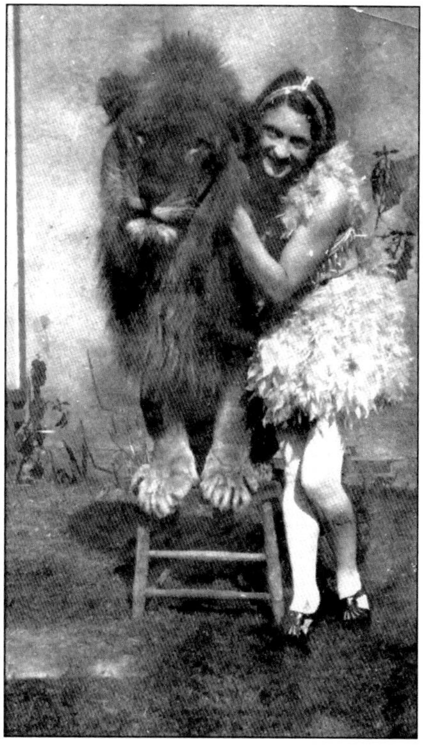

One day, while the John Robinson's Circus was showing in Pennsylvania, a lion escaped from its cage. The circus hands scurried about looking for the beast. They quickly found the big cat standing in a meadow peering across a stream. Using canvas sidewalls from a tent, the hands were able to corral the lion and safely return him to his cage. The crowd in the big top was unaware of what was going on.

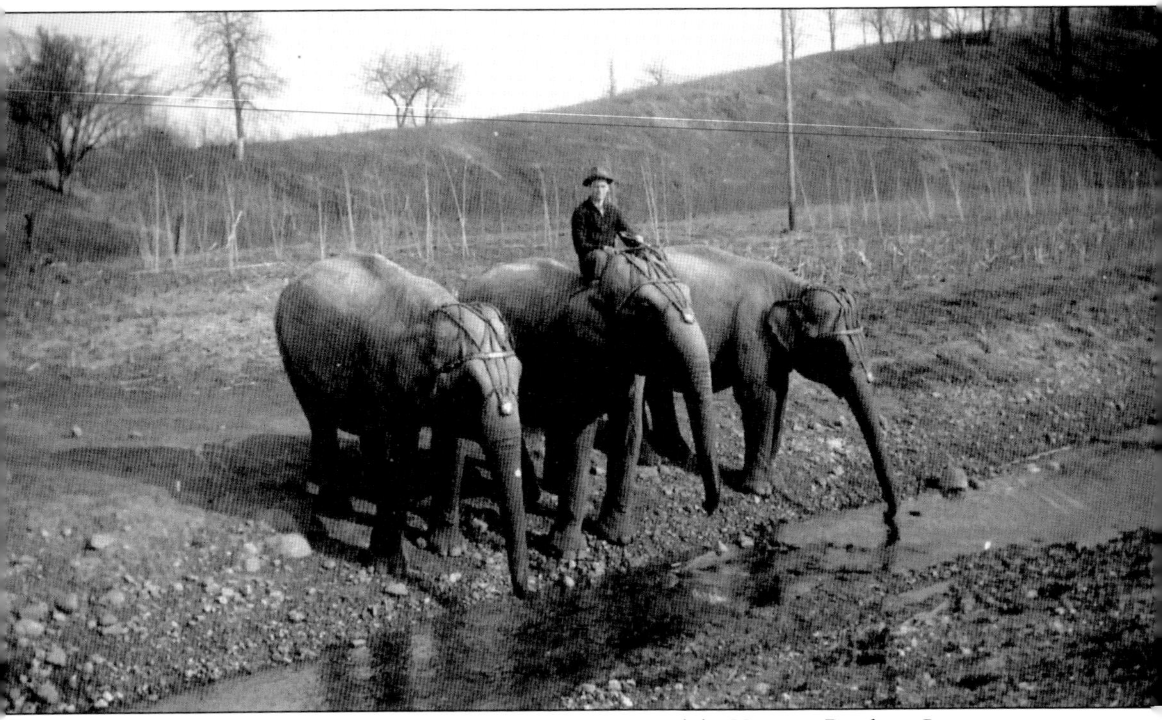

In August, the American Circus Corporation repossessed the Heritage Brothers Circus equipment in Kansas. The employees were paid off, and the equipment and animals were sent to Peru. Arthur Hoffman was furious and vowed to sue Jeremiah Mugivan. Hoffman filed a $20,000 suit against Mugivan in the South Bend federal court. Three witnesses were heard by the court, and the judge found the evidence submitted in the case contradictory. Some in the business at that time thought Mugivan wanted Hoffman back as manager of the Hagenbeck-Wallace sideshow and was willing to close Hoffman's show to get him back. The case was settled out of court about a year later, and Mugivan agreed to pay Hoffman $3,500 plus court costs. Hoffman stayed in the circus business until he retired in the 1950s, but he never worked for Mugivan again.

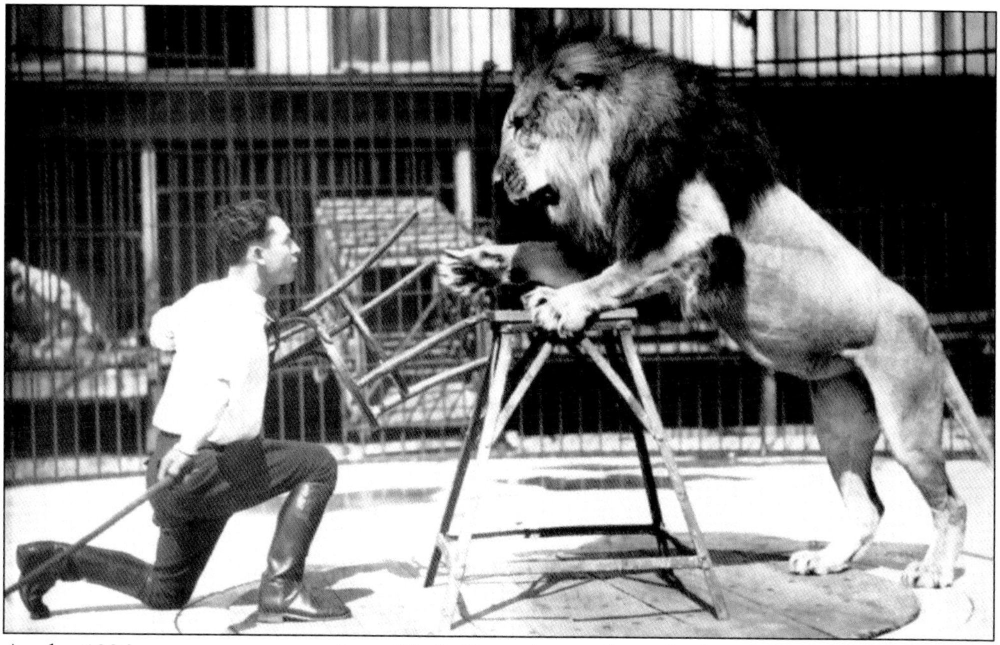

As the 1926 season came to a close, Clyde Beatty's popularity had grown, and he was quickly becoming a hero to the American youth. His peers at the Peru winter quarters thought he was green, foolish, and lacked the polish the seasoned trainers possessed. A thrill a minute was Beatty's mission each time he stepped into the ring. Beatty was as masterful at working the crowd as he worked the big cats.

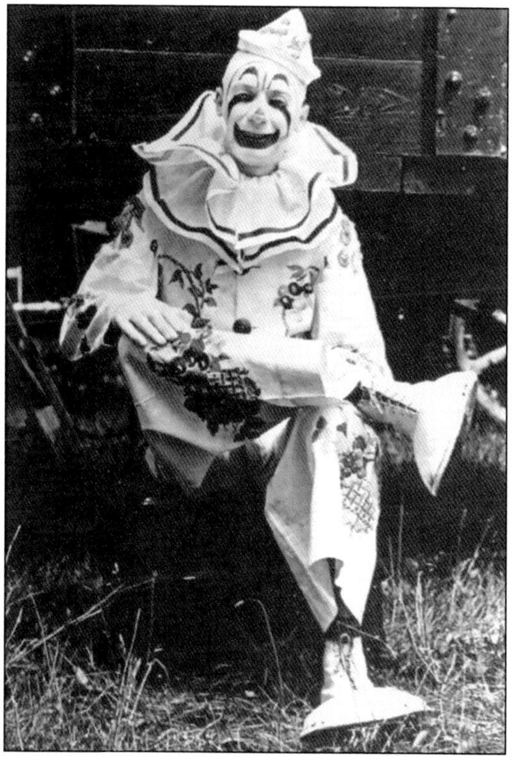

At the end of the 1926 season, the Sells-Floto and the Hagenbeck-Wallace Circuses wintered at the Peru winter quarters, and the John Robinson's Circus wintered again at the West Baden winter quarters. The winter quarters at Peru were still growing, and the circuses were operating like well-oiled machines. The American Circus Corporation was doing so well that Jeremiah Mugivan would boast that it would one day own the Ringling Brothers and Barnum and Bailey Circus.

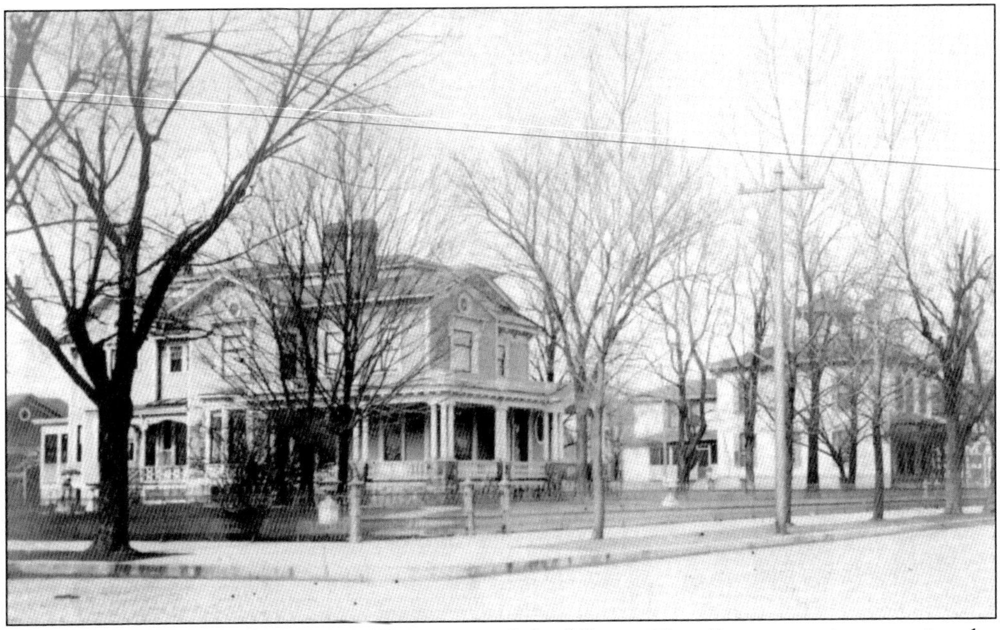

Profits were up during the Roaring Twenties, and the "Circus Kings" were starting to enjoy the fruits of their labor. Bert Bowers was living in Benjamin E. Wallace's old home (pictured) on Broadway in Peru, Jeremiah Mugivan was making plans to build a new home on East Main Street in Peru, and John Ringling had just finished building a new home in Sarasota, Florida, that he called Ca d'zan (House of John).

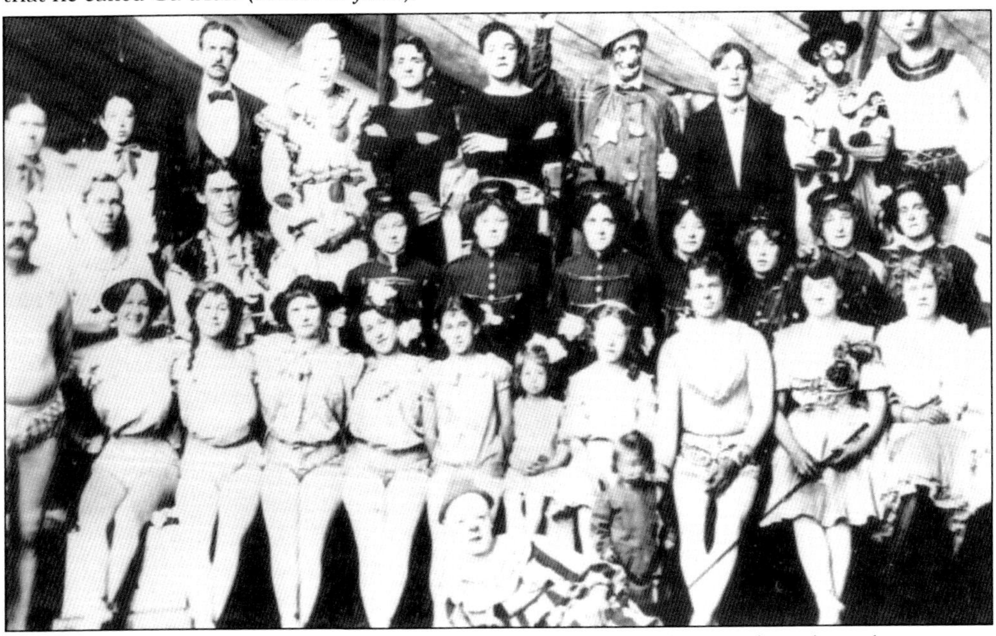

On December 3, 1926, Charles Ringling passed away, leaving John Ringling the only surviving brother. Charles was head of production for the Ringling Brothers and Barnum and Bailey Circus and had also just finished building a new home in Sarasota, Florida. Charles's wife Edith took a position on the board of directors, and with in-laws now in the family business, John found it hard to run the circus as he did when his brothers were alive.

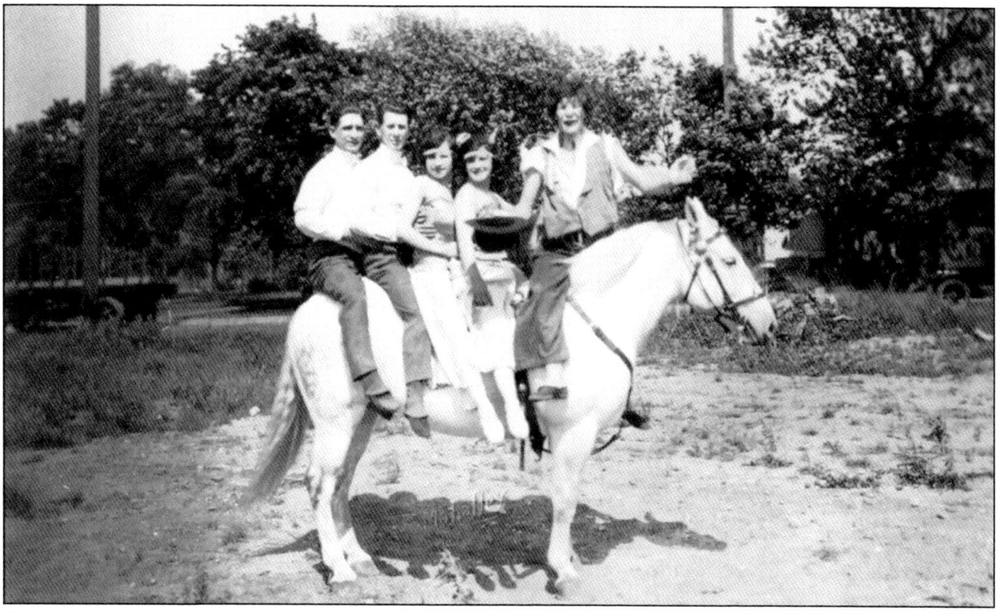

Upon arriving in Peru, performers began planning for the next season. Some developed a new routine or polished an old one. Some looked for a better-paying circus with better accommodations. The Albert Hodgini Troupe was one such act. Albert Hodgini and his family were equestrians and trouped with Ringling Brothers and the Sells-Floto Circus. In 1915 and 1916, Albert had his own circus called Hodgini's European with Jess H. Adkins as general manager. Albert had signed on to the Miller Brothers 101 Ranch for the 1927 season.

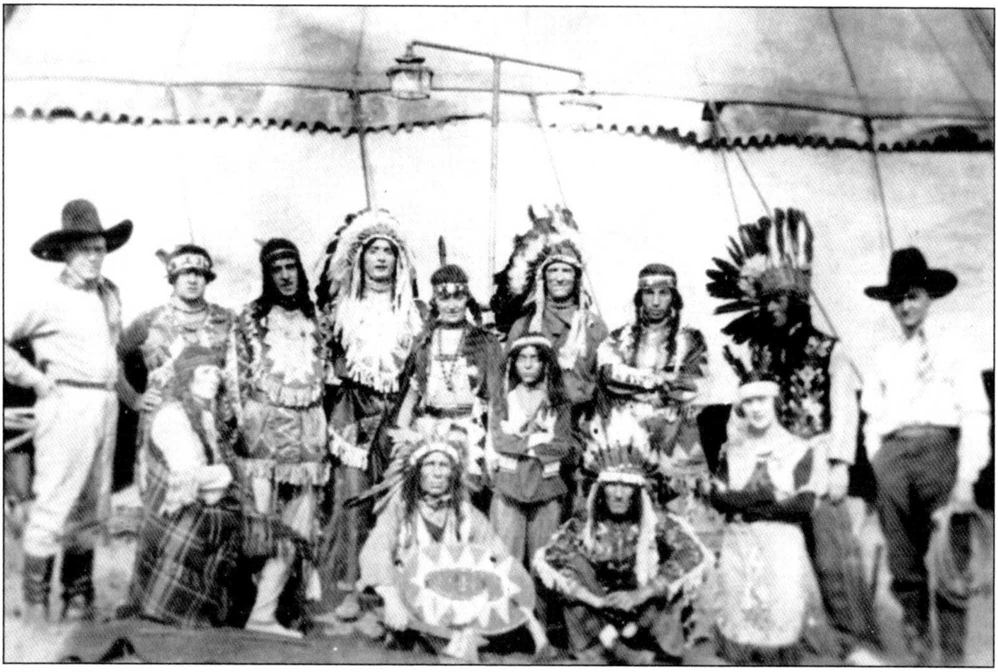

Albert Hodgini and his troupe performed a bareback Native American comedy routine that was a hit in the show. The act featured Otto Griebling, a skilled equestrian trained by Hodgini. Griebling is pictured above (standing, second from the left) dressed as Native American woman.

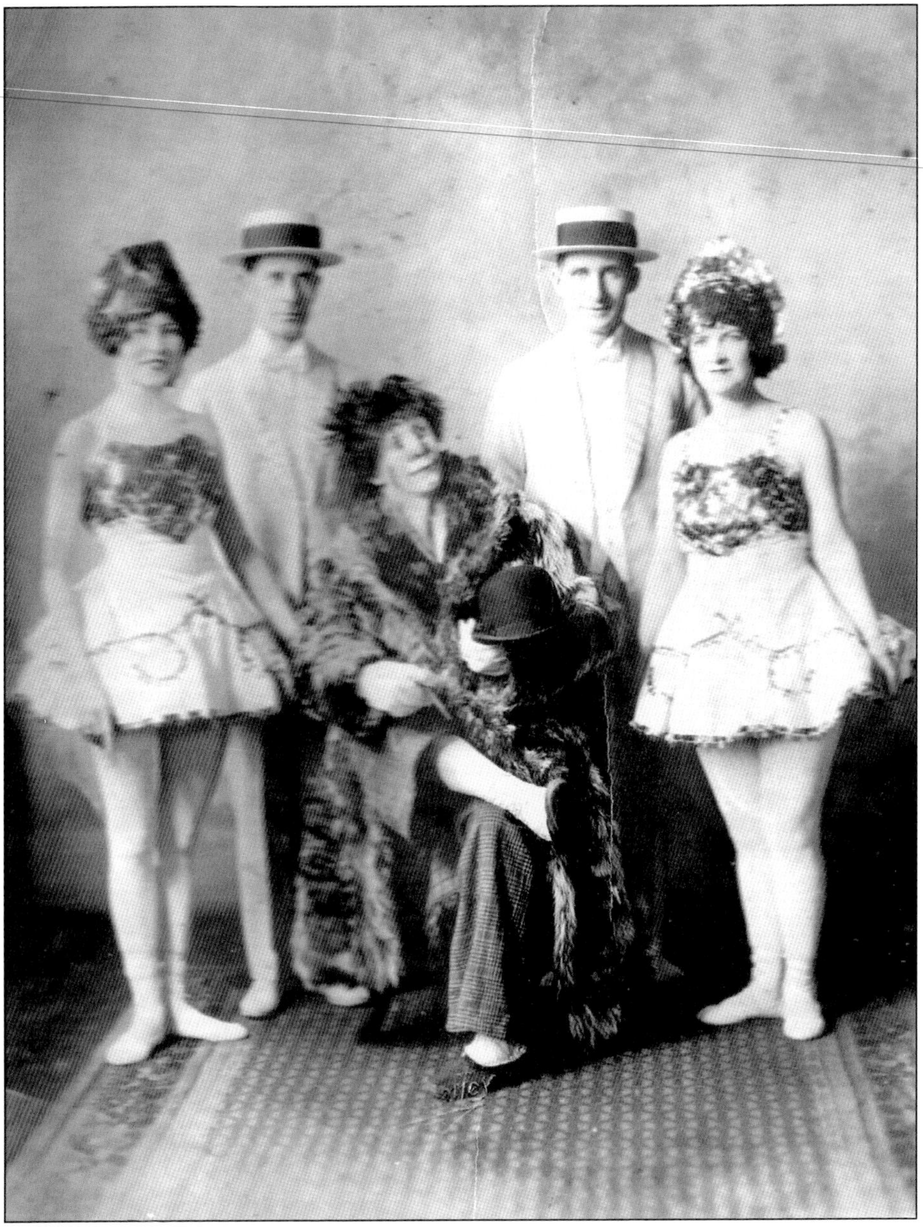

One of the best circus stories ever told is one of Albert Hodgini and Otto Griebling. Griebling came to America from Germany in 1911 and answered an advertisement placed by Hodgini for an apprentice equestrian. Griebling got the job, and Hodgini taught him to be an expert rider. One day, while the Hodginis were trouping with the Ringling Brothers and Barnum and Bailey Circus, the show made a stand in Madison, Wisconsin. Hodgini gave Griebling $5 and sent him to the store for two quarts of milk and two loaves of bread. While in town, Griebling decided to keep the money and leave the circus. He found work on a dairy farm in Madison for the next few years until the Ringling Brothers show came back to town. Griebling had grown tired of working on the dairy farm so he showed up at Hodgini's tent with two loaves of bread and two quarts of milk and the correct change from the $5. Griebling said, "All he did was carefully count the change." Hodgini allowed Griebling to stay, and Otto Griebling never left the circus life again.

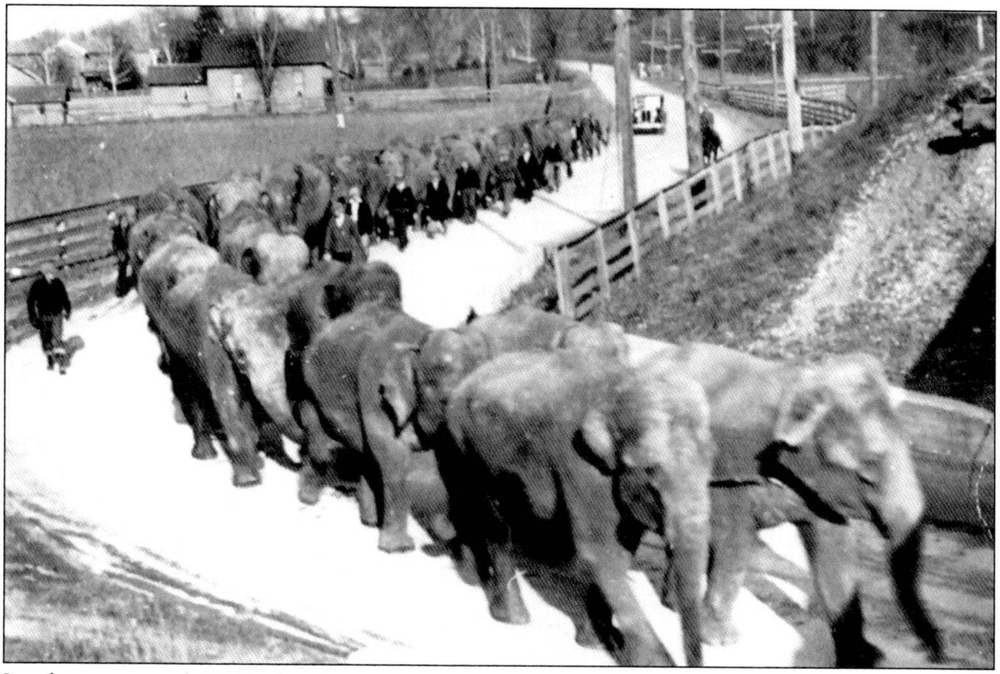

In the spring of 1927, the American Circus Corporation sent out the John Robinson's, Sells-Floto, and Hagenbeck-Wallace Circuses, leaving from their winter quarters on 30 railcars each. There would be no parades this year on any of the three "Peru circuses," as they were referred to in the business. By this time, much of the horse stock had been replaced by trucks and tractors and the circuses were running more efficient than ever.

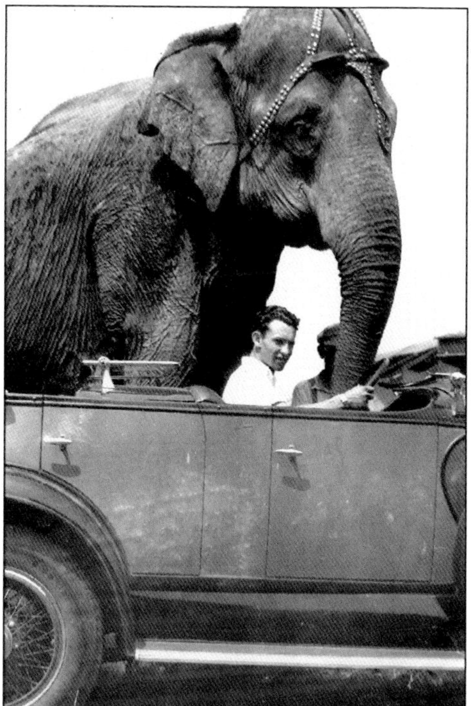

The 1927 season went without incident from weather, fire, or injury and, therefore, was very profitable for the American Circus Corporation. Emmett and Eva Kelly were again with the John Robinson's Circus performing their trapeze act. Mickey King's sister Antoinette Comeau joined the Sells-Floto Circus on tour. She would later marry Art Concello and become a legendary trapeze flyer as Antoinette Concello. On the Hagenbeck-Wallace Circus, 25-year-old Clyde Beatty was quickly becoming a star of the show.

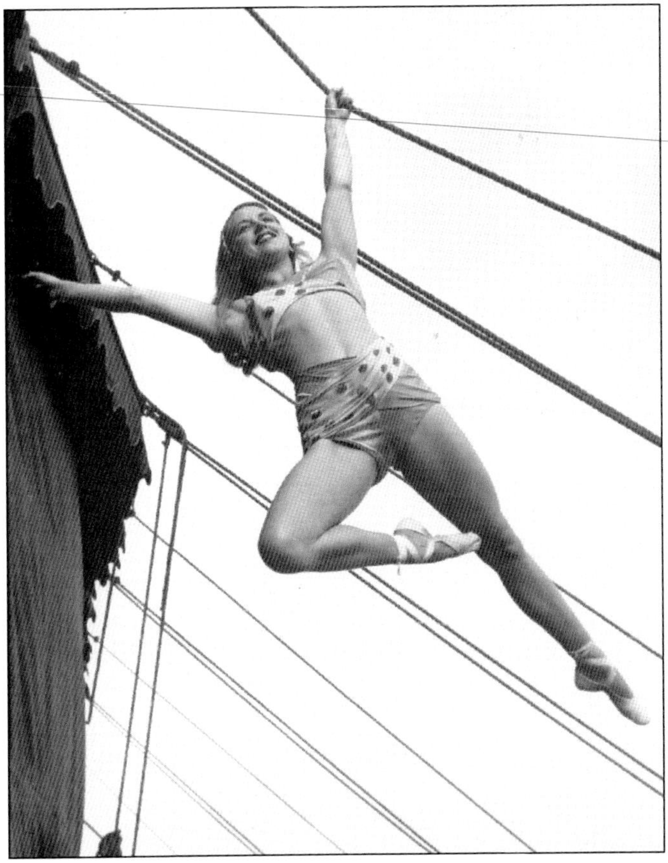

At the end of the 1927 season, John Ringling moved the Ringling Brothers and Barnum and Bailey Circus winter quarters from Bridgeport, Connecticut, to Sarasota, Florida. John and his brother Charles had been wintering in Sarasota since 1909 and had given much to the community. On Christmas Day 1927, the winter quarters was open to the public.

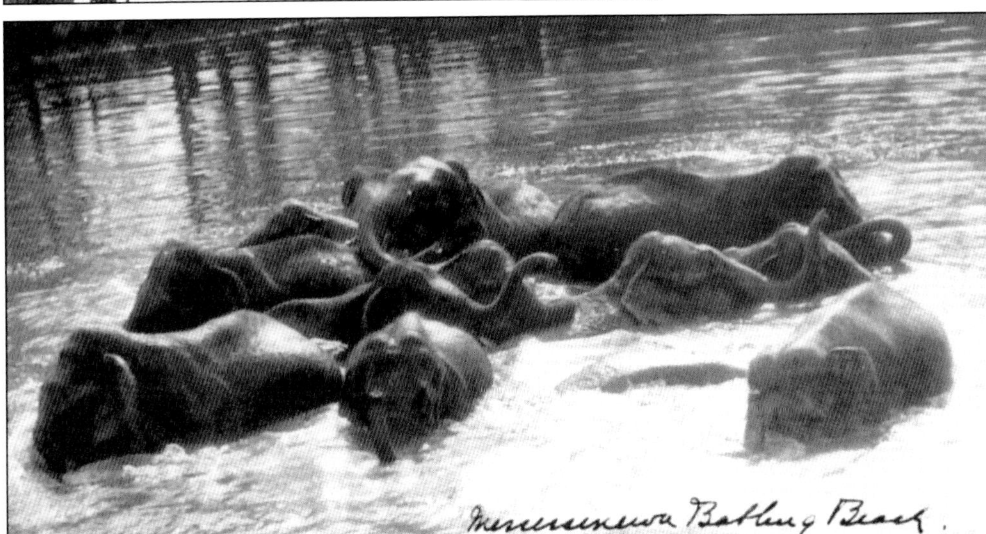


At the close of the 1927 season, the John Robinson's Circus wintered in West Baden, and the Sells-Floto and Hagenbeck-Wallace Circuses wintered in Peru. The Peru winter quarters had become a very popular tourist attraction during the off-season. Automobiles were no longer a novelty and were quickly replacing the streetcar. People were now taking leisurely drives by the winter quarters to see all the exotic animals.

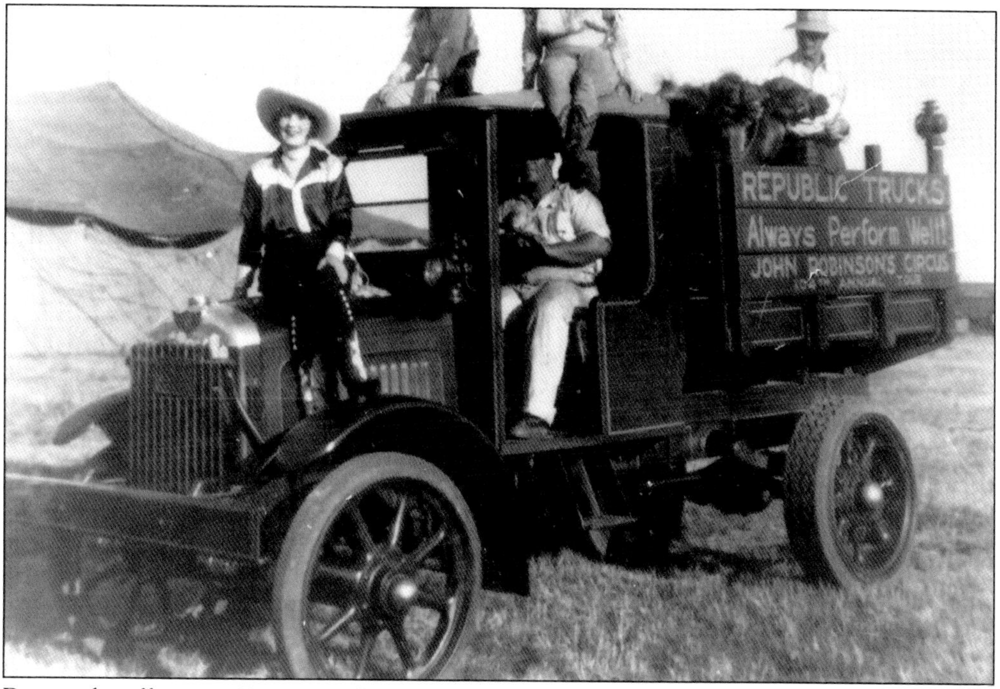


During the off-season, Emmett Kelly took a shot at Ringling Brothers show hoping to get his and Eva's double trapeze act on the bill to hopefully make more money. Eva was unhappy performing swinging ladders, and Emmett did not like being a whiteface clown. But when the John Robinson's Circus rolled out of Peru, Emmett and Eva were on the train. The John Robinson's, Sells-Floto, and Hagenbeck-Wallace Circuses traveled on 30 railcars during the 1928 season.

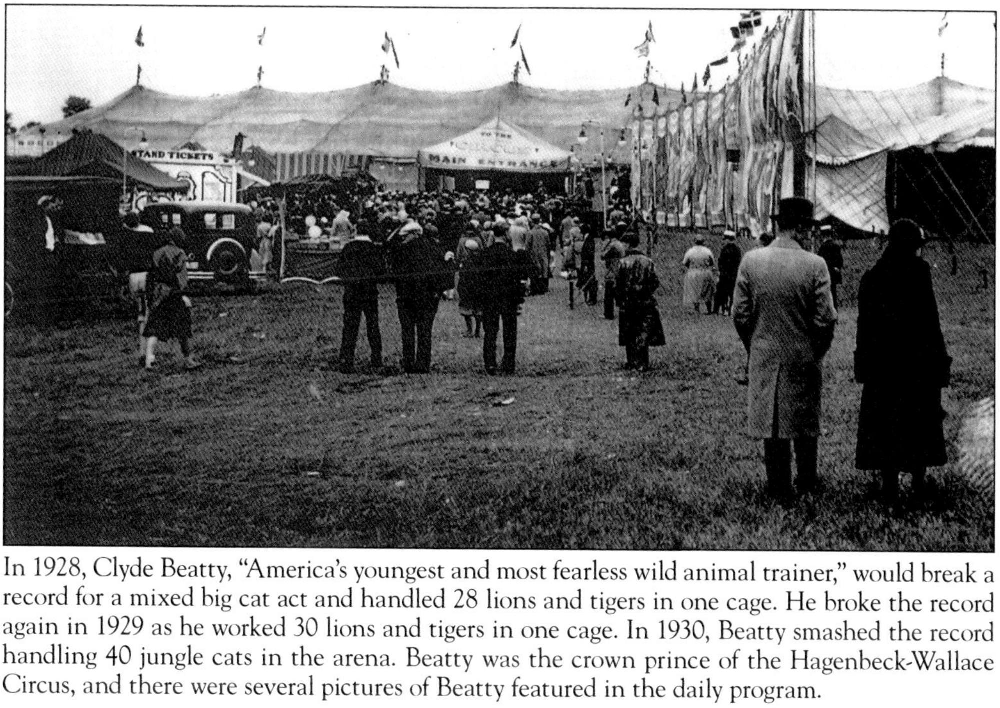


In 1928, Clyde Beatty, "America's youngest and most fearless wild animal trainer," would break a record for a mixed big cat act and handled 28 lions and tigers in one cage. He broke the record again in 1929 as he worked 30 lions and tigers in one cage. In 1930, Beatty smashed the record handling 40 jungle cats in the arena. Beatty was the crown prince of the Hagenbeck-Wallace Circus, and there were several pictures of Beatty featured in the daily program.

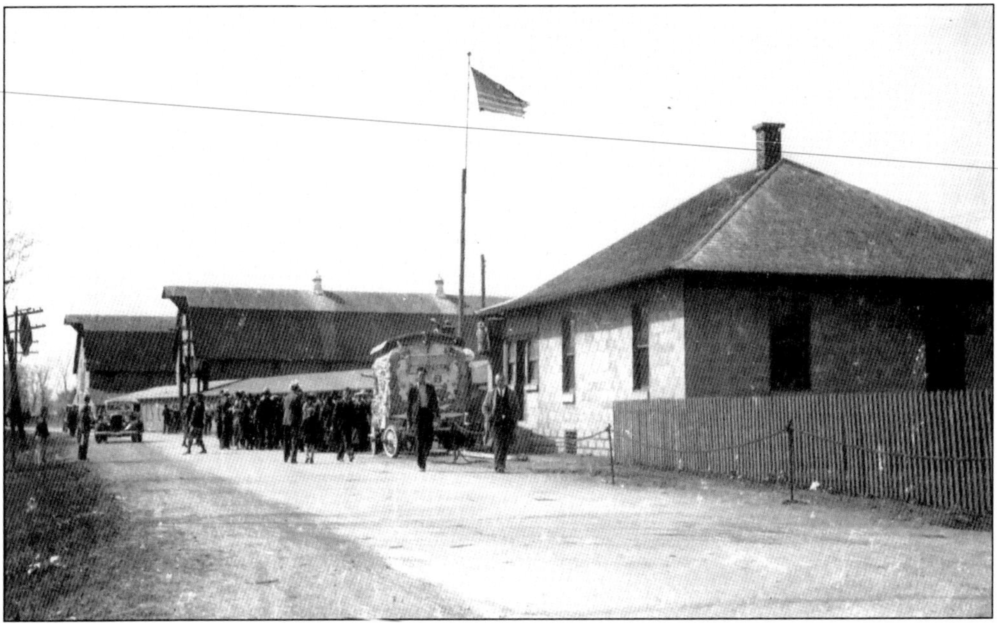

During the 1928 season, the American Circus Corporation continued to harass John Ringling's show at every opportunity. Ringling had learn to live with the competition and tolerated the first-to-the-money tactics. Jeremiah Mugivan, Bert Bowers, and Edward M. Ballard had plans to make the American Circus Corporation the largest circus holding company in the world.

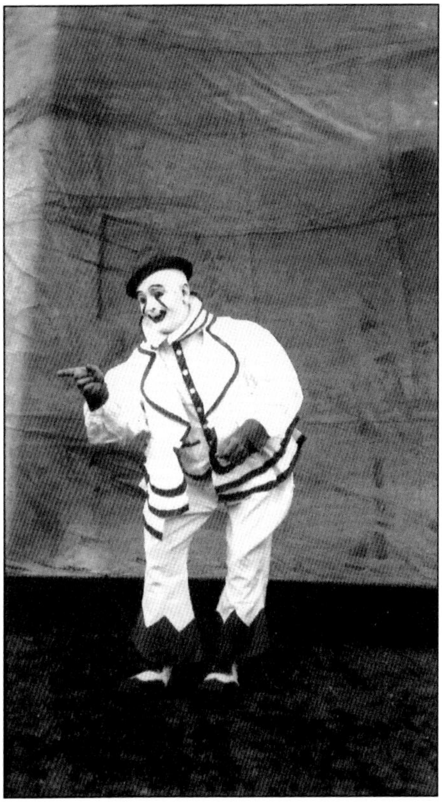

For the first time, at the end of the 1928 season, the John Robinson's, Sells-Floto, and Hagenbeck-Wallace Circuses wintered in Peru. The winter quarters at West Baden were closed. Over 4,000 people were now living and working for the American Circus Corporation. What happened next shocked the circus world.

# *Nine*

# Madison Square Garden in 1930

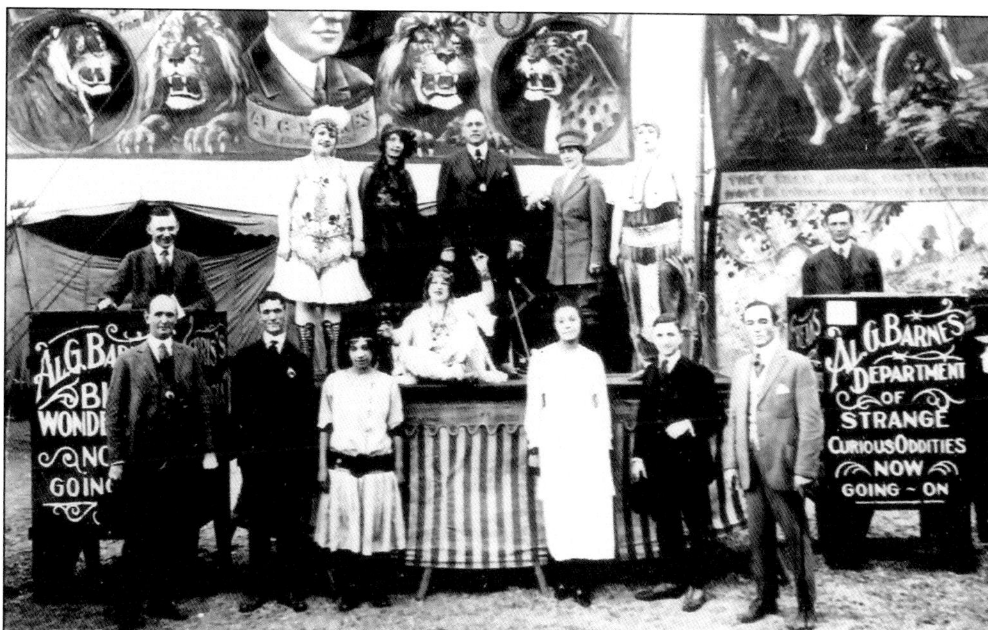


At the end of the 1928 season, H. B. Gentry purchased the Sparks Circus from Charles and Clifton Sparks. Unknown to the Sparkses, Gentry was acting as an agent for the American Circus Corporation. Charles was furious since he had always sworn he would never sell to Jeremiah Mugivan. In January 1929, the American Circus Corporation also bought the Al G. Barnes Circus. The American Circus Corporation's circus holdings were the largest in the world, consisting of 10 circus titles, over 150 railcars, and more than 2,000 animals. Peru was now "the Circus Capital of the World."

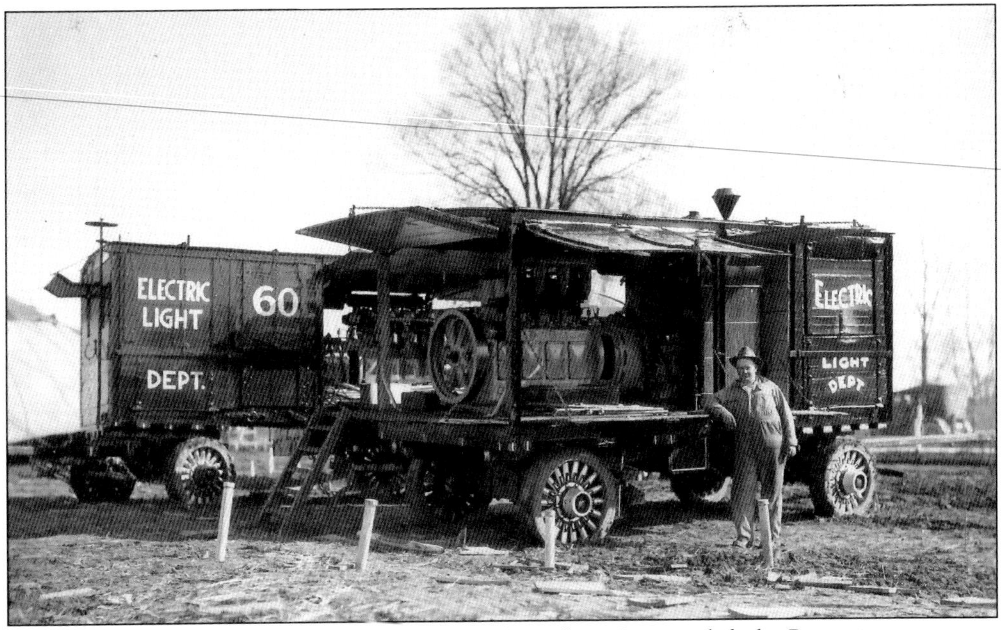


The John Robinson's, Sells-Floto, and Hagenbeck-Wallace Circuses left the Peru winter quarters in the spring of 1929. Each of the Peru circuses traveled on 30 railcars. The Sparks Circus left its quarters at Macon, Georgia, on 20 railcars, and the Al G. Barnes Circus left its quarters at Baldwin Park, California, on 30 railcars. Jeremiah Mugivan, Bert Bowers, and Edward M. Ballard expected 1929 to be their most profitable season ever.

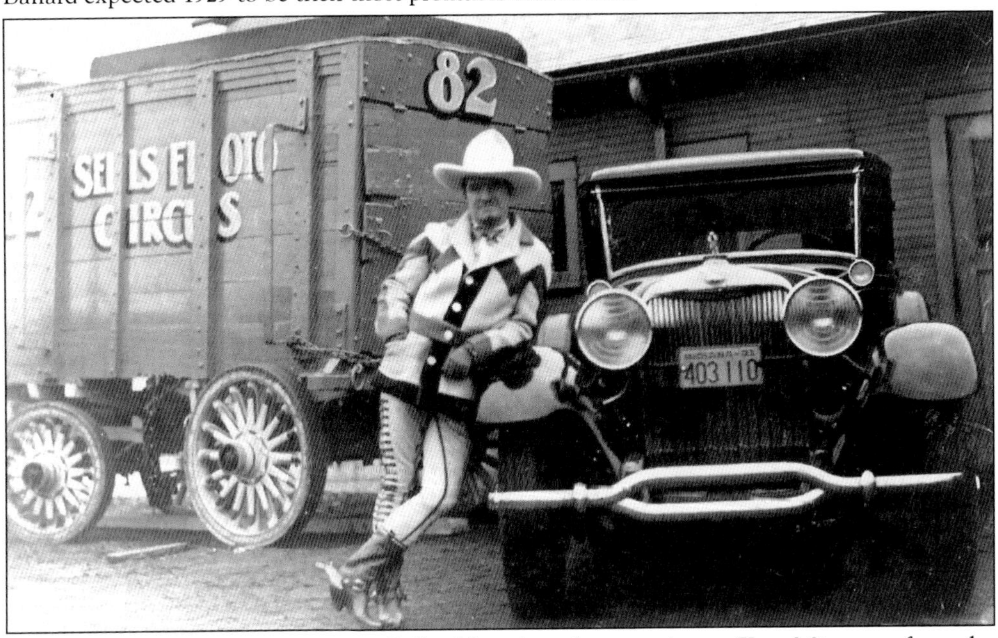


To ensure the corporation's success, Ballard hired cowboy movie star Tom Mix away from the Miller Brothers 101 Ranch. Mix was a superstar in 1929 and was paid $10,000 a week to perform in the Sells-Floto Circus. The show's wagons were painted to say, "Sells-Floto Circus and Tom Mix Himself." Mix and his "Wonder Horse" Tony were such a hit that eight more railcars were added to the show.

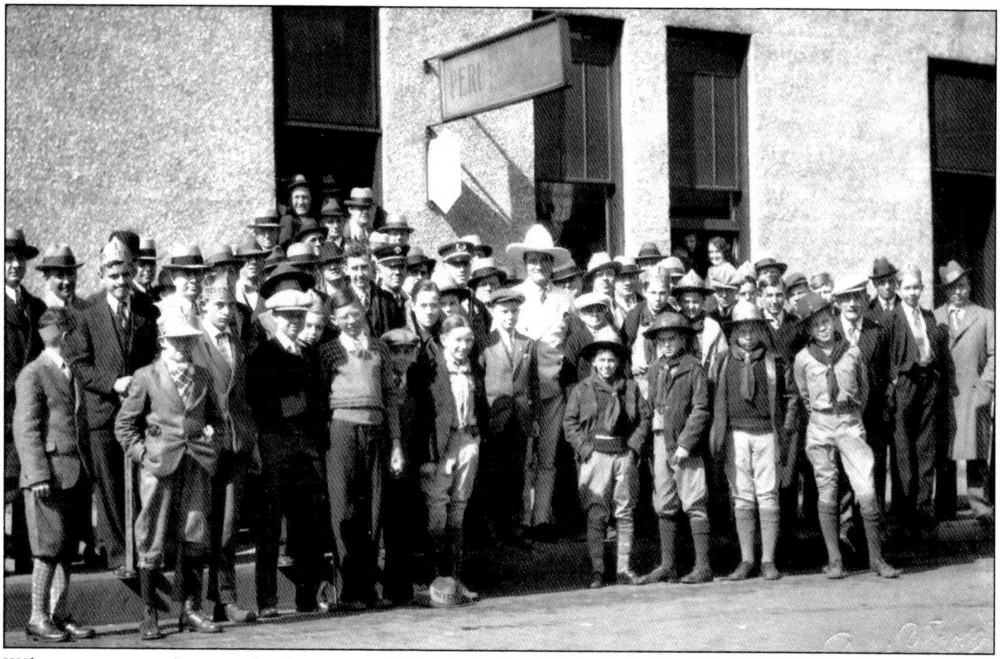

When not traveling with the circus, Mix stayed in Peru at the Bearss Hotel on Broadway and later in a private railcar at the circus railroad yards on Washington Street. Mix was very generous to the children of Peru; he always had a smile and a wave to the children who passed by the circus railroad yards. Mix was a hero to the children of America, and everyone knew from the smile on his face that he loved his job.

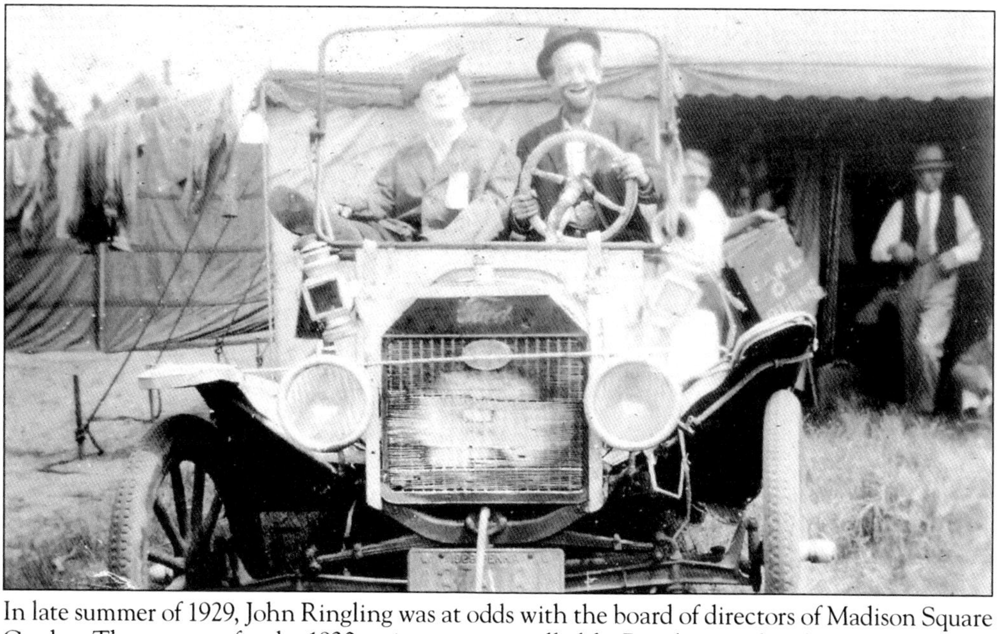

In late summer of 1929, John Ringling was at odds with the board of directors of Madison Square Garden. The contract for the 1930 spring opening called for Ringling to close his show on Friday nights for boxing exhibitions. Ringling was completely unwilling to close and lose revenue. The Ringling show was Madison Square Garden's biggest moneymaker, and Ringling knew it. Ringling had the garden up against the ropes.

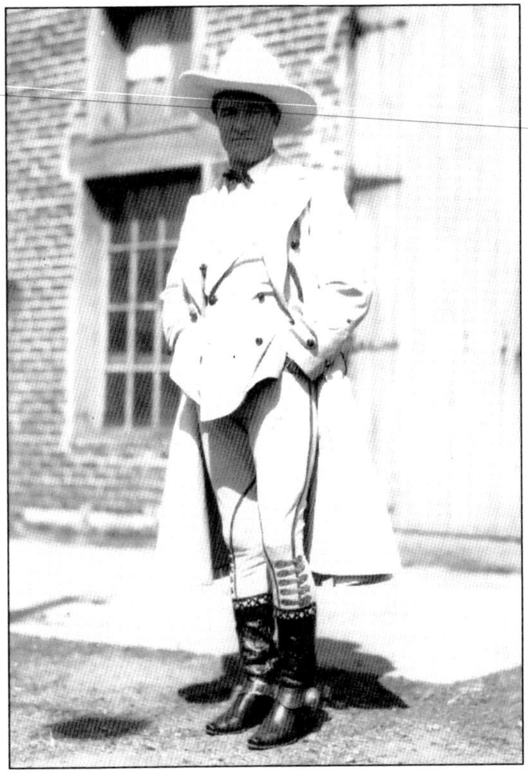

Jeremiah Mugivan saw a golden opportunity for the American Circus Corporation. He stepped in and offered to combine the Hagenbeck-Wallace and Sells-Floto Circuses and feature Tom Mix and Tony "the Wonder Horse." Mugivan added that the American Circus Corporation had no problem closing on Friday for boxing exhibitions.

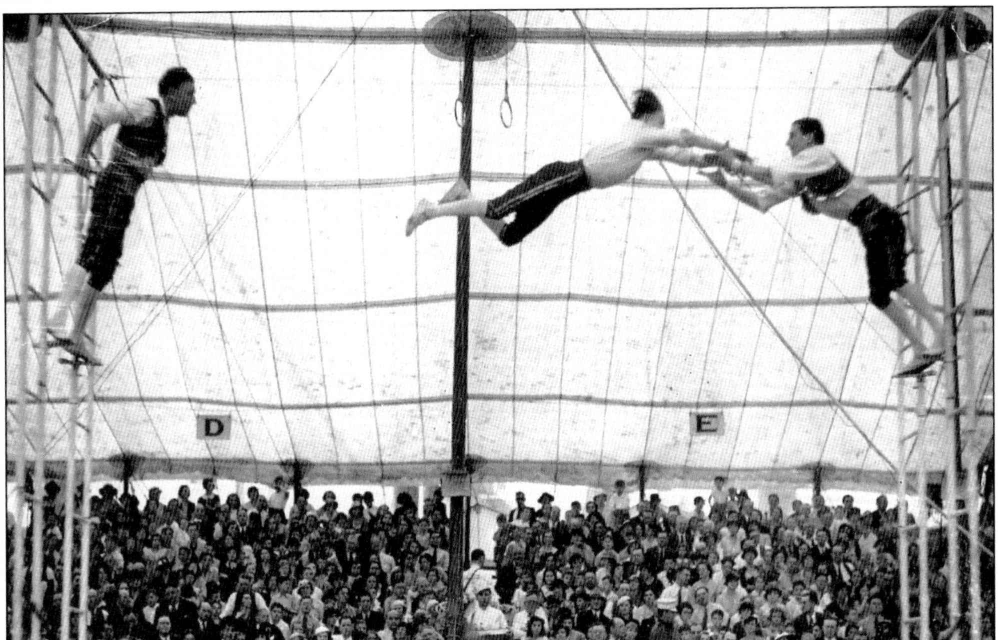


The news broke in the *New York Times*: "Ringling Circus Breaks with Garden. Showman Rejects New Lease, Refusing to Allow Boxing Bouts to Interfere Each Week . . . Garden Head . . . Makes Deal with Another Circus . . . Combination Consisting of the Sells-Floto Circus, the Hagenbeck-Wallace Animal Show."

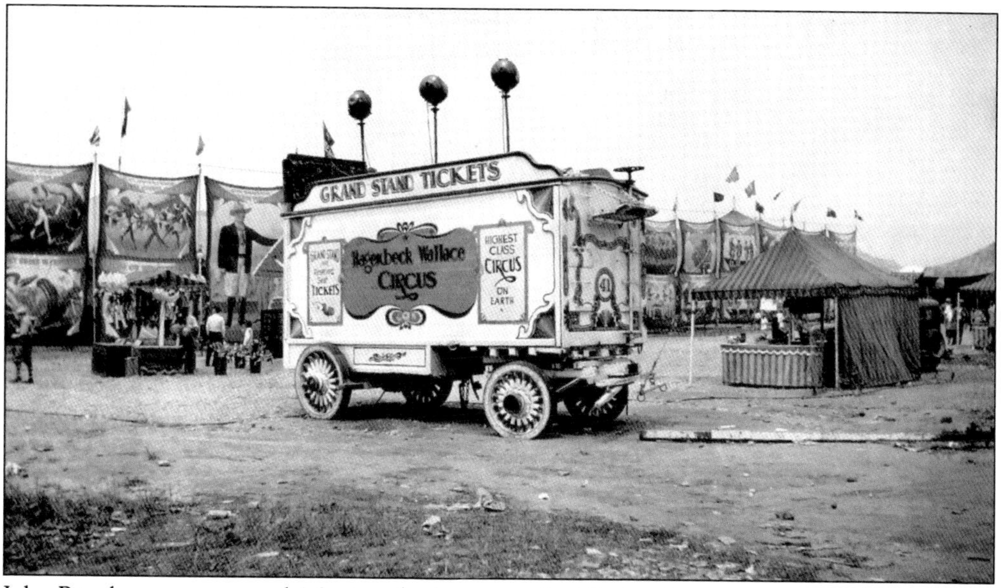


John Ringling was outraged. Mugivan had gone too far. To Ringling, it was a matter of tradition. Barnum and Bailey or Ringling Brothers and Barnum and Bailey Circuses has always opened at Madison Square Garden. Ringling stated, "We are going to open in the Garden, even if I have to buy those circuses."

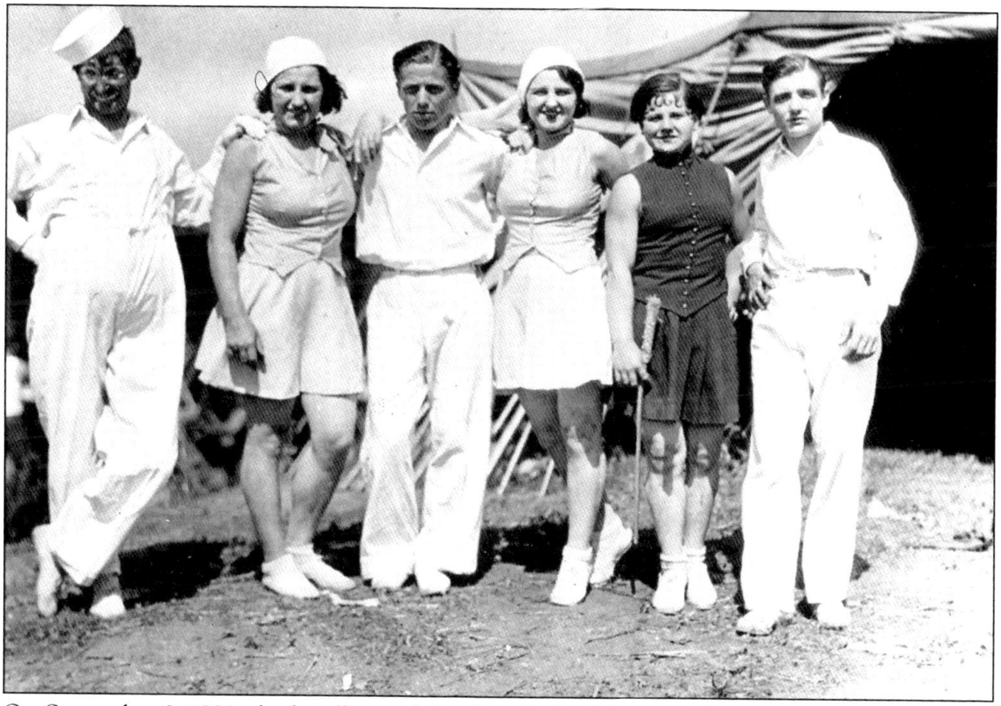

On September 9, 1929, the headlines of the *Peru Daily Tribune* read, "Peru Circuses Sold." The story stated that the sale included the Peru winter quarters with over 1,000 acres of land and numerous buildings. Mugivan said that he and his partners would sever all communications with the circuses when the deal was complete. It was later learned that Ringling had borrowed $1.7 million and made Mugivan a cash offer.

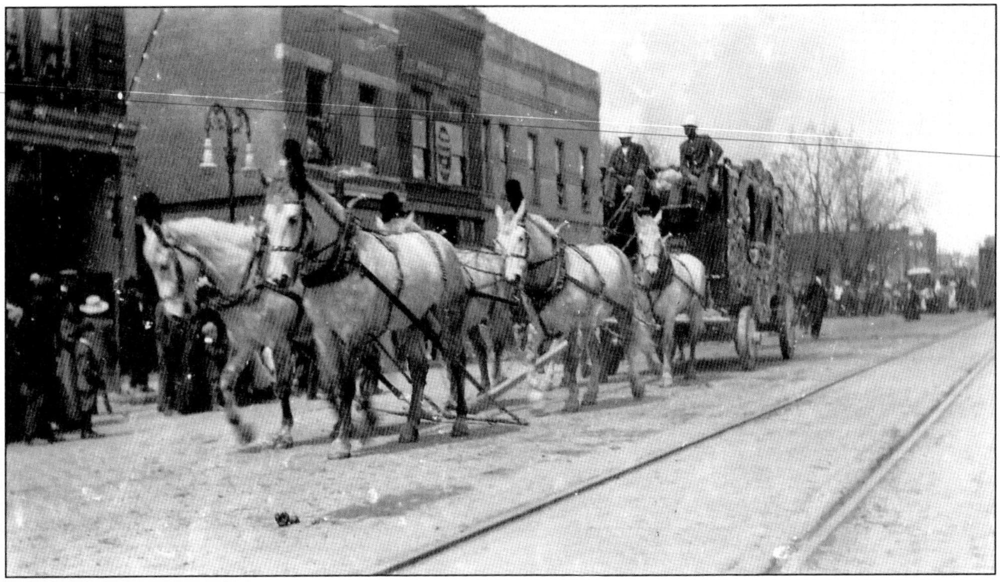

When the deal was completed, John Ringling sat back in his chair and said to his associates, "I'm playing the Garden next year." John Ringling was now the "Circus King," and along with that title, he now owned 10 more circus titles: Famous Robinson Circus, Sells-Floto Circus, Yankee Robinson Circus, Buffalo Bill's Wild West Show, Hagenbeck-Wallace Circus, John Robinson's Circus, Howe's Great London Circus, Van Amburg's Trained Wild Animals, Sparks Circus, and Al G. Barnes Circus.

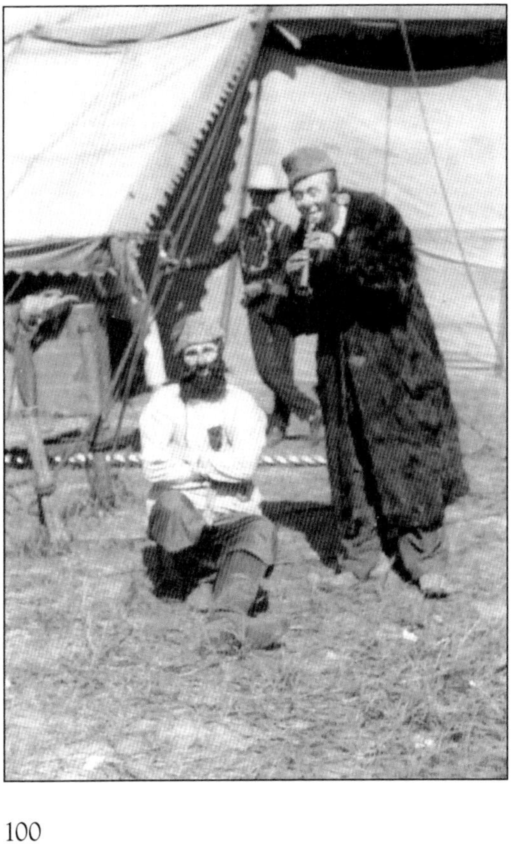

All five of the Peru circuses were on tour when they learned that the American Circus Corporation was sold to Ringling. No one knew what to expect. Thousands of employees wondered if they would finish the season or if there would be a 1930 season. Everyone from the circus manager to the roustabouts were in the dark.

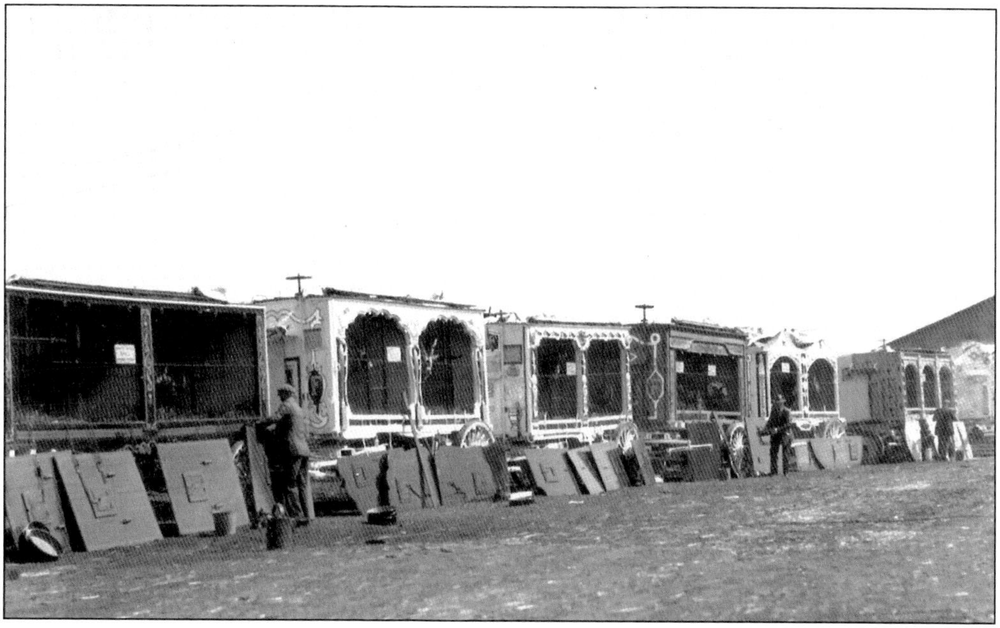

John Ringling arrived in Peru on September 12, 1929, to assess his new assets. From there, Ringling began visiting each of the Peru circuses on tour. After his inspection tour, everyone was relieved to learn that all the circuses were going out in 1930, and many acts were even signed for the next season on his inspection tour. Ringling had no way of knowing that his impulse purchase would soon come back to haunt him.

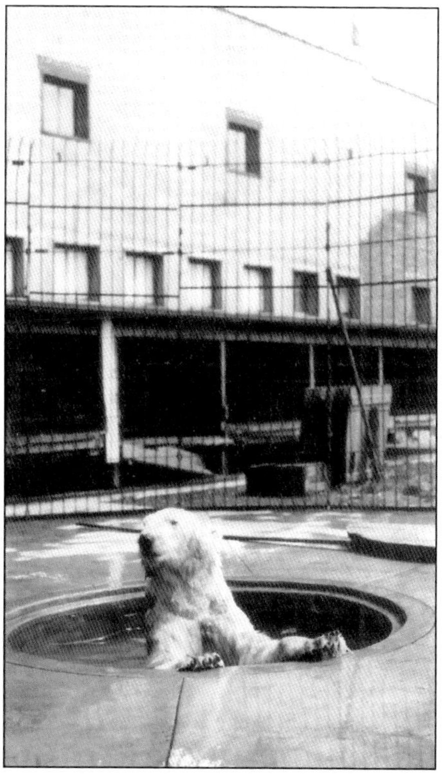

In October 1929, the stock market crashed and the nation slipped in to the Great Depression. Although the economy was weakening, Ringling was still preparing to send six circuses out on tour for the 1930 season. Since Ringling disliked animal acts, only the Hagenbeck-Wallace, Sparks, and Al G. Barnes Circuses would feature wild animals.

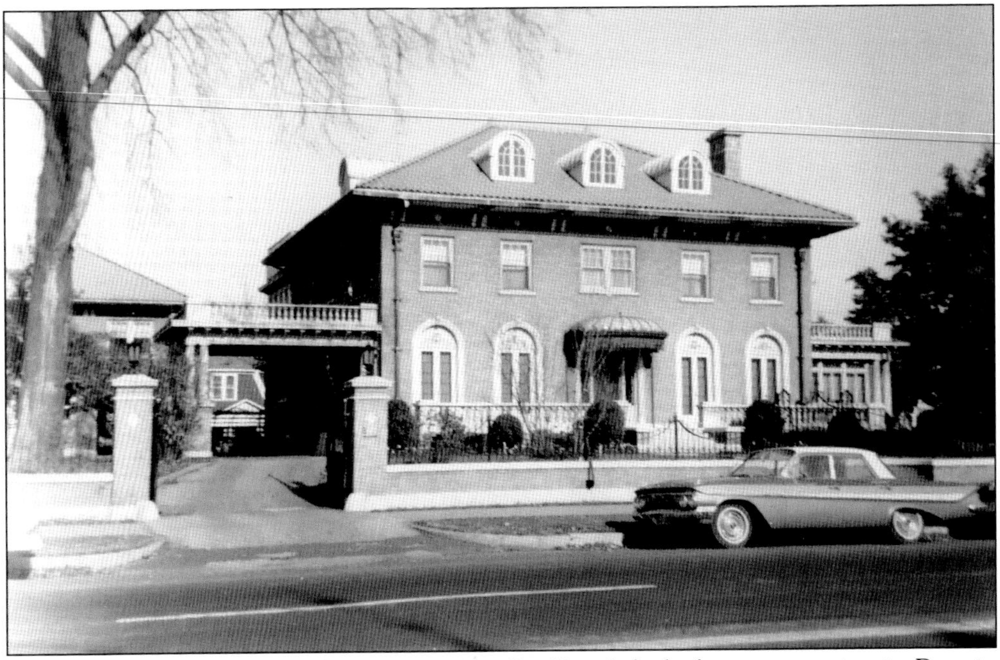

On January 23, 1930, Jeremiah Mugivan, "the Big Boss," died after an operation in Detroit. Mugivan was without a doubt the king of the white tops who ruled a circus empire. Mugivan's management skills, drive, and determination turned the American Circus Corporation into the largest circus holding company in the world. His generosity to his employees and to the city of Peru will be remembered for many generations.

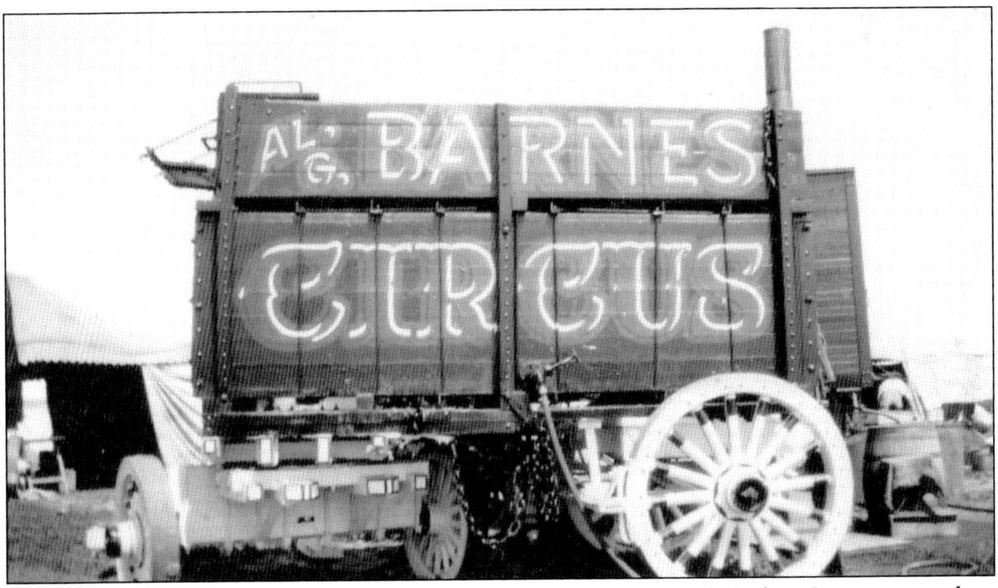


In the spring of 1930, the Ringling Brothers and Barnum and Bailey Circus opened at Madison Square Garden. As promised by John Ringling, the Sells-Floto, John Robinson's, and Hagenbeck-Wallace Circuses left the Peru winter quarters, and the Sparks and Al G. Barnes Circuses also left their winter quarters in Georgia and California for the season.

# *Ten*

# THE RECKONING

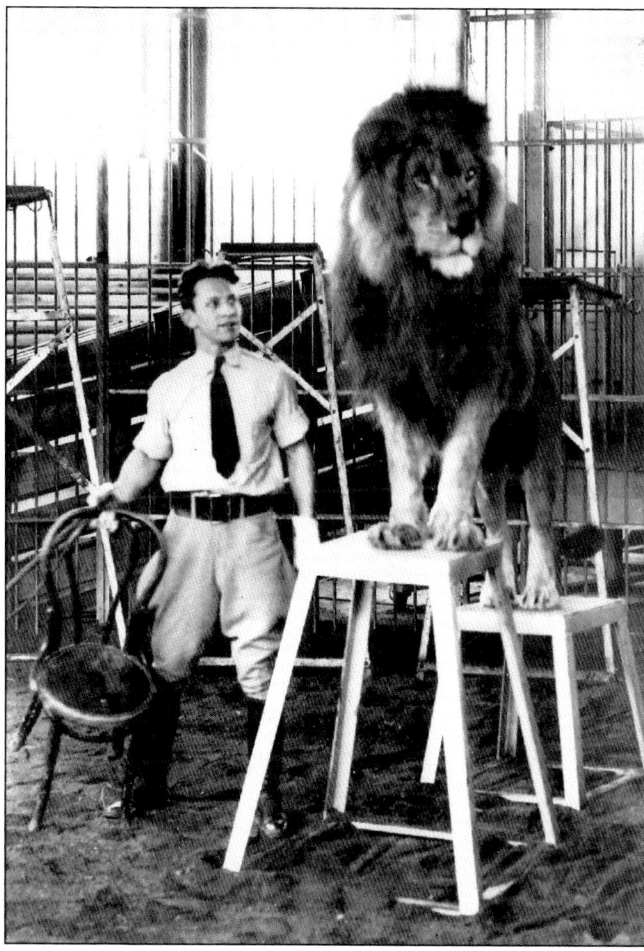

On April 24, 1930, when the Hagenbeck-Wallace Circus was in Kokomo, Clyde Beatty was rehearsing his act when one of his tigers suddenly attacked. The tiger ripped Beatty's right side open with a single blow and knocked him to the ground. The tiger then sunk his teeth deep into Beatty's right arm. A lion named Prince (who disliked the tiger) suddenly bolted from his seat and attacked the tiger. With just a few swipes from the paws of the mighty beast, the tiger ran for the tunnel. Prince had saved Beatty's life. Beatty struggled to his feet and ran all 32 cats to their cage, stepped outside the arena, and collapsed. The story of how Beatty's trusty lion Prince saved his life swept the country. Clyde Beatty and his loyal lion Prince became a household name overnight.

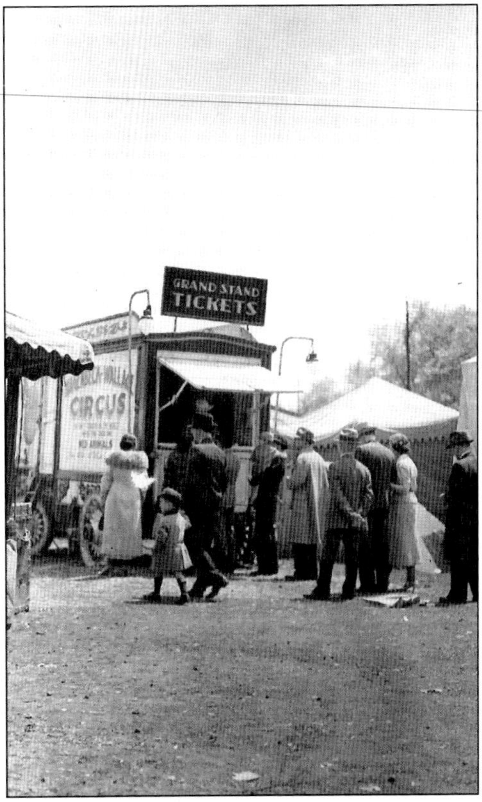


All six of John Ringling's circuses began to lose money by the end of summer. Circuses all across the country began heading to their winter quarters early, and some never survived the season. The Great Depression was taking a toll on America, and the circus was a luxury that few Americans could afford. Before the end of the 1930 season, all Ringling's circuses closed early and returned to their winter quarters.

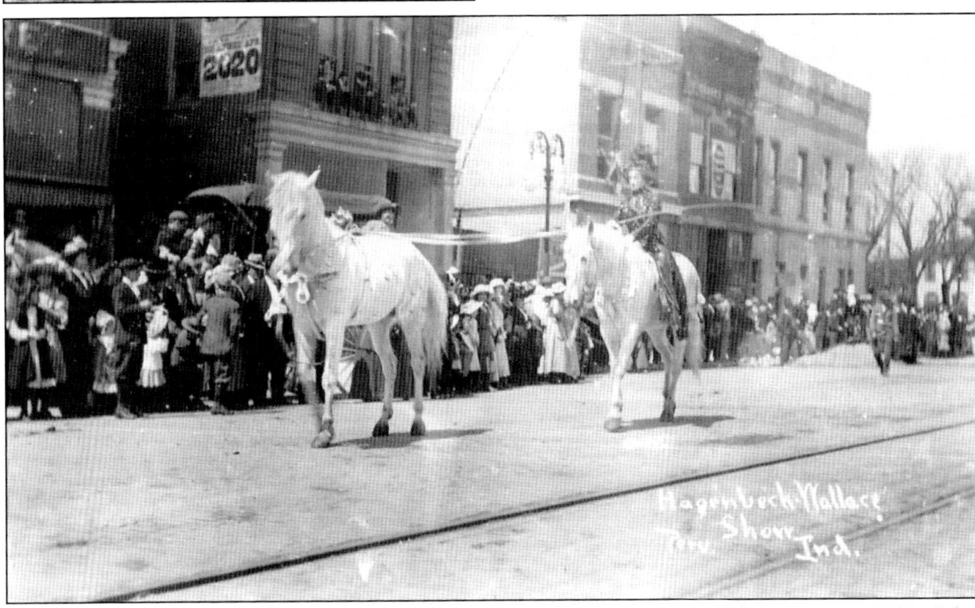


It was decided by John Ringling that the John Robinson's Circus would not tour in 1931. After 106 seasons of touring America, the John Robinson's Circus was shelved and would never tour again. The wagons and equipment were split up among the remaining Ringling circuses, and in the spring of 1931, only the Hagenbeck-Wallace and the Sells-Floto Circuses would leave Peru to tour.

The Ringling Brothers and Barnum and Bailey Circus opened at Madison Square Garden on April 2, 1931. To ensure the success of this engagement, John Ringling borrowed Clyde Beatty from the Hagenbeck-Wallace and billed Beatty's act as "the Greatest Wild Animal Act Ever Witnessed." Beatty's act was a hit, and after this engagement, Beatty returned to the Hagenbeck-Wallace for the 1931 season.

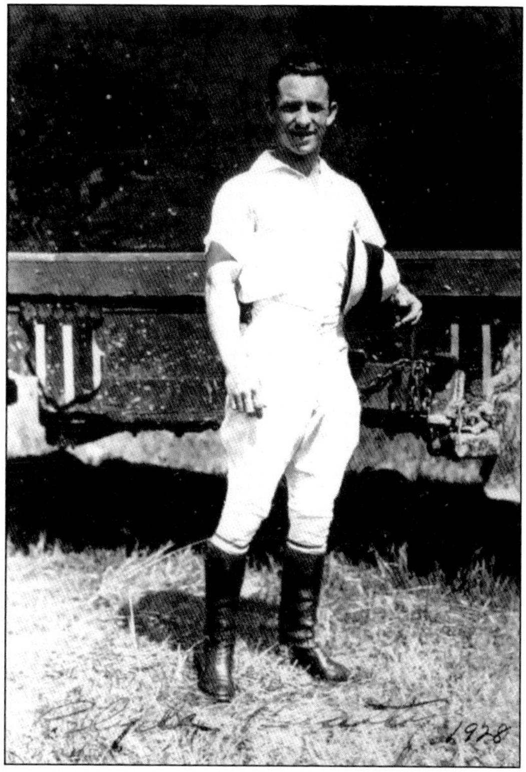


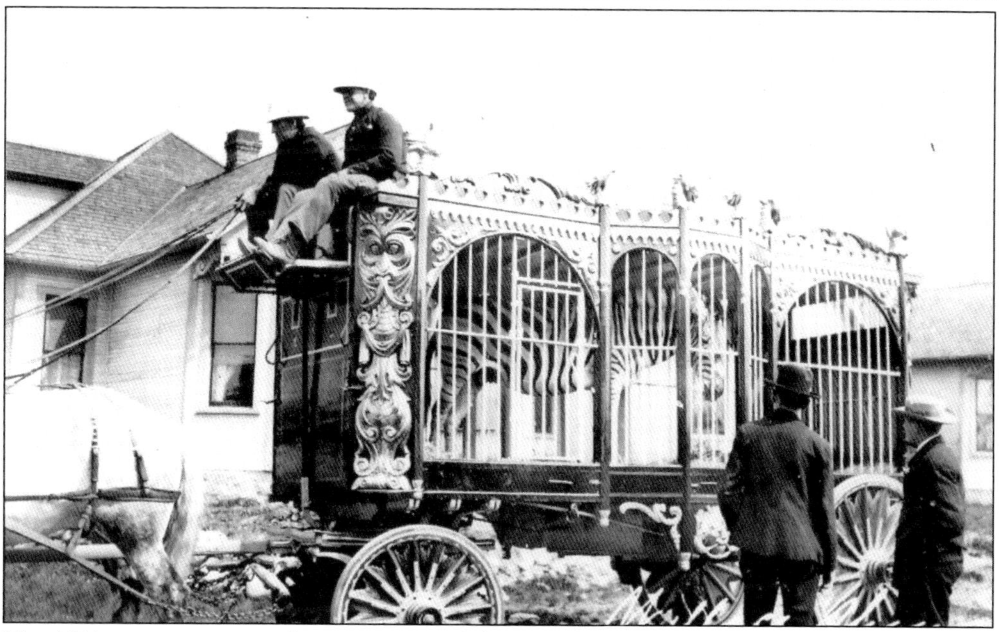

The 1931 season was very disappointing to John Ringling with all his circuses struggling. The Hagenbeck-Wallace was doing better than the others, but it was still a far cry from the profits of five years earlier. All five shows closed in early fall and returned to their winter quarters. The Ringling Brothers and Barnum and Bailey Circus closed on September 14, which was the earliest in its history.

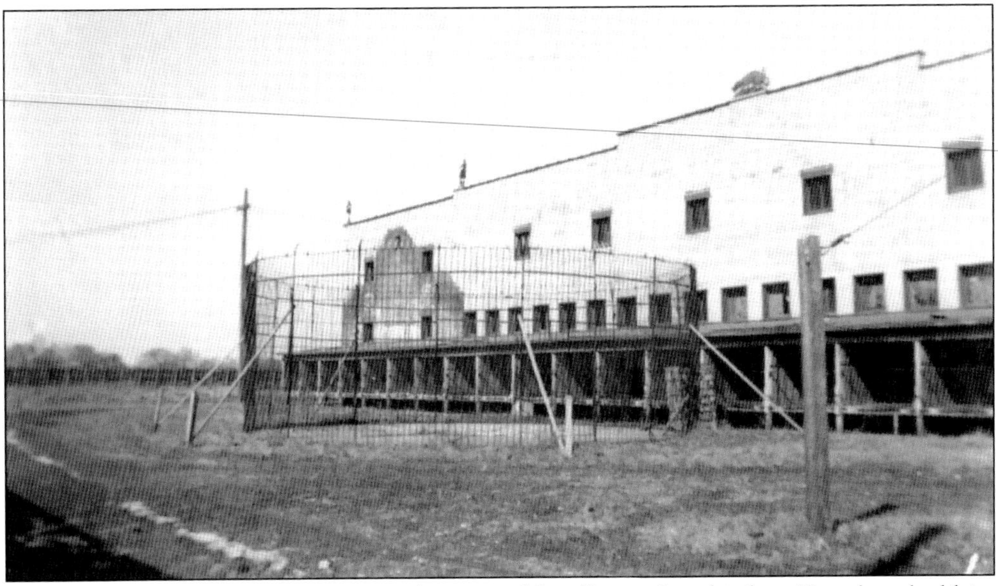

On January 23, 1932, Clyde Beatty made national headlines when his lion Nero knocked him down and bit his right leg while rehearsing in Peru. Within hours, Beatty suffered from jungle fever, for which there was no known cure. Many medications were tried but had no effect. Doctors from Peru and Chicago finally concocted a serum that proved successful and saved Beatty from certain death.

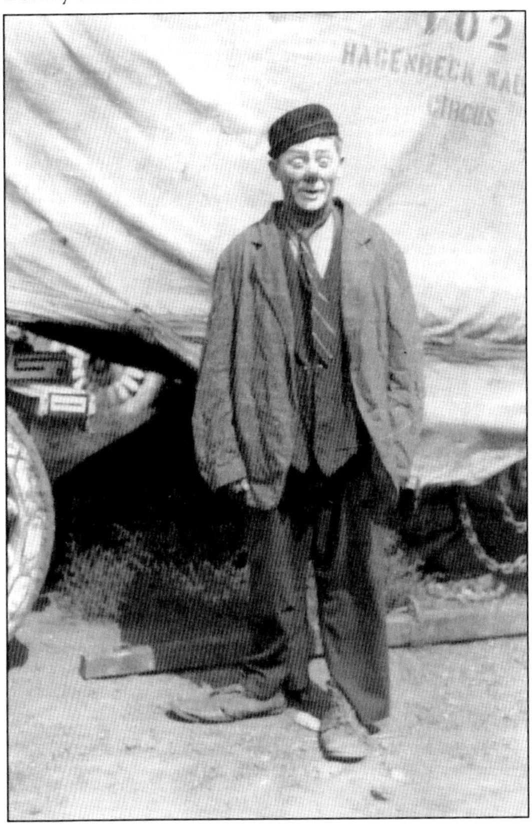

In the spring of 1932, Clyde Beatty again opened the Ringling Brothers and Barnum and Bailey Circus in Madison Square Garden then returned to tour with the Hagenbeck-Wallace Circus. In 1932, the Sells-Floto Circus left Peru on 30 railcars, and the Hagenbeck-Wallace left on 35 railcars. The Al G. Barnes Circus left its winter quarters in California for the season, but it was decided that the Sparks Circus would not tour and would remain at the winter quarters in Macon, Georgia.

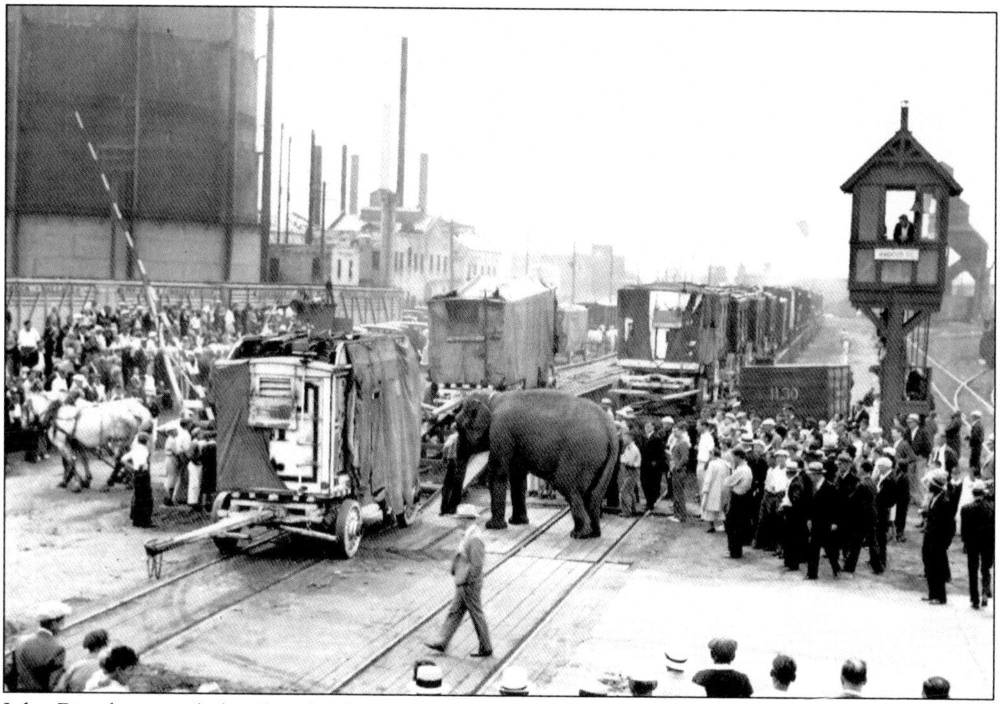

John Ringling was behind on his loan payment in 1932. His creditors and in-law partners stepped in and took control of the circuses. To prevent foreclosure, Ringling had to put all his property and assets up for collateral. They insisted Samuel W. Gumpertz step in as vice president and take over operations. Ringling remained president with a salary but no authority.

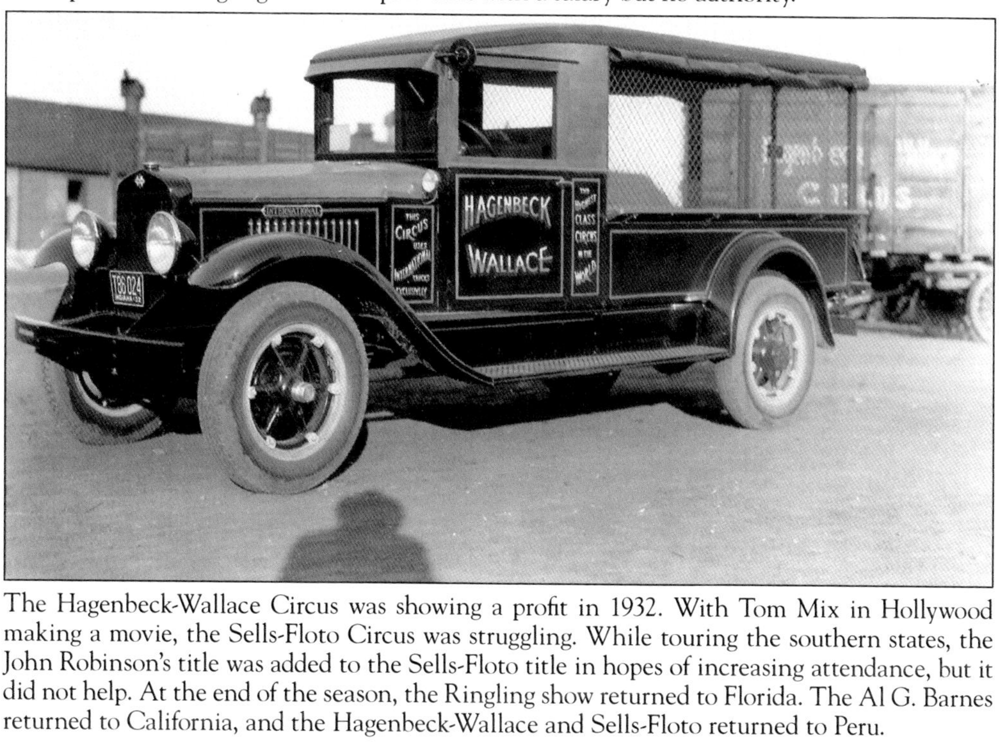


The Hagenbeck-Wallace Circus was showing a profit in 1932. With Tom Mix in Hollywood making a movie, the Sells-Floto Circus was struggling. While touring the southern states, the John Robinson's title was added to the Sells-Floto title in hopes of increasing attendance, but it did not help. At the end of the season, the Ringling show returned to Florida. The Al G. Barnes returned to California, and the Hagenbeck-Wallace and Sells-Floto returned to Peru.

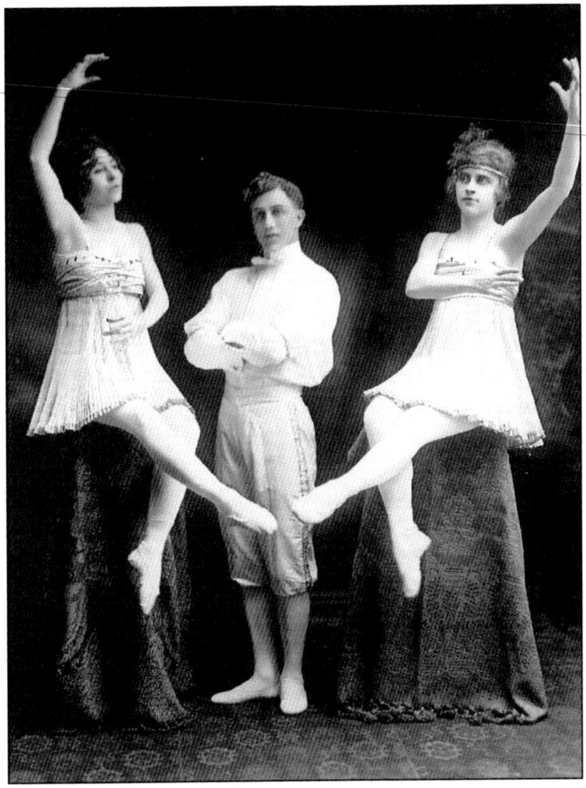

In the spring of 1933, only the Hagenbeck-Wallace Circus left Peru for the season. With the John Robinson's and Sells-Floto Circuses now shelved, hundreds of circus acts and employees were leaving Peru in search of work. Some found work on small truck circuses; others like the Albert Hodgini Troupe were off the road in 1933. Luckily, Emmett and Eva Kelly found work on the Hagenbeck-Wallace.

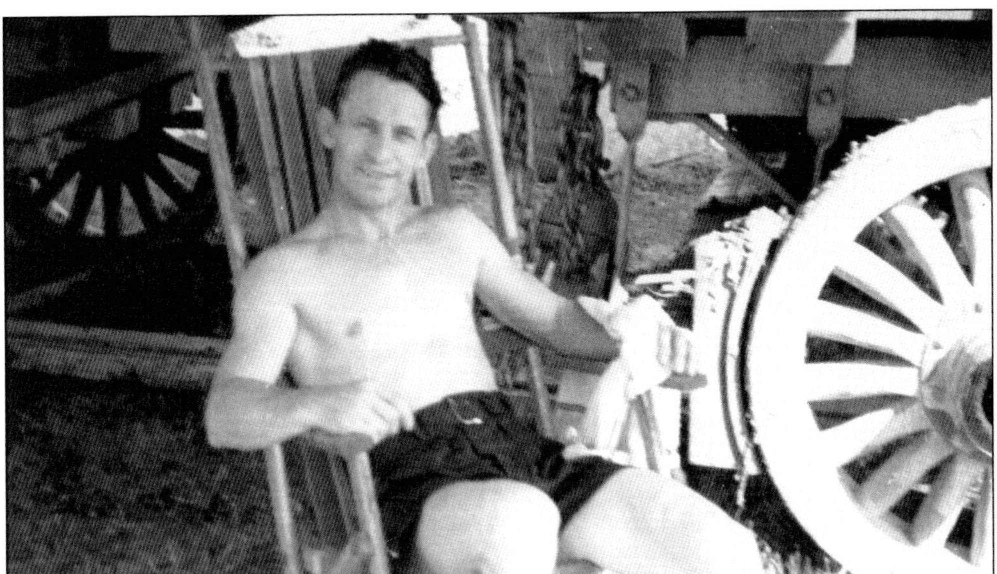

In 1933, the Ringling Brothers and Barnum and Bailey Circus, Hagenbeck-Wallace, and the Al G. Barnes Circus were the only three rail circuses in America. Clyde Beatty opened the Ringling show in Madison Square Garden before rejoining the Hagenbeck-Wallace show. On May 1, 1933, Beatty's first Hollywood movie, *The Big Cage*, was released, costarring Mickey Rooney. The movie was a hit with the fans but not with Samuel W. Gumpertz, the new Ringling manager.

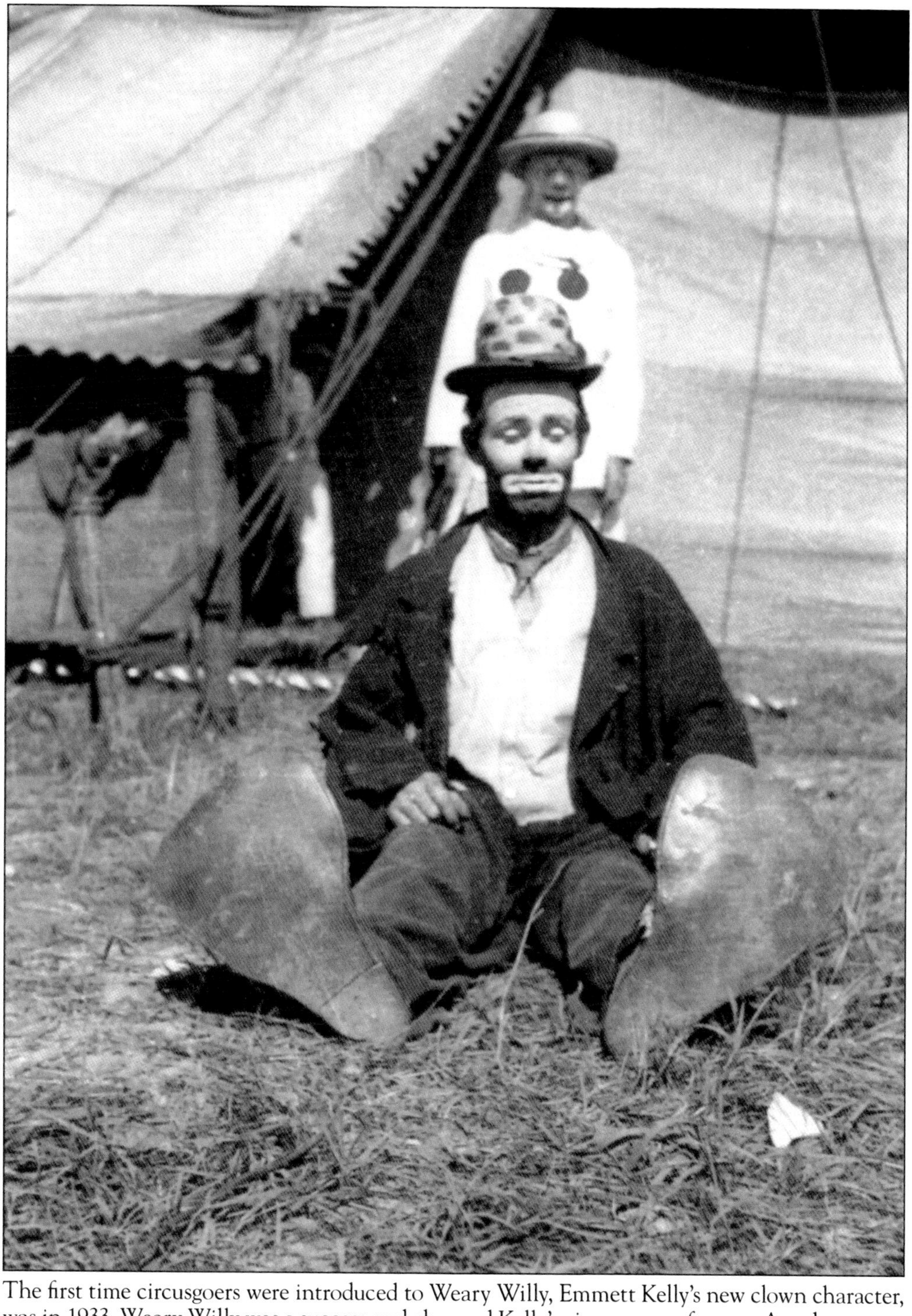

The first time circusgoers were introduced to Weary Willy, Emmett Kelly's new clown character, was in 1933. Weary Willy was a success and changed Kelly's circus career forever. Another tramp clown on the Hagenbeck-Wallace was Otto Griebling. Griebling began clowning after a serious accident. He felt that if he could be funny as an acrobatic equestrian he could also be funny as a clown.

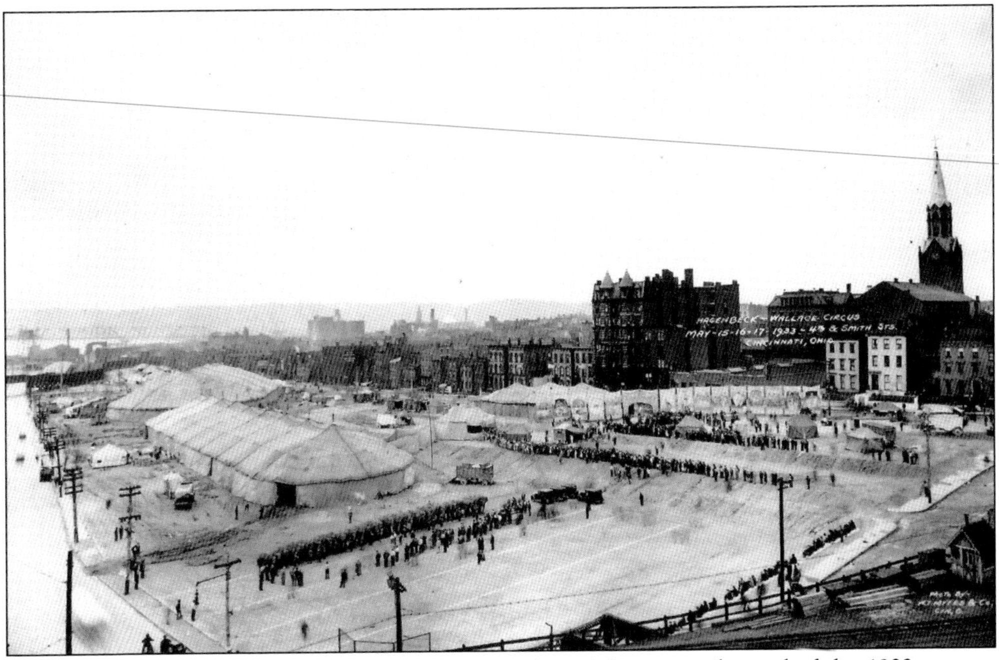


The Al G. Barnes Circus wintered in Baldwin Park, California, at the end of the 1933 season. The Ringling Brothers and Barnum and Bailey Circus went to Sarasota, Florida, and the Hagenbeck-Wallace Circus returned to Peru. The Hagenbeck-Wallace had featured several test street parades during the tour that proved to increase ticket sales. Samuel W. Gumpertz agreed to let manager Jess H. Adkins parade during the 1934 season.

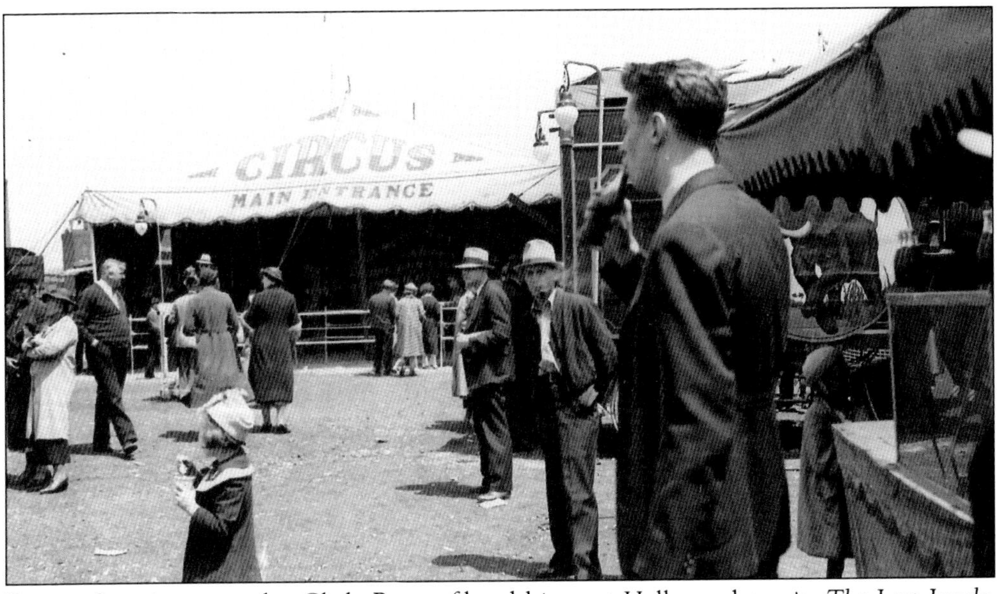


During the winter months, Clyde Beatty filmed his next Hollywood movie, *The Lost Jungle*. Beatty and Ringling manager Samuel W. Gumpertz were still at odds over Beatty's public appearances and movie deals. The Ringling show opened the 1934 season in Madison Square Garden featuring Clyde Beatty. Gumpertz promised that the 1935 season would open with an all new feature act.

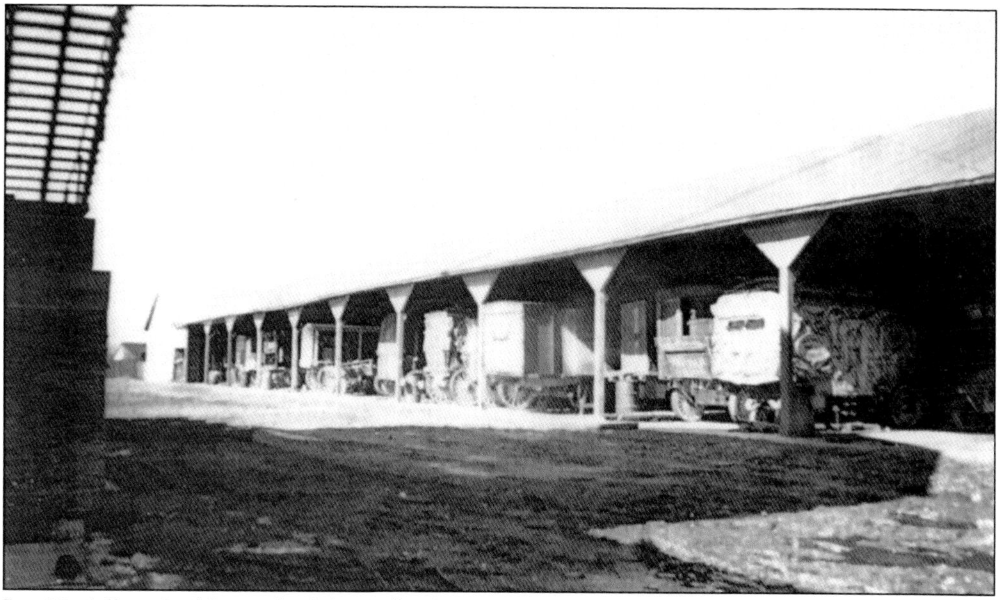

Jess H. Adkins had his pick of the Sells-Floto Circus and John Robinson's Circus wagons stored at Peru. He had them repainted and ready to parade by spring. The Hagenbeck-Wallace left Peru in the spring of 1934 on 48 railcars. The Al G. Barnes left its winter quarters for the season, and the Ringling shows also took to the rail. They were the only circuses to travel by rail this season.

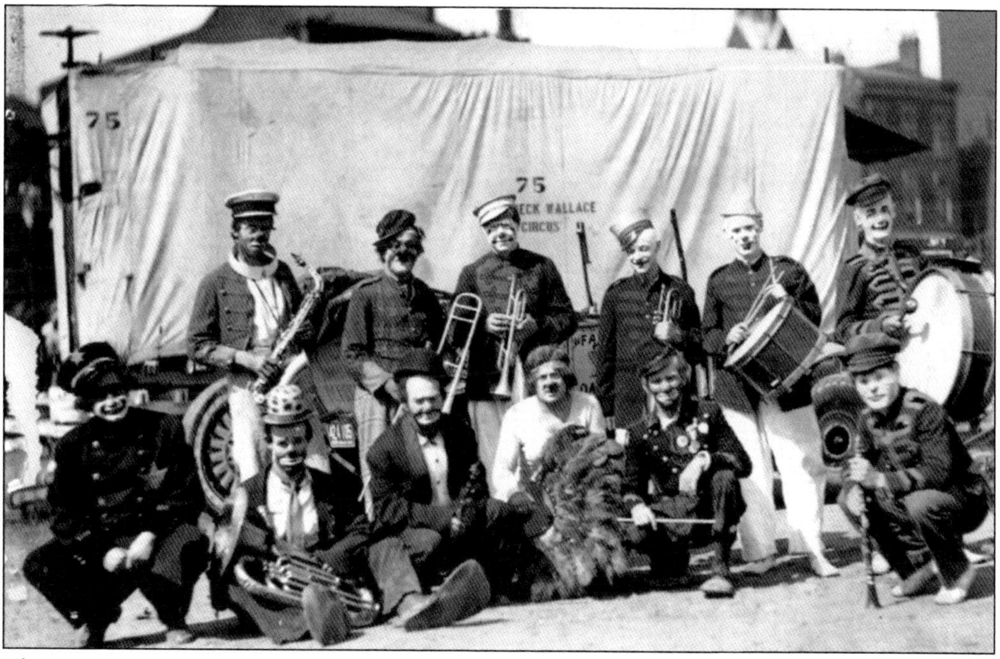


The country was showing signs of recovery from the Great Depression. All three Ringling shows were seeing better attendance than they had seen since the crash. The Hagenbeck-Wallace Circus was having one of the best years in its history. Clyde Beatty's new movie serial *The Lost Jungle* was released, and now Beatty was no longer just a skilled showman; he was becoming a real movie star.

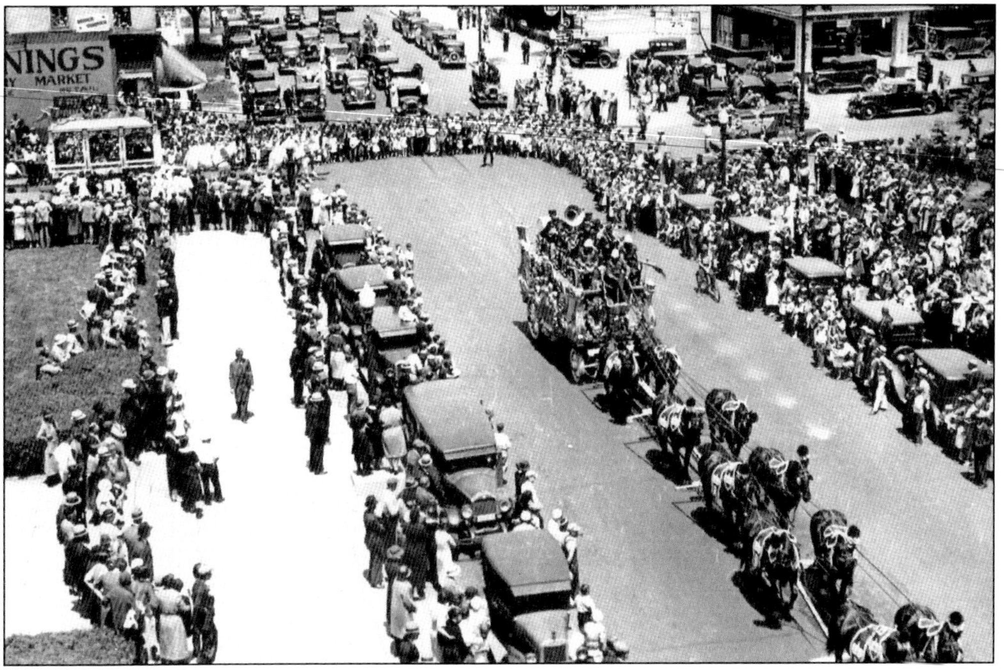

At the end of the season all three Ringling shows returned to their winter quarters. The Hagenbeck-Wallace Circus earned a better profit than even the much larger Ringling Brothers and Barnum and Bailey Circus show. The daily parades had paid off, and things were beginning to look better until the unexpected happened. After arriving at the Peru winter quarters, Jess H. Adkins, manager of the Hagenbeck-Wallace, resigned and took Clyde Beatty with him.

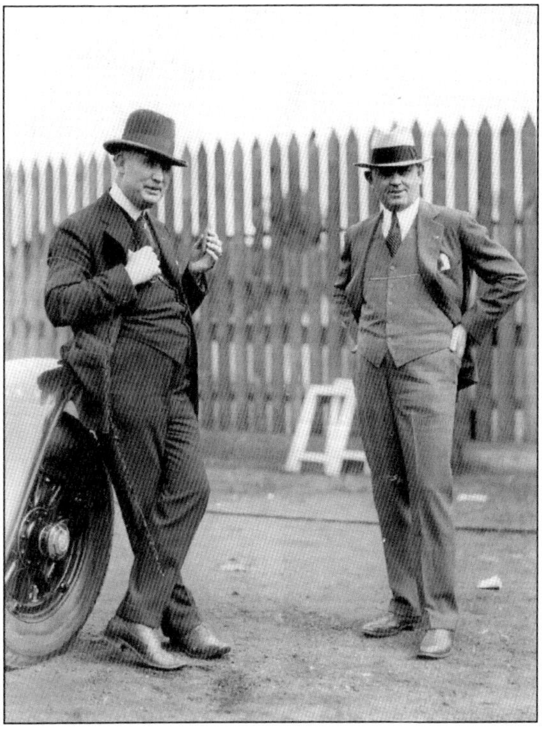

Jess H. Adkins and former Sells-Floto manager Zack Terrell had plans to start their own circus. The men formed the Indiana Circus Corporation and bought the Rochester Bridge Company building in Rochester to use as a winter quarters. The two men spent the winter of 1934–1935 putting together a circus and hiring acts. Many of the acts came from the Hagenbeck-Wallace Circus.

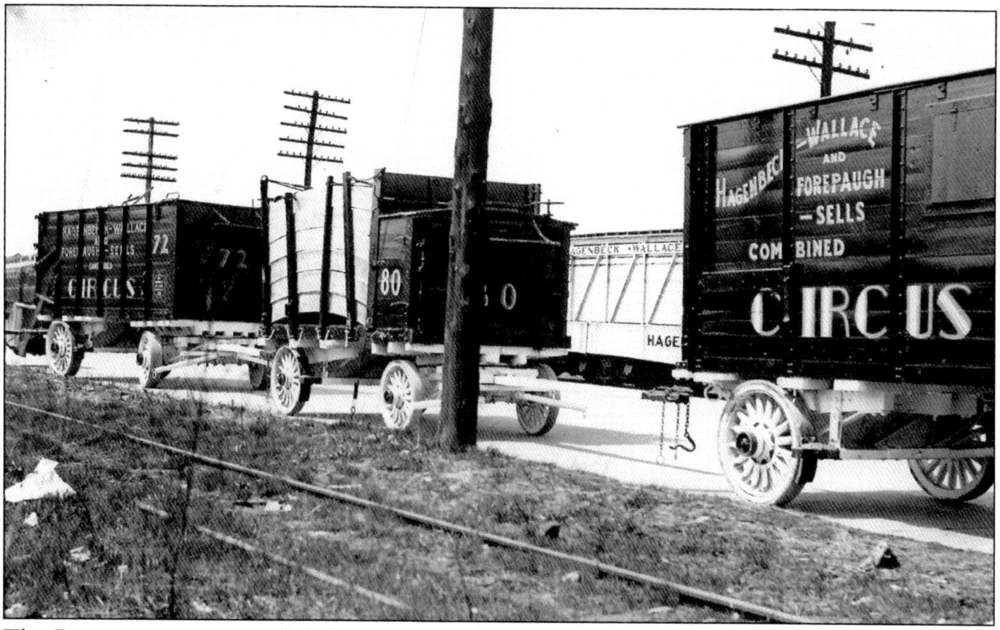


The Peru circus runaways left Rochester on 35 railcars as Cole Brothers–Clyde Beatty Circus and opened on April 20, 1935, at the Chicago Coliseum. The Ringling Brothers and Barnum and Bailey, Al G. Barnes, and Hagenbeck-Wallace Circuses were the only other shows traveling by rail. The Hagenbeck-Wallace would troupe with only 35 railcars in 1935 and feature a new title, Hagenbeck-Wallace–Forepaugh-Sells Combined Circus.

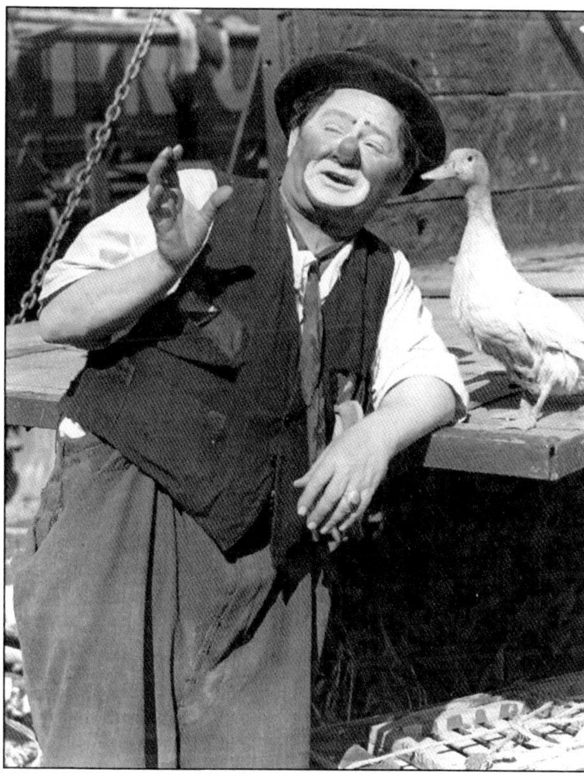

Ringling management once again decided not to feature daily parades with its circuses although several were featured on the Hagenbeck-Wallace–Forepaugh-Sells Combined Circus. With seasoned acts like Clyde Beatty, Allen King, Emmett Kelly, Otto Griebling, and the Albert Hodgini Troupe, the new Cole Brothers show was doing very well. At the end of the season, all four rail shows returned to their winter quarters.

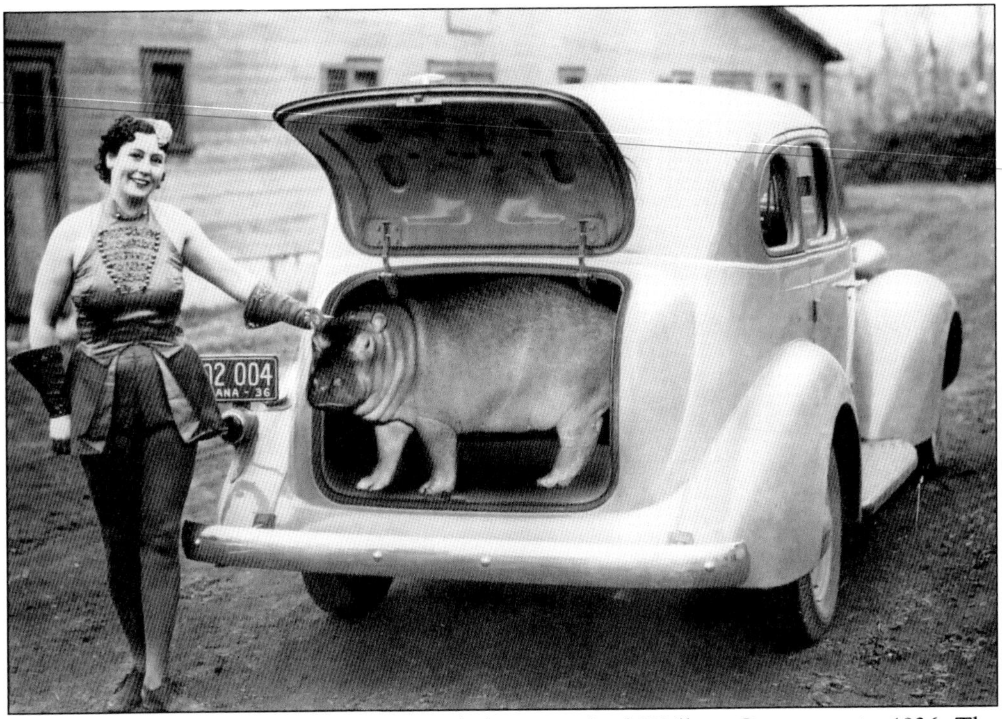

Ringling management decided not to send the Hagenbeck-Wallace Circus out in 1936. The Hagenbeck-Wallace had toured America for 52 consecutive years, and for the first time in 20 years, no circuses left Peru. Only three circuses traveled by rail this season; the Ringling Brothers and Barnum and Bailey, Cole Brothers–Clyde Beatty, and Al G. Barnes Circuses. About 60 truck shows toured in 1936, which included the Tom Mix Circus.

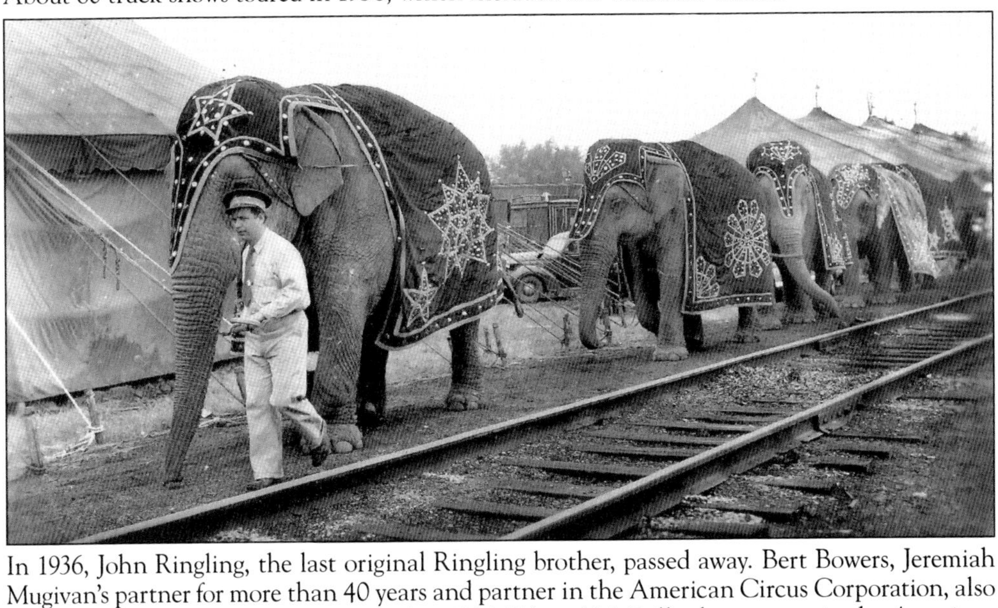

In 1936, John Ringling, the last original Ringling brother, passed away. Bert Bowers, Jeremiah Mugivan's partner for more than 40 years and partner in the American Circus Corporation, also passed away from an illness. In November 1936, Edward M. Ballard, a partner in the American Circus Corporation, was shot and killed in Hot Springs, Arkansas. The last of the old-time showmen were gone.

*Eleven*

# THE LAST HURRAH

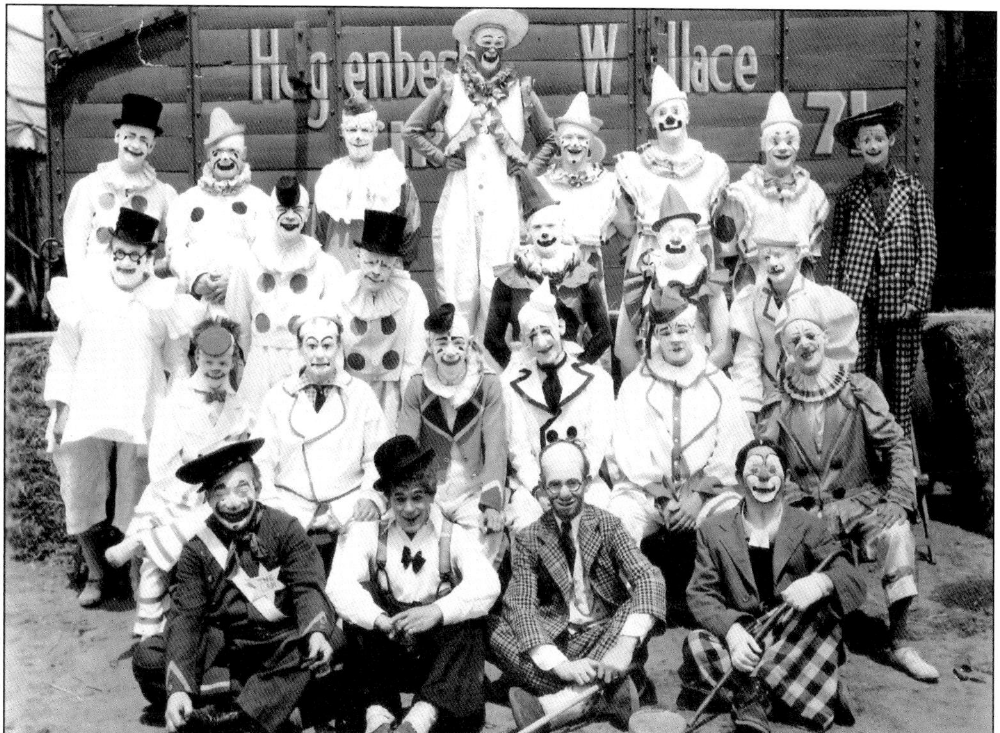

In the spring of 1937, the Cole Brothers–Clyde Beatty Circus hit the rails on 40 railcars. The Ringling Brothers and Barnum and Bailey Circus traveled on 90 railcars, and the Al G. Barnes Circus added the Sells-Floto title to its show hitting the rails on 30 cars. The Hagenbeck-Wallace Circus that was off the road in 1936 was leased to Eddie Arlington and Frank Hatch, who opened the show in the Chicago Coliseum. After the opening stand, Arlington and Hatch transferred the show to Howard Y. Bary.

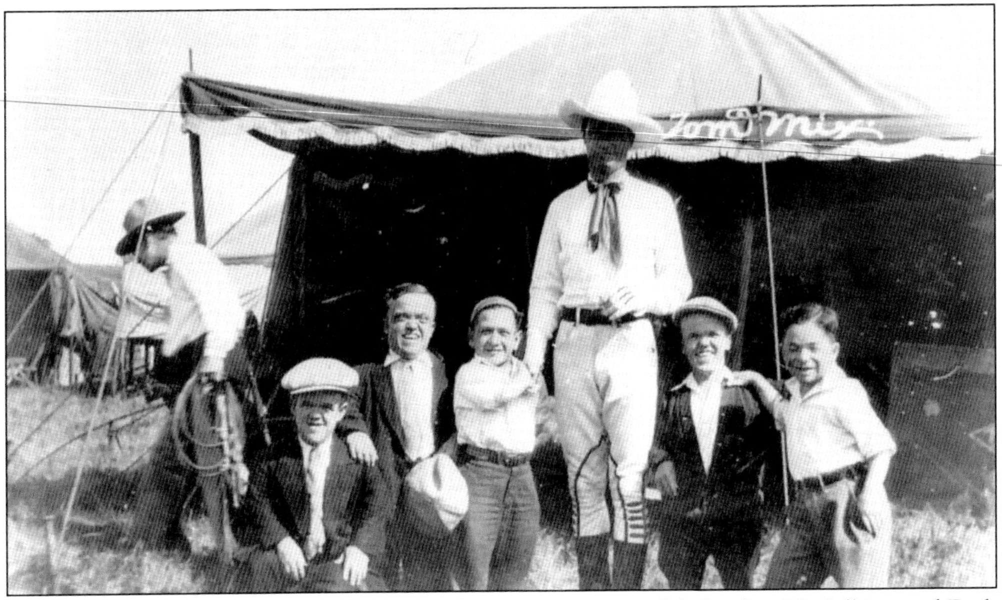


The rail and truck shows did well in 1937. They were so successful that Jess H. Adkins and Zack Terrell began planning a second rail circus for the 1938 season. The Tom Mix Circus had been doing well the last few years and was touring on more than 60 trucks. Mix's show was the first truck show to tour from coast to coast in one season.

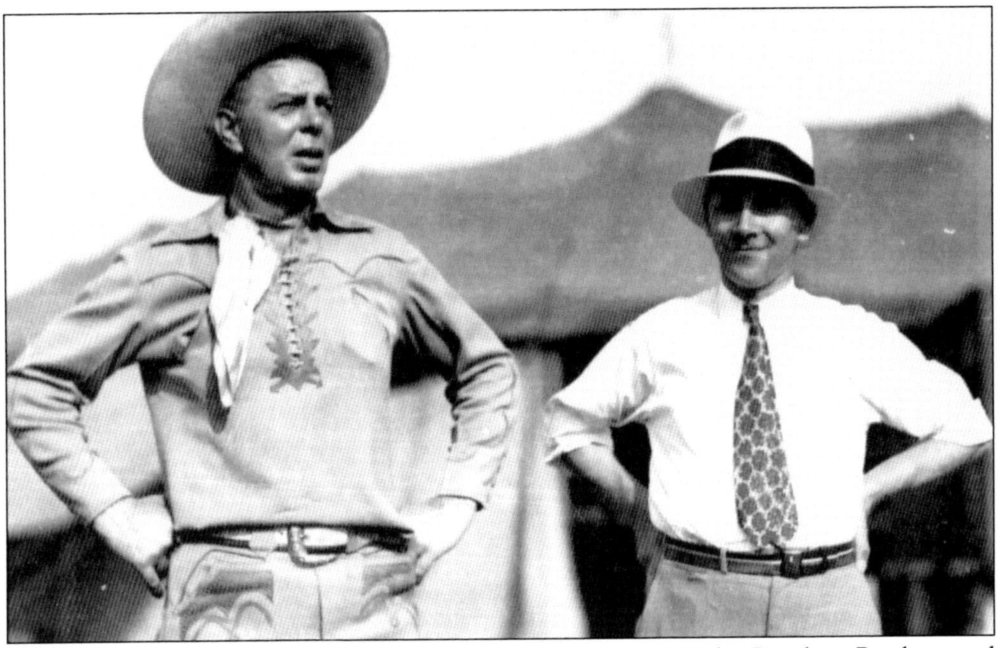

John Ringling North, nephew of John Ringling, was managing the Ringling Brothers and Barnum and Bailey Circus by the end of the 1937 season. In late 1937, North bought a disfigured gorilla and named him Gargantua. North also contracted Terrell Jacobs to work the big cats. Adkins and Terrell were planning their new circus to be titled Robbins Brothers. To help ensure its success, they hired cowboy movie star Hoot Gibson for the season.

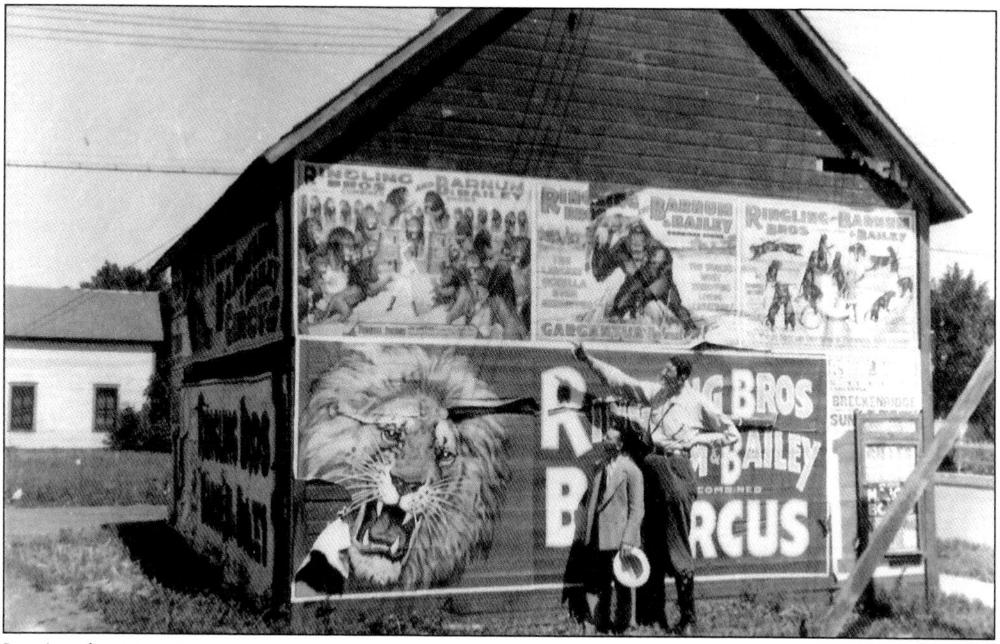


In April 1938, Ringling opened in Madison Square Garden featuring Terrell Jacobs, "the Lion King," and also featuring Gargantua the Great. The Al G. Barnes–Sells-Floto Circus hit the rails on 30 cars, and Howard Y. Bary took the Hagenbeck-Wallace Circus out of Peru on 25 railcars. The Cole Brothers–Clyde Beatty Circus left Rochester on 30 cars, and the new Robbins Brothers Circus left Rochester on 15 railcars.

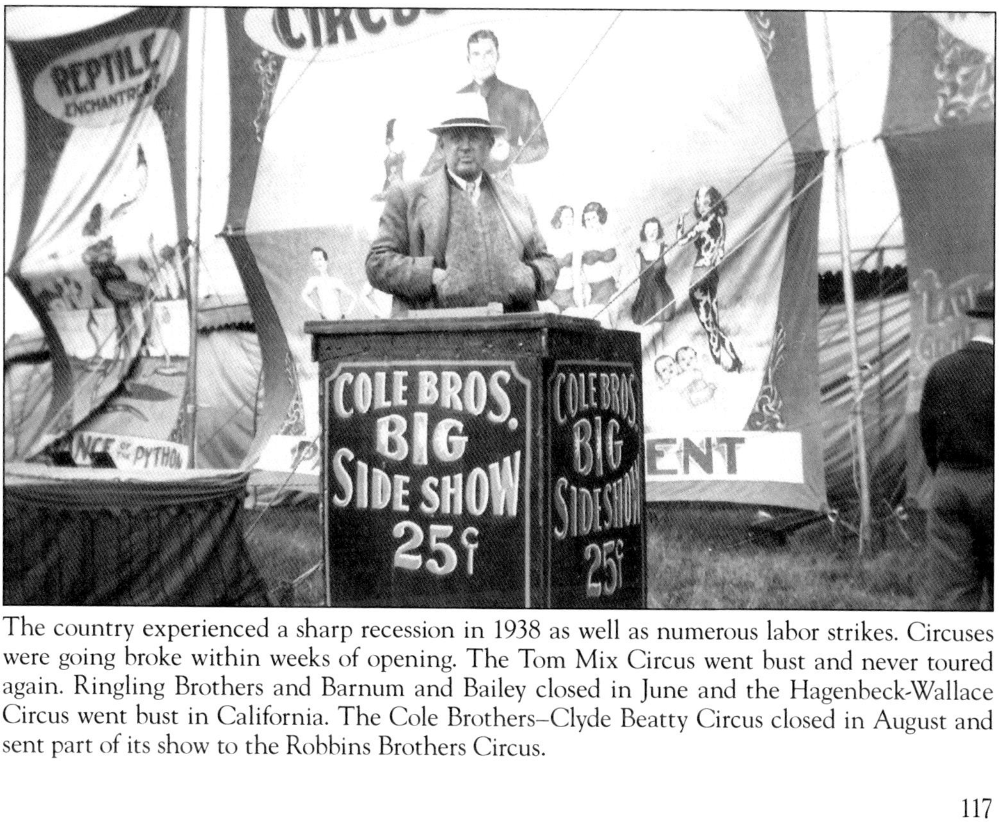


The country experienced a sharp recession in 1938 as well as numerous labor strikes. Circuses were going broke within weeks of opening. The Tom Mix Circus went bust and never toured again. Ringling Brothers and Barnum and Bailey closed in June and the Hagenbeck-Wallace Circus went bust in California. The Cole Brothers–Clyde Beatty Circus closed in August and sent part of its show to the Robbins Brothers Circus.

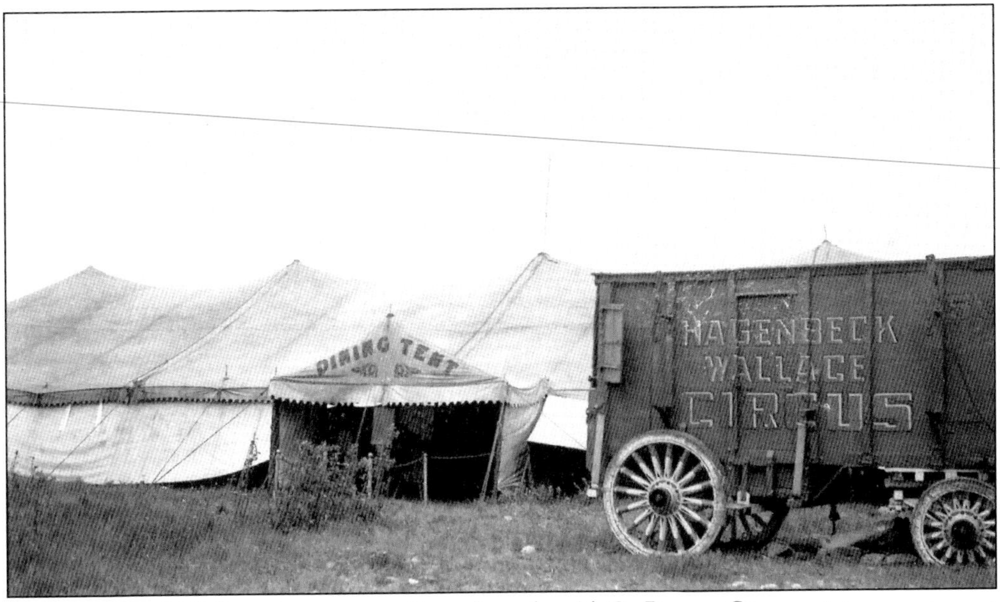


The Hagenbeck-Wallace Circus was shipped to the Al G. Barnes Circus winter quarters at Baldwin Park, California. John Ringling North sent an agent to sell off the circus equipment as well as the Al G. Barnes winter quarters. The Hagenbeck-Wallace had toured America for over half a century. It was the pride of Peru and the crown jewel of the American Circus Corporation, and now it could only parade in the hearts of America.

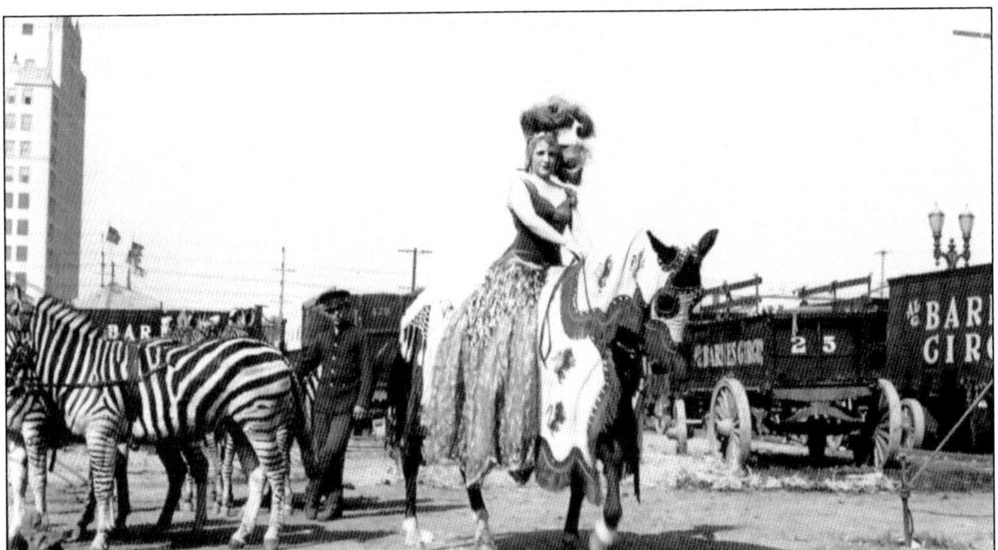

John Ringling North sent 21 railcars to join the Al G. Barnes–Sells-Floto still touring. The title now read Al G. Barnes–Sells-Floto and John Robinson's Combined Circus Present Ringling Brothers and Barnum and Bailey's Stupendous New Features. At the end of the season, the show was sent to Ringling's winter quarters in Sarasota, Florida, and the Al G. Barnes was shelved.

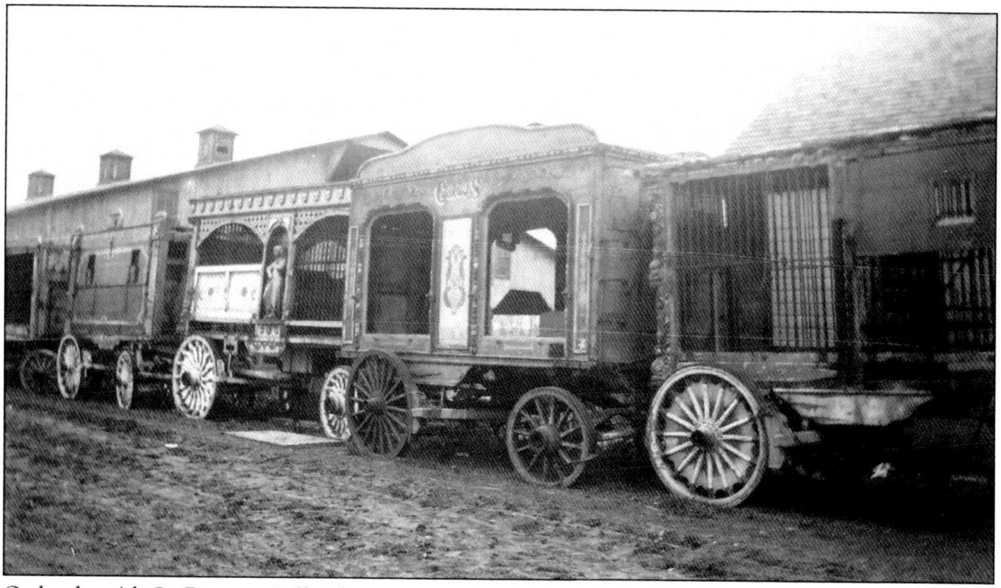

Only the Al G. Barnes–Sells-Floto and the new Robbins Brothers Circus finished the 1938 season. The recession and labor strikes put an end to many of America's beloved circuses. The Ringling Brothers and Barnum and Bailey Circus once again barely escaped financial ruin. The Peru winter quarters was nothing more than a storage facility that housed wagons and equipment that were part of the biggest circuses in the country a few years earlier.

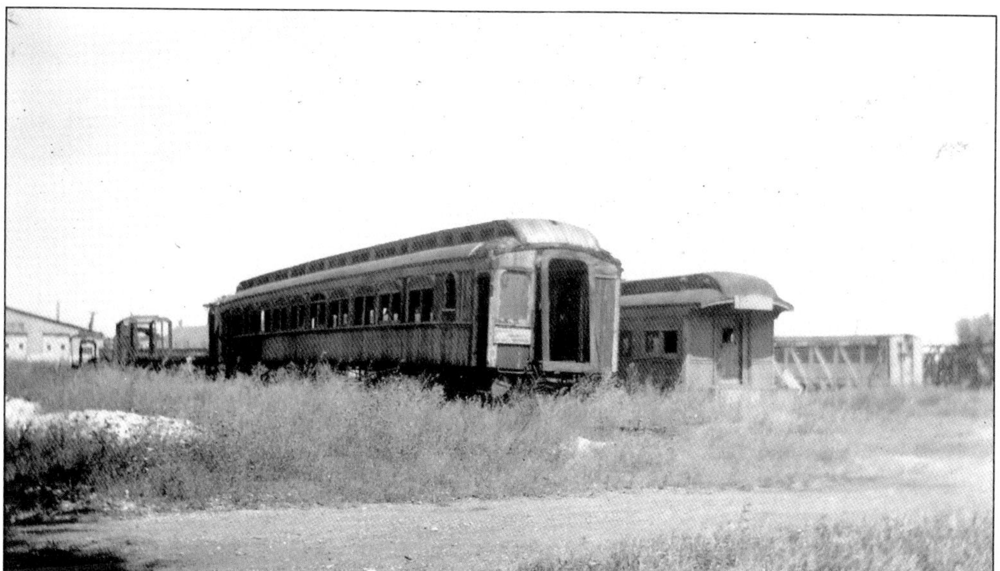

The Peru circus rail yards at Washington Street were full of stored railcars. Some would be sold off and others dismantled and cut up for scrap. The 1930s destroyed the circus industry. Circus families began leaving Peru looking for work wherever they could find it. Some would leave the circus life altogether.

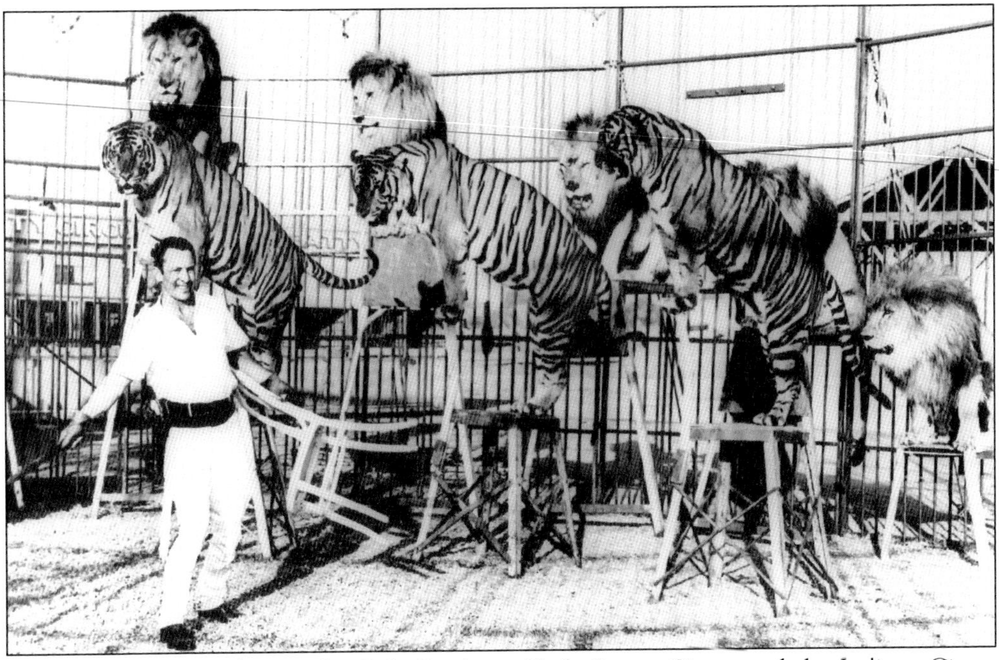

Upon arriving in Rochester, the Cole Brothers–Clyde Beatty Circus and the Indiana Circus Corporation filed for bankruptcy, as did the Robbins Brothers Circus. Jess H. Adkins and Zack Terrell began reorganizing for the 1939 season and incorporated the Hoosier Circus Corporation and the Cole Brothers Circus. Clyde Beatty booked with George Hamid's Million Dollar Pier in Atlantic City, New Jersey, for the 1939 season.

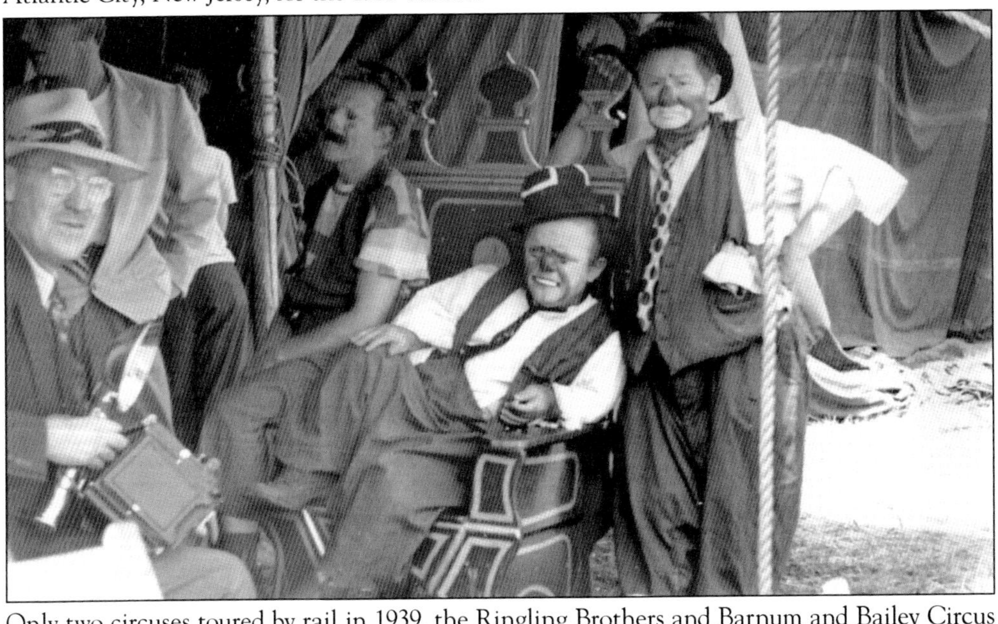

Only two circuses toured by rail in 1939, the Ringling Brothers and Barnum and Bailey Circus on 80 railcars, featuring Terrell Jacobs and Gargantua the Great, and the new Cole Brothers Circus on 20 railcars. Adkins and Terrell put together the new circus in the same fashion that Jeremiah Mugivan and Bert Bowers did 20 years earlier, which was without movie stars and superstars—just good old solid circus and animal acts.

On February 20, 1940, fire broke out in the winter quarters of the Cole Brothers Circus. Circus animals ran free in the streets of Rochester, and damages totaled $150,000. By the time the fire was extinguished, John Ringling North agreed to allow the Cole Brothers show to move its animals to the Peru winter quarters. Zack Terrell left immediately for Sarasota, Florida, to negotiate the purchase of equipment stored at Peru. Pictured here is Terrell Jacobs after the fire.

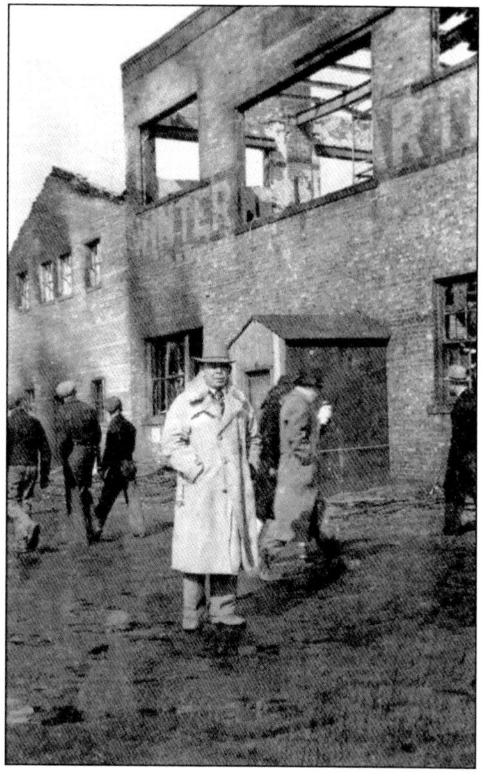

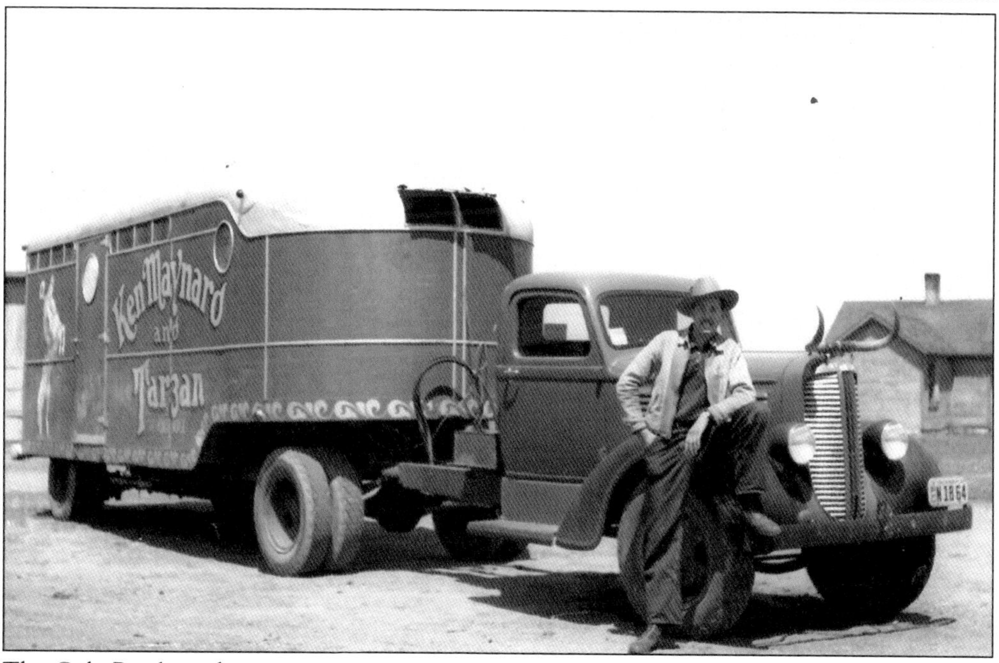


The Cole Brothers show was now preparing and training for the 1940 season at the Peru and Rochester winter quarters. John Ringling North agreed to sell Adkins and Terrell whatever they needed to open their show. On May 3, 1940, the Cole Brothers Circus opened in Rochester featuring cowboy movie star Ken Maynard.

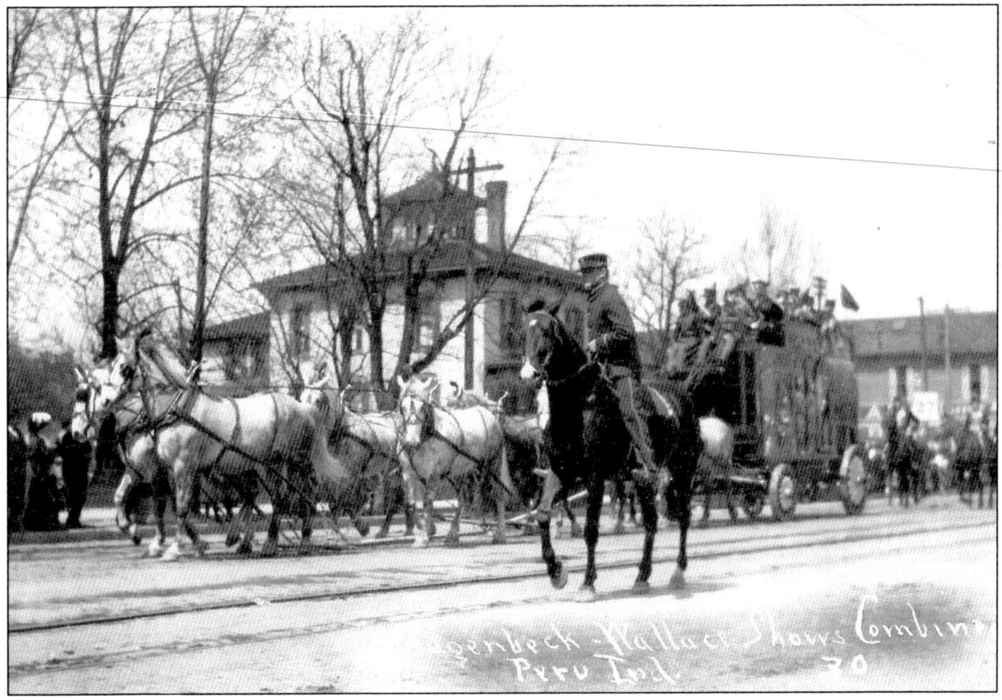


On June 25, 1940, Jess H. Adkins died of a heart attack at the age of 54 while touring with the Cole Brothers Circus. After college, Adkins had made a career of managing circuses in one capacity or another. His work on the Hagenbeck-Wallace and Cole Brothers Circuses became legendary. His funeral was attended by a multitude of circus owners and performers. The showman was laid to rest in Mount Hope Cemetery in Peru.

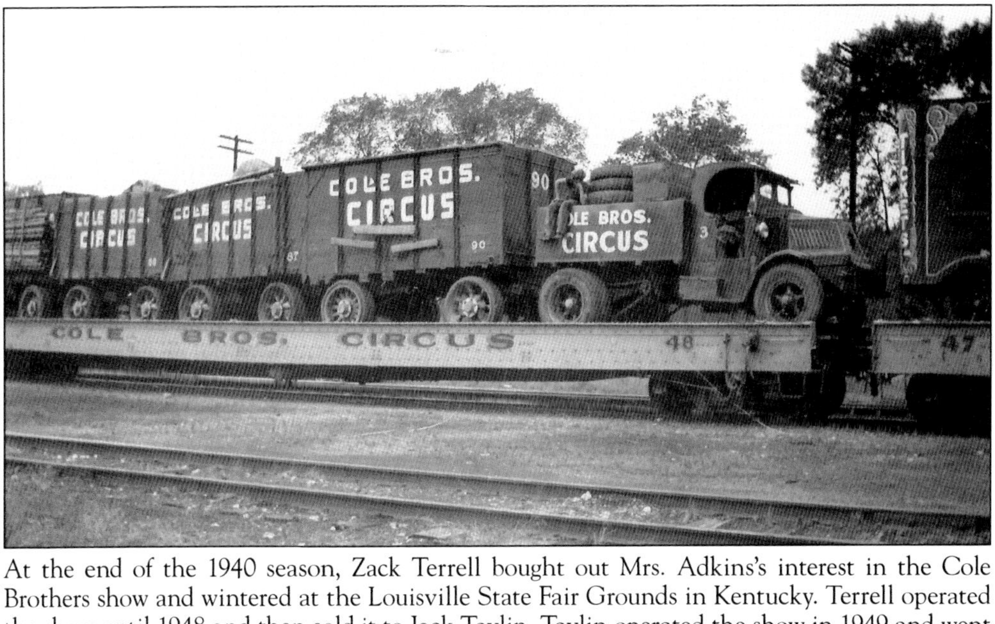


At the end of the 1940 season, Zack Terrell bought out Mrs. Adkins's interest in the Cole Brothers show and wintered at the Louisville State Fair Grounds in Kentucky. Terrell operated the show until 1948 and then sold it to Jack Tavlin. Tavlin operated the show in 1949 and went bankrupt. The Ringling Brothers and Barnum and Bailey Circus was now the sole survivor of the great American circuses.

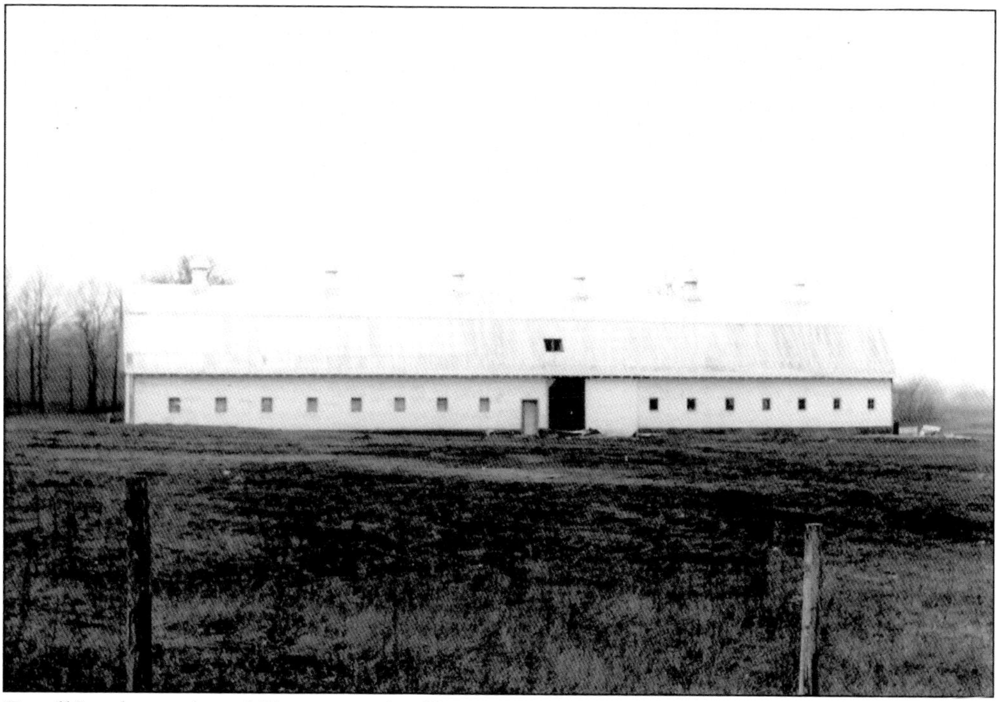

Terrell Jacobs purchased 13 acres south of Peru in 1940 to create a winter quarters for his animals. Over the next few years, Jacobs booked his act with circuses, carnivals, and special events. By 1942, Jacobs had built a second barn on the property that included cages for his lions, tigers, and other animals as well as an indoor arena.

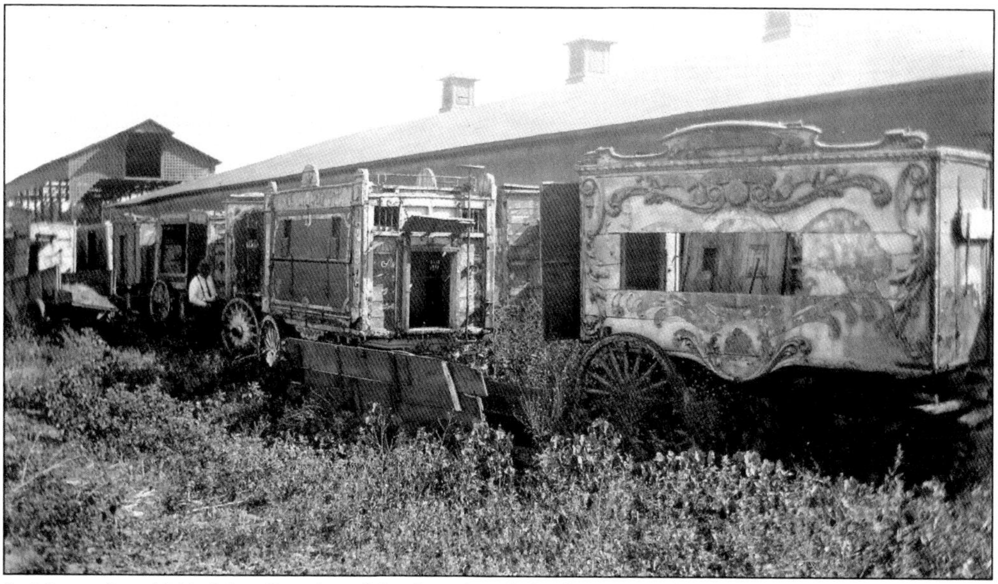

In November 1941, John Ringling North ordered the burning of the wagons stored at the Peru winter quarters. Some of the wagons had been stored for more than 10 years, and many had rotted and were missing parts. The circus world had changed, and the wagons were obsolete. North was preparing to permanently close the winter quarters and sell it off for farming.

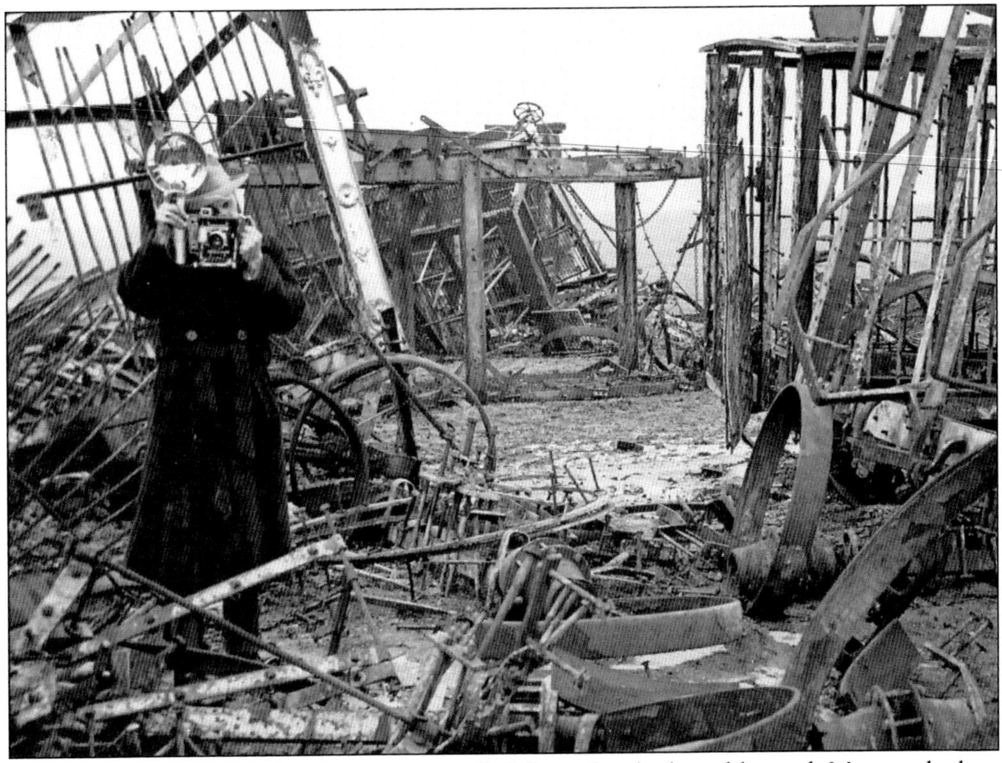

On November 21, 1941, the wagons were pulled from the sheds and burned. Many onlookers begged the workers to spare some of the wagons, wheels, and carvings, but they had strict orders to burn them all. The last inventory list shows 137 wagons, of which 10 went to Sarasota, 1 to Terrell Jacobs, 4 to the Cole Brothers Circus, and 1 to the Ringling Brothers and Barnum and Bailey Circus, leaving 121 wagons destroyed.

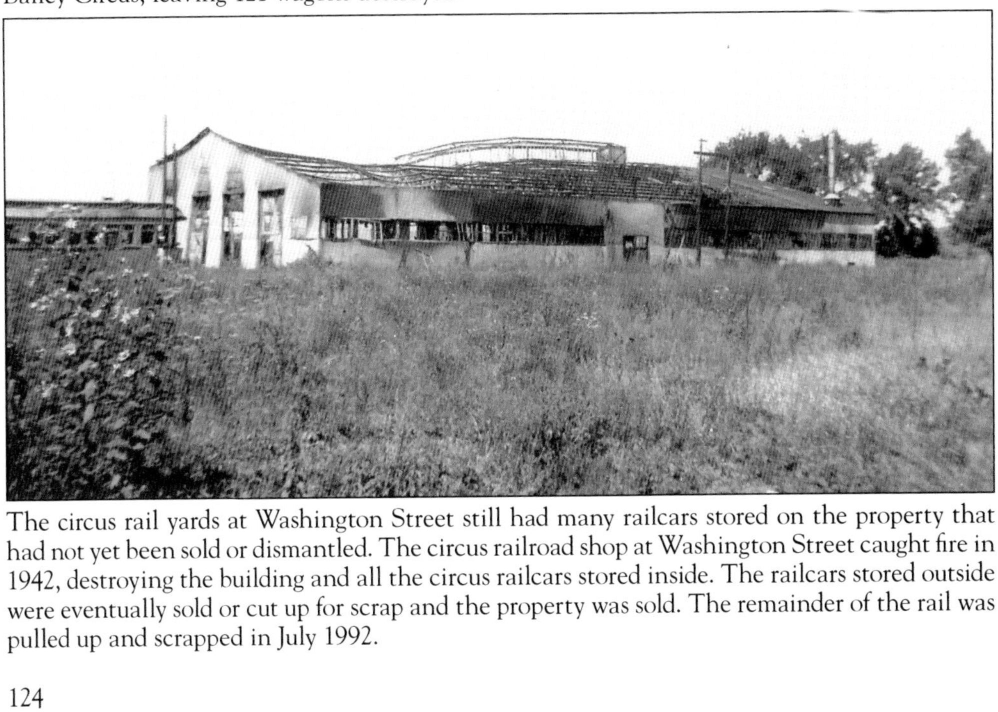

The circus rail yards at Washington Street still had many railcars stored on the property that had not yet been sold or dismantled. The circus railroad shop at Washington Street caught fire in 1942, destroying the building and all the circus railcars stored inside. The railcars stored outside were eventually sold or cut up for scrap and the property was sold. The remainder of the rail was pulled up and scrapped in July 1992.

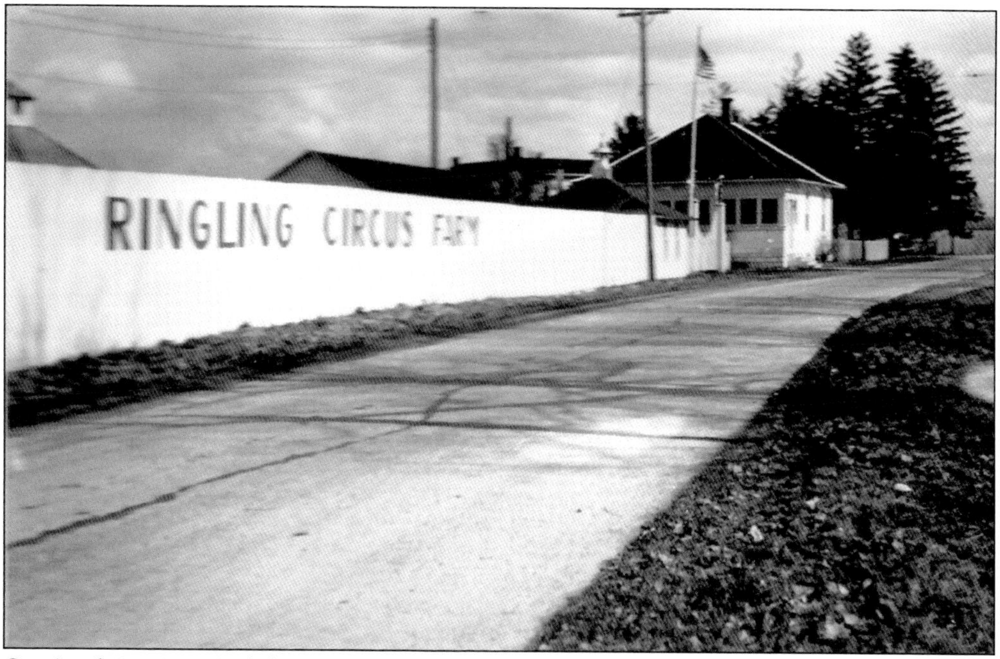


On April 8, 1944, 5 of the 10 wagons that John Ringling North reserved from the original inventory list were loaded up on two railcars and shipped to Sarasota, Florida. The property was then sold, and thus came the end of a 60-year era that saw the beginning and end of many of the biggest and greatest American circuses that ever toured the country.

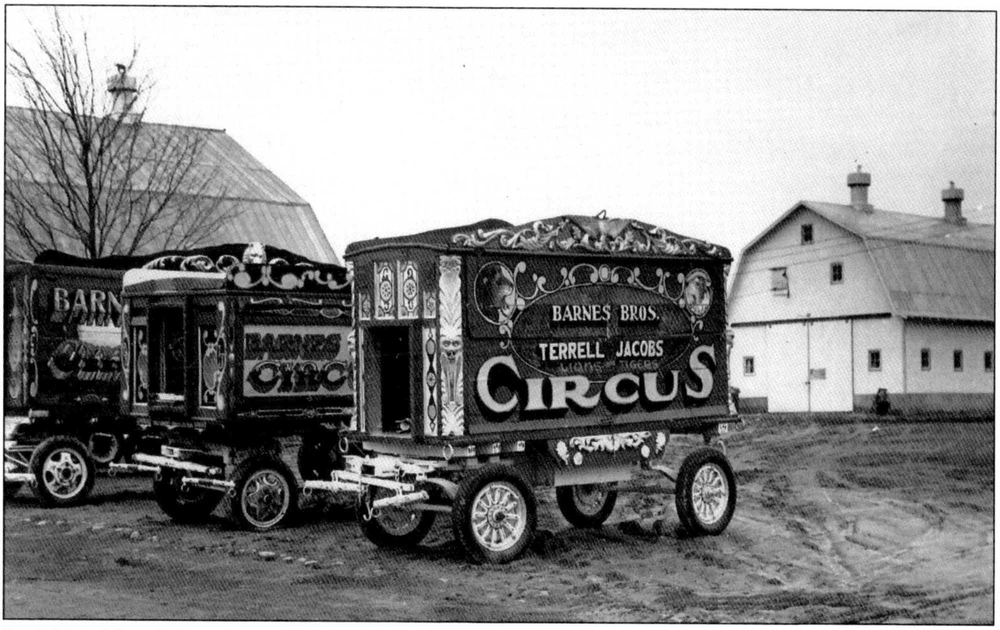


In 1944, Terrell Jacobs put out his own truck circus called the Terrell Jacobs Wild Animal Circus. The following year, Terrell and his wife Dolly divorced and sold all their assets to Arthur M. Wirtz of the Chicago Stadium. Wirtz formed the Barnes Brothers Menagerie Inc. and hired Terrell to work the act. The wagons read Barnes Brothers–Terrell Jacobs Lions and Tigers. This act worked the annual spring circus in the Chicago Stadium for the next several years.

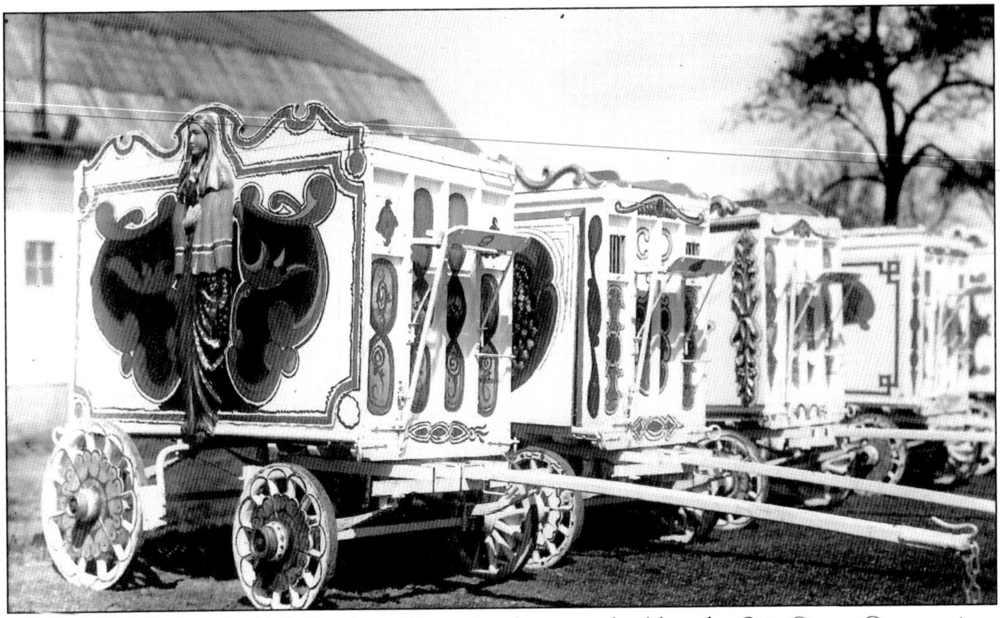

January 1950 found the Cole Brothers Circus bankrupt and sold to the Otis Circus Corporation, which was suspected to be owned by Arthur M. Wirtz. In February, Barnes Brothers merged with Otis, and the Barnes and Cole equipment was sent to Chicago and opened at the stadium as Hopalong Cassidy Presented by Cole Brothers Circus. The show wintered at the Barnes-Jacobs winter quarters in Peru.

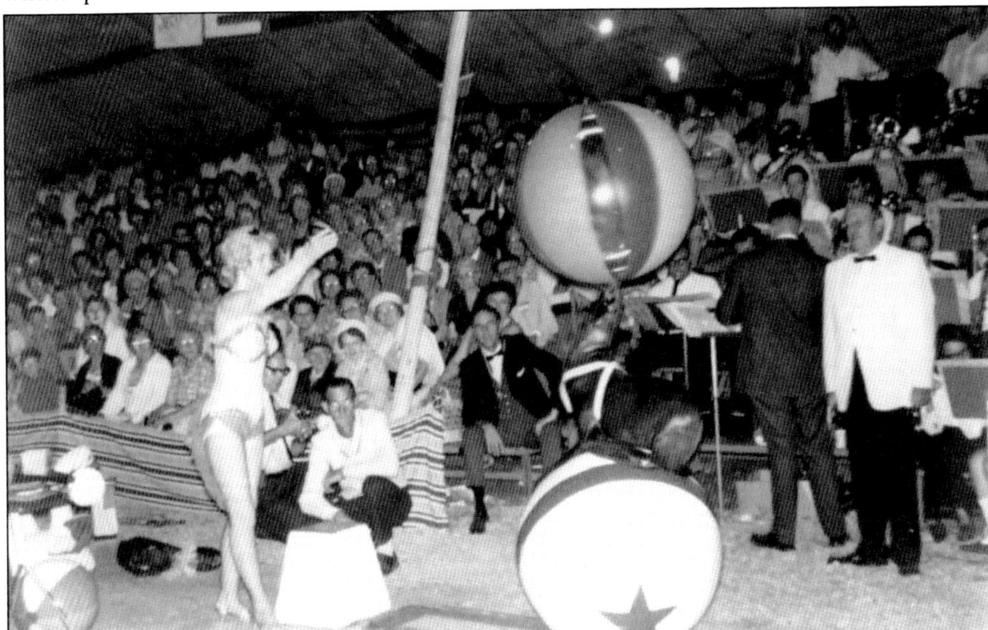

The Cole Brothers Circus worked the Chicago Stadium again in 1951. Soon after, Terrell Jacobs bought his act back from the Otis Circus Corporation and moved it to a farm in Twelve Mile. Otis used the Cole Brothers Circus title until 1955. In the mid-1950s, Paul and Dorothy Kelly bought the Barnes-Jacobs winter quarters, animals, and equipment and booked elephant, seal, and goat acts for many years. Dorothy and her son Ed still live on the property.

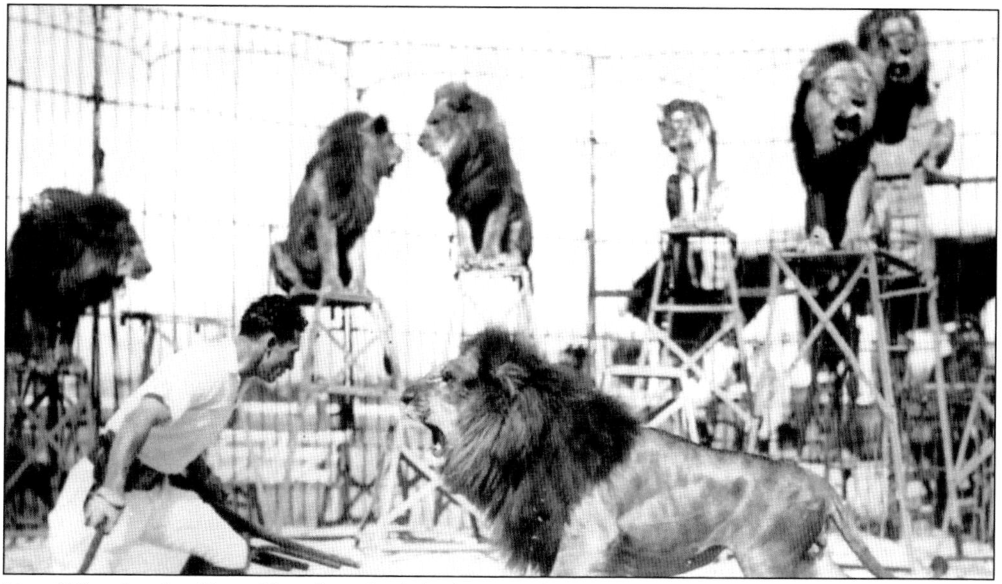

Terrell Jacobs, the "Lion King," worked the big cats for 16 circuses over 40 years before his death in 1957. Emmett Kelly and Otto Griebling found great fame as clowns with the Ringling Brothers Barnum and Bailey Circus. Clyde Beatty was a star in the arena, the movies, and television until his death in 1965. Mickey King, who ran away and joined the circus, spent her life performing with circuses around the world and then retired in Peru.

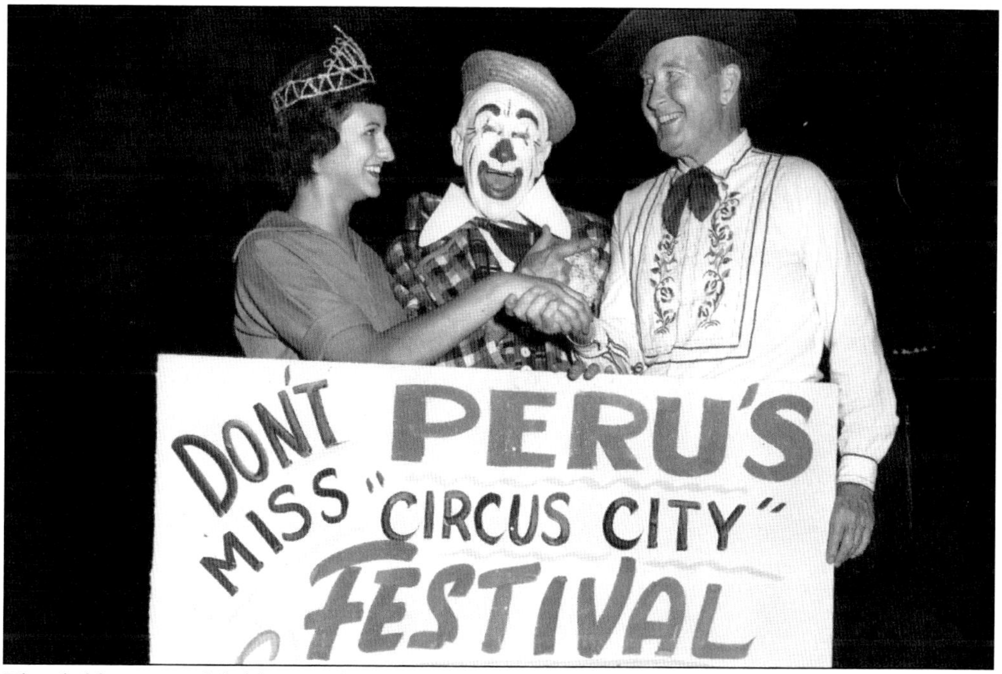


The children, grandchildren, and great-grandchildren of many circus greats still live in Peru. The Circus City Festival Inc. founded by retired circus professionals in 1959 living in Peru preserves their heritage. The Peru winter quarters is home to the International Circus Hall of Fame. In July each year, circus performances can be seen at each location, just as they were done under the old white tops.

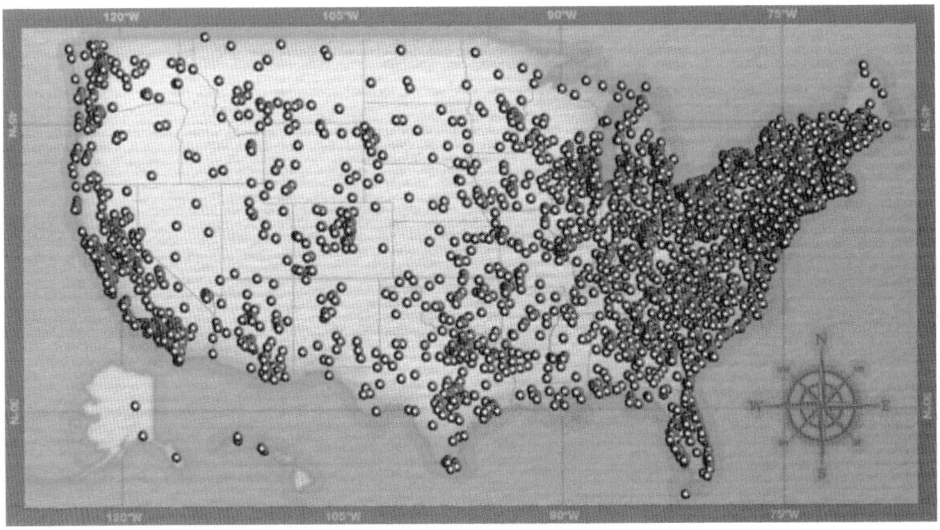